6/94   OFFICIALLY NOTED

Discarded by
Santa Maria Library

97   98   01   09   10

y

Twayne's English Authors Series

EDITOR OF THIS VOLUME

Sarah W. R. Smith

Tufts University

John Keats

TEAS 334

John Keats

Courtesy of The National Portrait Gallery, London

JOHN KEATS

By WOLF Z. HIRST
University of Haifa

TWAYNE PUBLISHERS
A DIVISION OF G. K. HALL & CO., BOSTON

Published in 1981 by Twayne Publishers,
A Division of G. K. Hall & Co.
All Rights Reserved

Printed on permanent/durable acid-free paper and bound
in the United States of America

Frontispiece credit: sketch of John Keats by Charles Brown,
courtesy of the National Portrait Gallery

Library of Congress Cataloging in Publication Data

Hirst, Wolf Z.
John Keats.

(Twayne's English authors series ; TEAS 334)
Bibliography: p. 176–83
Includes index.
1. Keats, John, 1795–1821—Criticism and inter-
pretation. I. Title. II. Series.
PR4837.H5 1981   821'.7   81–1938
ISBN 0–8057–6821–1   AACR2

To Esther

Contents

About the Author

Wolf Z. Hirst studied modern languages under a state scholarship at Oxford University, and education at Cambridge University, England, from 1950 to 1954, receiving his M.A. from Oxford in 1957. He worked as a graduate assistant, under a university fellowship in comparative literature, and as instructor in the German and English departments at Washington University, St. Louis, from 1961 to 1964, and he was awarded a Ph. D in comparative literature, with a dissertation on "Old Testament Influences on the Romantic Hero Figure in England, France, and Germany," in 1965. Since 1964 he has been a member of the English department at the University of Haifa, Israel, serving as chairman of the department from 1966 to 1968 and teaching mainly courses in the development of drama and in romantic poetry, including graduate seminars on John Keats. He has published articles on Byron and Keats.

Preface

The aim of this book is to give the student of Keats a comprehensive and scholarly account of the poet's works. While providing a picture of the critical consensus on Keats's major poems and his artistic achievement in general, I have also tried to reinterpret his work in a manner that may at least occasionally stimulate new discussion and research. By not focusing exclusively on a particular subject such as Keats's sensuous imagery or his preoccupation with the poetic process, with self-consciousness, or with dreams and visions (which, no doubt, are all central to Keats's poetry) I have been able to encompass more works than most books of similar length while yet doing minimal justice to all major poems. Limitation of space, however, has prevented me from pursuing various points of interest and special problems. For these I have had to refer the interested scholar to other studies, only a few of which I could list again in the Selected Bibliography.

I have used the recent edition by Jack Stillinger for the texts of the poems. The letters are quoted from Hyder Edward Rollins's two-volume edition, which retains Keats's idiosyncrasies of spelling and punctuation. Although I have no doubt been influenced by numerous Keats scholars I feel I owe most to the critical works of Walter Jackson Bate, Harold Bloom, Douglas Bush, Morris Dickstein, Robert Gittings, John Jones, John Middleton Murry, David Perkins, E. C. Pettet, Stuart Sperry, Jack Stillinger, and Earl Wasserman.

Thanks are due to the University of Haifa for a research grant, to the British Council for supplying numerous photostats from abroad, and to Susan Barrie and Marion Gold for typing the manuscript. I want to thank Irving Saposnik for encouraging me to undertake the present study and William Freedman, Bernard Knieger, Murray Roston, and Miora Weinberger for reading the draft and offering many valuable suggestions. I also must express my profound gratitude to Douglas Bush and E. C. Pettet, who most kindly agreed to read the manuscript without knowing me, and who both commented no less meticulously than my friends and colleagues. Finally, I wish to acknowledge my indebtedness to Sarah W. R. Smith for her extremely useful editorial comments.

WOLF Z. HIRST

University of Haifa

Chronology

1795   John Keats born in London (31 October), eldest son of Thomas and Frances Keats.

1797   Birth of George Keats (28 February).

1799   Birth of Thomas (Tom) Keats (18 November).

1803   Birth of Frances Mary (Fanny) Keats (3 June). John and George enter the Clarke school at Enfield (August).

1804   Father killed by a fall from his horse (16 April). Mother marries William Rawlings (June 27). Children stay with grandparents.

1805   Death of grandfather (8 March). Grandmother moves with children to Edmonton.

1808   Frances Keats returns to her children.
or
1809

1810   Death of Keats's mother from tuberculosis after long illness (March). Grandmother establishes trust fund for children and appoints Richard Abbey as one of the guardians.

1810   Keats leaves school. Apprenticed to Thomas Hammond,
or   surgeon and apothecary at Edmonton. Continues to see
1811   Cowden Clarke.

1814   First known attempts at verse, including "Imitation of Spenser." Death of grandmother. Fanny taken to the Abbeys (December).

1815   Enters Guy's Hospital, London, as medical student (1 October).

1816   Begins work as dresser at the hospital (3 March). First published poem, "O Solitude!" appears in Hunt's *Examiner* (5 May). Receives apothecary's certificate (July 25). John and Tom visit Margate (August). Meets Hunt, Haydon, and Reynolds. Lodges with George and Tom in London. Writes sonnet on "Chapman's Homer," "I stood tip-toe," and "Sleep and Poetry." Decides not to practice medicine (October-

December). Hunt's article on Shelley, Reynolds, and Keats printed in *Examiner* (1 December).

1817 Publication of first volume, *Poems* (3 March). Moves to Hampstead (March). Begins *Endymion* on Isle of Wight. Studies Shakespeare closely (April). Goes on to Canterbury. Meets Isabella Jones at Bo-Peep near Hastings (May). Stays with Bailey at Oxford (September). Visits Stratford-on-Avon (October). Letters on the "truth of Imagination" (22 November), and "negative capability" (21 December).

1818 Revises and copies *Endymion*. Attends Hazlitt's lectures (January–February). At Teignmouth nursing Tom (March–May 4 or 5). Writes verse epistle to Reynolds (25 March). *Endymion* published by Taylor and Hessey. Finishes "Isabella" (April). Composes "Ode to Maia." George marries Georgiana Wylie (May). John takes leave of George and Georgiana at Liverpool (June). Walking tour through Lake District and Scotland with his friend Charles Brown (25 June–7 August). Meets Fanny Brawne. Appearance of hostile reviews of *Endymion* in August issue of *Blackwood's*, and, belatedly, in April issue of *Critical Quarterly*. Nurses Tom. Begins *Hyperion* (August–December). Death of Tom (1 December). Moves to Wentworth Place. Perhaps arrives at an informal understanding with Fanny Brawne (25 December).

1819 Visits Chichester and Bedhampton with Brown. Writes "Eve of St. Agnes" (January) and "Eve of St. Mark" (February). The Brawnes move to Wentworth Place (3 April). Copies "La Belle Dame sans Merci" and "Ode to Psyche" (April). Probably writes "Ode on Indolence," "Ode to a Nightingale," "Ode on a Grecian Urn," "Ode on Melancholy" (April–May). Finishes journal-letter to George and Georgiana containing passage on "vale of Soul-making" (3 May). On Isle of Wight with Brown. Works on *Otho the Great, Lamia, Fall of Hyperion* (June–August). At Winchester (August–October) composes "To Autumn" (19 September). Has abandoned *Fall of Hyperion* (21 September). Begins *King Stephen* and *The Jealousies (The Cap and Bells)*. Possibly makes last additions to *Fall of Hyperion* (November–December). Probably engaged to Fanny (25 December).

1820 George's visit (January). Suffers hemorrhage and sees his "death-warrant" (3 February). Moves to Kentish Town (May). At Hunt's house (June–August). *Lamia* volume published

Chronology

(July). Nursed by Mrs. Brawne and Fanny (August). Sails for
Italy (18 September). Reaches Rome (15 November).

1821   Dies (23 February). Shelley's *Adonais: An Elegy on the Death
of John Keats* published (July).

CHAPTER 1

Introduction

I *Biographical*

THE tombstone of John Keats in the Protestant cemetery in Rome bears the following inscription: "Here lies One Whose Name was writ in Water." The words were requested by the poet as he lay dying of consumption in February 1821. Yet not long before, in his last year of health, within the span of the twelve months from September 1818 to September 1819, Keats had composed most of the poems for which he is remembered—probably greater poetry than has ever been written by a man of twenty-three.

The poet's early childhood seems to have been prosaic enough. He was born in London, the eldest child of Thomas and Frances Keats, on 31 October 1795. It has generally been assumed that Thomas Keats was the head ostler and livery stable keeper at the Swan and Hoop, an inn belonging to John Jennings, his father-in-law, but we know for certain only that by 1802, when Jennings rented a house in Enfield thirteen miles north of London, Thomas Keats was managing the inn and stables for his wife's father. John Keats had three brothers, George, Tom, and Edward (who died in infancy), and a sister, Fanny. From August 1803 John and George, and later Tom, lived as boarders at John Clarke's school at Enfield.

John had not been there a year when the first in a series of events occurred which must have profoundly shaken the lives of the children. In April 1804 their father was killed by a fall from his horse. Only two months later their mother remarried. Their grandfather died in March 1805 after drafting a will which complicated the family finances for the next twenty years. The children were living separately from their mother at the latest by the summer of 1805 when Alice Jennings, the beloved grandmother (an early sonnet gives evidence of John's attachment to her), moved from Enfield to Edmonton, two or three miles nearer to London, and took the children to live with her. By 1806 Keats's mother had left her second husband and was rumored to be living with another man at Edmonton. Tuberculosis, the disease which was soon to kill her (and later Tom at the age of nineteen, John at twenty-five, and eventually George when he was almost forty-five) took the life of her brother, Lieutenant Midgley Jennings, the uncle admired by the three boys, probably near the end of 1808. When some time afterwards she returned to her mother and her children, she had only a short time to live. Robert Gittings argues that Keats's determination "to carry off all the prizes in literature" (the words of Keats's tutor) was motivated by his sense of responsibility as the oldest male in the family and a desire to gain the approval of his sick mother.[1] Fourteen-year-old John nursed his mother and guarded her jealously during the later stages of her illness. Of Keats's reaction to his mother's death (March 1810) Edward Holmes, a school-fellow, wrote many years later: ". . . he gave way to . . . impassioned & prolonged grief—(hiding himself in a nook under the master's desk)" (*Keats Circle*, II, 165). Aileen Ward suggests that Keats's divided loyalty between his mother and grandmother "helps to explain a division in his nature which appeared later in many forms, one being a tendency to be drawn towards two quite different types of women—flirtatious young beauties and serious young ladies sexually much less challenging, often several years older than himself." [2] The poet's letters are silent about a mother who, according to George, "was extremely fond of him and humoured him in every whim" (*Keats Circle*, I, 288), but when he once does mention the early loss of his parents, he cryptically hints at still "earlier Misfortunes," and there are curious references to Hamlet and Ophelia,[3] which tempt us to speculate upon the poet's suspicion about his mother's sexual morals and to conjecture an Oedipus complex he never outgrew. One thing is certain: the shocks of his mother's hasty remarriage, her defection, her lingering illness, and her death found indirect expression in Keats's writings.

After so many misfortunes in their family the Keats boys may have looked upon the Clarke school as their second home. Here John came under the beneficent influence of Charles Cowden Clarke, the headmaster's son, and received a more liberal education than was customary at the time. Despite his short stature, about which he remained sensitive throughout his life (*Letters*, I, 301, 342; II, 61, 213), during most of his school days John seems to have been known better for his pugnaciousness than for his assiduity. "He would fight any one—morning, noon or night," Holmes recollected, at the same time testifying to John's "generosity of disposition" (*Keats Circle*, II,

163–65). Stories are told of how he once defended his brother against an usher at school, and how later he protected a kitten or a puppy against its tormentor and became known as "the little fellow who licked the butcher-boy" (*Keats Circle*, I, 325; II, 147, 152). In his last year and a half at school, however, he read voraciously and won book prizes given for voluntary extra work such as the translation of the *Aeneid*, early proof of his self-discipline and perseverance. When he was apprenticed to Thomas Hammond, a surgeon in Edmonton, he remained in contact with Cowden Clarke, who presided over his continued studies in literature and subsequently over his first attempts in poetry. After completing a year's training at Guy's Hospital in London and qualifying for the practice of medicine by passing the apothecary's examination (25 July 1816), he announced to his guardian Richard Abbey that he intended to gain his "Living by exercising" his "Abilities as a Poet" (*Keats Circle*, I, 307). Keats is not known ever to have regretted his choice of poetry over medicine, but on the other hand he could still write in May 1818: "I am glad at not having given away my medical Books" (*Letters*, I, 277).

Keats's acceptance of poetry as his vocation was largely prepared by his entry, following Cowden Clarke's introduction, into the literary circle of Leigh Hunt; and an article in Hunt's *Examiner* (1 December 1816) praising Keats alongside his friend John Hamilton Reynolds and his friendly rival Shelley was said to have "sealed his fate" (*Keats Circle*, II, 211). In March he moved to the suburb of Hampstead to be close to Hunt. Though Keats's first volume of *Poems*, published in March 1817, was ignored by the public, it was greeted enthusiastically by his friends. He was especially encouraged by Clarke, Hunt, Reynolds, the painter Benjamin Robert Haydon, who promoted his interest in painting and sculpture, and later by the solicitor Richard Woodhouse, the first collector of Keatsiana, who reassured him in moments of crisis. Lectures by the critic William Hazlitt and discussions and correspondence with Reynolds, the future clergyman Benjamin Bailey, and with Woodhouse helped to develop his critical theories. Keats met Wordsworth a few times in December 1817 but was less impressed by his personality than by his poems, in particular "Tintern Abbey," the "Immortality Ode," and the excerpt from *The Recluse* published as "Prospectus" to *The Excursion* in 1814.

Shortly after the failure of his first volume Keats found another publishing firm, that of John Taylor and James Augustus Hessey. Begun on the Isle of Wight in April and finished at Burford Bridge in November 1817, *Endymion* was published by Taylor and Hessey in April 1818. Since the author was a friend of the liberal Leigh Hunt, he was viciously attacked by *Blackwood's Edinburgh Magazine* (August) and by the *Critical Quarterly* (September). The reviews stopped sales. Keats was undoubtedly embarrassed by the financial difficulties thus aggravated and he may well have been offended by the personal nature of the attacks, but he was too sensible and self-confident a judge of his own work to have been paralyzed by extravagantly hostile criticism; despite later reports by friends about outbursts against the reviewers, we should accept his considered judgment: "My own domestic criticism has given me pain beyond what Blackwood or the Quarterly could possibly inflict" (*Letters*, I, 374), and we must believe his disclaimer (in a *Lamia* volume preserved at Harvard) of an announcement by his publishers that the poem *Hyperion* was left fragmentary because of the reception given to *Endymion*.

Nevertheless after the poet's death a myth arose that he was killed by the reviewers. Byron's gibe in *Don Juan* that Keats let himself "be snuffed out by an article" (canto xi, stanza 60) and Shelley's figure in *Adonais* of the shepherd, "Like a pale flower by some sad maiden cherished" (line 48, an allusion to "Isabella"), fostered the legend about the sentimental and effeminate poet. The public gradually learned that Keats died of consumption, not adverse criticism, and George Keats's insistence that "John was noble and manly" (*Keats Circle*, I, 314) is generally accepted today, but there still remains a misconception about Keats's poetry. Although standard nineteenth-century epithets like "babyish effeminacy" and "nauseous sweetness"[4] have become rare nowadays, some critics write yet about supposedly excessive softening, blurring, and romanticizing in Keats. These critics seem to mistake portrayal of weakness for weakness.

All of Keats's courage was required in March 1818 when he went to Teignmouth in Devonshire to take George's place in nursing Tom, who by that time had contracted the family disease. Early in May John took Tom back to Hampstead. George married Georgiana Augusta Wylie at the end of May and emigrated with her to America in June. John escorted the newlyweds to Liverpool, and continued, in the company of his friend Charles Brown, on a walking tour through the Lake District and Scotland. When he returned to Hampstead he found that Tom's condition had deteriorated. "I am obliged to write, and plunge into abstract images to ease myself of his countenance his voice and feebleness," the poet confessed (*Letters*, I, 369). The "abstract images" were those of his projected epic *Hyperion*. Although we cannot assume that Keats, with his medical training, then knew that he was to die of tuberculosis himself, the spectacle of his wasting brother, reinforced by recollections that his uncle and his mother had died of the disease, may well have intensified premonitions of an early death even before the appearance of any symptoms.

Tom died on the first of December 1818. Upon his brother's death Keats moved into lodgings with Brown at Wentworth Place, Hampstead. These lodgings had been occupied by a widow, Mrs. Brawne, and her son and two daughters during the summer. In a letter to George and Georgiana of 16 December Keats mentions Mrs. Brawne and her daughter Fanny for the first time; and the latter he describes as "beautiful and elegant, graceful, silly, fashionable and strange" and goes on to say that they have a little "tiff now and then—and she behaves a little better" (II, 8). The date and circumstances of their first meeting are hotly disputed, but most probably Keats had met Fanny at the home of Dilke, a friend (and later a neighbor) at Wentworth Place, in the autumn of 1818. Despite the ambivalent attitude expressed in the letter of 16 December, he then seems already to have been in love with Fanny, and the two may have reached an informal understanding on Christmas Day. "The Eve of St. Agnes," Keats's magnificent love story in verse, was written at Chichester in January 1819. (The subjects for this poem and the fragmentary "Eve of St. Mark" were apparently suggested by the enigmatic Mrs. Isabella Jones, whom he had met in May 1817.) [5] In April the Brawnes became Keats's neighbors when they took over the part of Wentworth Place occupied by the Dilkes; and from April to September he wrote most of his greatest poems. The haunting ballad "La Belle Dame sans Merci," included in a letter to George and Georgiana on April 21, and the celebrated spring odes[6] may all have been composed while only a wall separated the poet from his beloved. Yet Keats felt he had to tear himself away from her in order to write, and in doing so he inflicted upon himself excruciating torments of jealousy. The fine verse narrative *Lamia* took most of the summer when he was again staying on the Isle of Wight. At the same time he was collaborating with Brown on the tragedy *Otho the Great* and trying to rework his majestic *Hyperion* fragment into *The Fall of Hyperion: A Dream*. The perfect ode "To Autumn" was composed at Winchester in September. He returned to London in October and wrote four promising scenes for a tragedy, *King Stephen*, and an

unfinished satire, *The Jealousies (The Cap and Bells)*. In the work of
this year we easily recognize the ecstasies of love and agonies of
jealousy the poet expressed in his letters to Fanny Brawne, but we
can only speculate on how far the relationship between the two
reinforces the recurrent Keatsian theme of apparent fulfillment followed by disillusion.

Keats's creative life came to an end as the symptoms of tuberculosis
appeared. In October 1819 one of his friends, the painter Joseph
Severn, found him in a bad state, and by 22 December we have
Keats's own testimony in a letter to his sister: "I have been and
continue rather unwell" (II, 238). On 3 February 1820 he suffered a
severe hemorrhage which he recognized as his "death-warrant"
(*Keats Circle*, II, 74). In May he moved to Kentish Town near
Hampstead; in June, following another hemorrhage, to Hunt's home
at Hampstead; and in August back to Wentworth Place, where he was
nursed by Fanny and her mother. July saw the publication of his third
volume, *Lamia, Isabella, The Eve of St. Agnes and Other Poems*,
containing, after the three title poems, the works in the following
order: "Ode to a Nightingale," "Ode on a Grecian Urn," "Ode to
Psyche," "Fancy," "Bards of Passion . . . ," "Lines on the Mermaid
Tavern," "Robin Hood," "To Autumn," "Ode on Melancholy," and
Hyperion: A Fragment. Favorable reviews of this volume did little to
console Keats, who had been told that his only hope of recovery lay in
a journey to Italy. He was now without financial resources, George
having visited London in January to retrieve his share of Tom's estate
and neither he nor George knowing about the inheritance left them
by their grandfather. The expenses for the sojourn in Italy were
generously met by Keats's publishers in return for the expectation of
future sales of his poems. On 18 September 1820 the poet sailed for
Italy attended by Severn. The separation from Fanny Brawne was
shattering. "I can bear to die—I cannot bear to leave her," Keats
wrote Brown from Italy (II, 351). On 23 February 1821 Keats died in
Severn's arms in their rooms in the Piazza di Spagna in Rome. In his
Life of Keats (*Keats Circle*, II, 94) Brown gives us the poet's last
words as he received them from Severn. They were: "I shall die
easy—don't be frightened—be firm, and thank God it has come!"

II   *Themes and Images*

Keats's decision to abandon medicine gives the clearest indication
of how much poetry means to him and at the same time may help to

explain some of the doubts and conflicts pervading his poems and letters. "I find that I cannot exist without poetry—without eternal poetry" (I, 133) is one of the numerous statements on the subject in the letters, and in one way or another most of Keats's poems deal with poetry or the poetic process. As in many of the poems, in several letters (I, 141, 169, 242; II, 69–70, 179) self-confidence is tinged with self-doubt. But any hesitations about his vocation sound less convincing than the following two judgments, both delivered in connection with the adverse critical reception of *Endymion:* "I would sooner fail than not be among the greatest" and: "I think I shall be among the English Poets after my death" (I, 374, 394). The repeated protestations that he hopes to benefit mankind, presumably through his art (I, 267, 271, 293, 387), may reflect attempts to prove to himself that by abandoning his medical career he has not betrayed his humanitarian aspirations, that he is one of "those to whom the miseries of the world / Are misery, and will not let them rest" (*The Fall of Hyperion*, i.148–49). For even as he praises "fine writing," Keats takes it for granted that "fine doing" is superior (*Letters*, II, 146). Humanitarian considerations make him place "philosophy" (in the widest sense of the word) above "poetry" and "the human friend Philosopher" above "a fine writer" (II, 80–81, 139). We must bear in mind Keats's subsequent express hope that he has become a more philosophical poet (II, 116) when we reflect upon his pronouncements on "negative capability," the ability of not "reaching after fact & reason" (I, 193), his preference of imagination over consecutive reasoning and sensations over thoughts (I, 184–85), and his assertion that "axioms in philosophy are not axioms until they are proved upon our pulses" (I, 279).

Occasionally Keats's poetry achieves precision of doctrine at the expense of living poetic power. "Poesy," he states in "Sleep and Poetry," "should be a friend / To sooth the cares, and lift the thoughts of man" (246–47). But, more typically, a few lines earlier he gives us a magnificent, richly evocative figure presenting poetry as "might half slumb'ring on its own right arm" (237). In this sculpture of strength and poise, the poet expresses his thoughts and intuitions about the artistic process in the manner which he knows best, in the language of sensation. From a description like the impatiently buzzing honey-bee or the heart as the mind's Bible (I, 232; II, 102–103) we see that even in his letters Keats conveys his meaning most effectively when he uses figurative language.

Ripening is Keats's master-metaphor, which he sometimes uses for intellectual growth in general (*Letters*, I, 214, 231) and more often to represent the poetic process. The harvest of poetry is presided over by Apollo, sun-god and god of poetry.[7] The poet draws his nourishment from the objects of sense around him; he is, as it were, rooted in the earth: "The flower must drink the nature of the soil / Before it can put forth its blossoming" ("Spenser, a jealous honorer of thine"). He repeatedly seeks to escape from the fever and fret of human misery and the pallor of mortality to the refuge of leafy luxury in shady bowers, where his burning forehead is relieved by a refreshing breeze and his parching tongue by cool drink. But the sanctuaries of nature soon cease to satisfy, and the poet aches for wings to fly into a higher realm, in which he often lights upon another bower.

Like much literature of the Romantic period, Keats's poetry reflects the tension between actuality and ideal perfection, the here and the beyond, mortality and immortality, time and eternity, the reality principle and longing for the absolute, a longing repeatedly symbolized by the union between a mortal and an immortal (*Endymion*, "La Belle Dame sans Merci," "Ode to Psyche," *Lamia*). The recurrent pattern is one of dream and awakening, flight on the wings of imagination into a higher order of reality followed by a disillusioned return to the ordinary, everyday world. Only at the end of *Endymion* does the hero's dream come true, when he approaches the heavenly Cynthia through an earthly maiden for an eternal reunion. But even in this romance, in which yearnings to transcend earthly limitations are satisfied, Keats obtrudes thoughts about the futility of all human endeavor.

Ultimately anchored in the actual, Keats's quest for infinitude differs from the infinite voyages of the other High Romantics and of his own imitators, from Byron's "wanderers o'er Eternity" (*Childe Harold*, canto III, stanza 70) or Tennyson's unyielding mariner, who "cannot rest from travel" and would "sail beyond the sunset" ("Ulysses," 6, 60) to pursue an eternally receding horizon. At times Keats uses a shore-sea dichotomy to represent the contrast between the finite and the infinite, between reality and aspiration. In the sonnet "To Homer" he compares his attempt to bridge the gap between actuality and desire to a person sitting "ashore" and longing for "deep seas." An inexhaustible potential is suggested by the Pacific in another sonnet, "On First Looking into Chapman's Homer," the "ocean dim, sprinkled with many an isle" of "Sleep and Poetry" (306), or the uncloying "wideness" in "On the Sea." As for the poet "on the shore / Of the wide world" ("When I have fears"), earth has become

too narrow for Endymion standing alone "Upon a misty, jutting head
of land" (II. 163) until, choosing a real woman over a phantom, he bids
farewell to "visionary seas" whose very "shore / Of tangled wonder"
has become menacing (IV.653–55). The "perilous seas in faery lands
forlorn" of "Ode to a Nightingale" (70) are the boundless stretches of
imagination from which the poet is about to be driven back to the
shores of reality.

But within the confines of temporal life everything "Cloys with
tasting" ("Fancy," 15) or else is brought to an end by death. Happiness on earth is thus inseparable from sorrow, pain from pleasure.
The paradox is a favorite one among Romantic poets: we remember
the "aching joys" of Wordsworth's "Tintern Abbey" (84), the "delicious pain" of Shelley's *Epipsychidion* (452), and the "sweet pain" of
his *Adonais* (80) beside Keats's own "sweetness of the pain" in
"Welcome joy, and welcome sorrow" (23) and in "What can I do to
drive away" (54). In his early poetry this motif appears as a sentimental pursuit of "the joy of grief" ("Fill for me a brimming bowl,"
24), a "sweetly sad" melody and a "pleasing woe" ("To Lord Bryon"),
or "sweet desolation—balmy pain" ("I stood tip-toe," 162), and in
Endymion as love's "grief contain'd / In the very deeps of pleasure"
(II.823–24). The theme of joy blended with woe gradually develops
into the mood of anticipating fulfillment and disillusion in the same
breath (conveyed, for example, by the characteristic Keatsian figure
"he will seize on trickling honey-combs" in *Endymion*, II.150), or it
becomes a "Happy gloom" (*Endymion*, IV.537) suggesting the Cave
of Quietude's calm following despair. *Hyperion* integrates the paradox of simultaneous "joy and grief" (II.289), "pain and pleasure"
(III.66) into its theme of the conquest of time. In the great odes this
paradox grows in complexity from the "pleasant pain" of creation in
"Psyche" (52), through the fusion of the poet's numbness, heartache,
and happiness in the nightingale's song, to the mixed joy of human
passion menaced by subsequent surfeit and sorrow in the "Grecian
Urn." "Ode on Melancholy" defines the joy-pain paradox as the
essentially human feature linked to the inescapable facts of mutability and human consciousness.

Keats's most explicit statement on earthly happiness ("what must it
end in?—Death") is followed by an analogy often implied in the
poetry:

For instance suppose a rose to have sensation, it blooms on a beautiful
morning it enjoys itself—but there comes a cold wind, a hot sun—it can not

escape it, it cannot destroy its annoyances—they are as native to the world as itself: no more can man be happy . . . (II, 101)

The conventional combination of beauty with ephemerality in flowers has become axiomatic only because it has been proved upon his pulses. The central theme in Keats is an assault upon time, the futile attempt to defeat death and decay.

III   The Triumph of Time

With a growing distrust of the imagination Keats's onslaughts on temporality begin to weaken. While his early work is dominated by an illusioned escapism, his poetry soon balances the craving for transcendence against a recognition of the inevitability of progression and change. In his final affirmation of natural process ("To Autumn") we hear only faint echoes of revolt against the human condition.

In the earliest poetry Keats does not face conflict or time and change. In the sonnet "O Solitude!" (his first published poem) the poet escapes to "boughs pavillion'd" from the "jumbled heap / of murky buildings," but such bowers simply provide refuge from the noise of civilization. Yet already in "I stood tip-toe" and "Sleep and Poetry," both completed towards the end of 1816, he rebels against his finite condition. In "Sleep and Poetry" "a bowery nook / Will be elysium" (63–64) by giving the poet an illusion of heaven on earth and intoxicating his senses till he imagines "Wings to find out an immortality" (84). In the poem's dialectic between infinite desire and recognition of human limitations, this overreaching, reminiscent of Icarus and Faustus, is countered by an inevitable downfall: "let the hot sun / Melt my Dedalian wings, and drive me down / Convuls'd and headlong!" (302–304). Keats therefore anticipates that his work will henceforth move from "the realm . . . / Of Flora, and old Pan" to "the agonies, the strife / Of human hearts" (101–25), from romance toward involvement in real life, from escape to self-confrontation, from luxurious indulgence to painful conflict. Keats will eventually abandon romance but not the romance environment, escapism but not the impulse to escape, indulgence but not the luxuriance of "sleep[ing] in the grass" of his "leafy world" (102, 119). When, in the mature poetry, we come upon figures like Apollo on his bowery island, the poet in the "embalmed darkness" of an arbor in "Ode to a Nightingale" (43) or "cool-bedded in the flowery grass" in "Ode on Indolence" (52), and Cupid and Psyche "couched side by side / In deepest grass, beneath the whisp'ring roof / Of leaves and trembled blossoms" ("Ode to Psyche," 9–11), the scenes are integrated into wider pictures which also include the strife of human hearts with its agony, perplexity, fever-fit, and loss.

"Sleep and Poetry" expresses the central Keatsian conflict pointedly by pitting a chariot which symbolizes the life of the imagination against "A sense of real things" (157), the world of empirical everyday existence. After *Endymion* Keats's love stories (the ballad "La Belle Dame" and the verse narratives "Isabella," *Lamia*, and, by implication, "The Eve of St. Agnes") invariably end in disaster and death when "real things" invade a romantic dream world. This opposition between the illusory and the real, imagination and consecutive reasoning, the quest for immortal bliss and an awareness of the limitations of mortality culminates in the symbolic debate of the great odes and the dramatic clash between the different characters of *Lamia*. In the latter the gulf between the temporal and a divine world is as wide as ever, and the victory of cold reality over illusion is final. Yet while its story follows "La Belle Dame" in the disastrous escape pattern from nature into the supernatural, *Lamia* also censures "cold philosophy" (II.230): "a moment's thought is passion's passing bell" (II.39). More obviously than in "La Belle Dame," the "Nightingale," and the "Grecian Urn," *Lamia* demonstrates a mortal's inability to sustain a visionary experience so easily undermined by self-consciousness. The poem's unresolved conflicts establish an equilibrium between the claims of prosaic actuality and the timeless world of imagination, between philosophy and the rainbow.

Time and eternity are symbolically reconciled in Moneta's sublime countenance "deathwards progressing / To no death" in *The Fall of Hyperion* (i.260–61). A poet who can "see as a God sees" and revives immortals by retrieving them from their timeless realm has conquered his "own weak mortality" (i.304, 389). But for Keats mortality reasserts itself. On 19 September 1819 he informs Reynolds that he has just composed a poem on the beautiful season and the stubble fields he saw on his Sunday walk ("To Autumn"). A few lines later he writes that he has "given up Hyperion" (the revised version of the ambitious project he has had in his mind since 1817) because of its "Miltonic inversions . . . Miltonic verse cannot be written in an artful or rather artist's humour. I wish to give myself up to other sensations" (II, 167). Not only style is involved. Of all the major poems the serene and flawless ode "To Autumn" expresses the least resistance to mutability. Keats may have come to realize that in the

Hyperions he has been producing "the false beauty proceeding from art" and not raising "the true voice of feeling" (II, 167) inasmuch as he has been trying to exchange Milton's doctrine for a proposition of his own: that timeless beauty and a poet's imagination can save mortals from the limitations of time. For it is a theme belied by what he has felt on his pulses. Despite poetry he remains fettered to the natural order in which "youth grows pale, and spectre-thin, and dies" ("Ode to a Nightingale," 26), since the mutable world recaptures mortals who try to escape it. All living things decay and the beauty of "a morning rose," "the rainbow of a salt sand-wave," "the wealth of globed peonies," or a lady's "peerless eyes" ("Ode on Melancholy," 15–20) make Keats all the more acutely aware of their ephemerality. The harvested fields around Winchester on the "soft-dying day" described in the last stanza of "To Autumn" now show the futility of his attempt to arrest the flow of time. A swath of unreaped grain "and all its twined flowers" (18) is a picture which the poet is tempted to rescue from time into the realm of art, but he finds this magnificent autumn scene to be a beauty that has died after all and been replaced by the new splendor of the rosy "stubble-plains" (26). Here he not only accepts but embraces the relentless triumph of time and natural process. Romance and the vain hope of the *Hyperions* have been finally left behind.

IV   *Style and Artistry*

Whereas Keats's ideas evolve gradually, almost imperceptibly, in a mind opening its leaves "like a flower . . . passive and receptive— budding patiently under the eye of Apollo" (*Letters*, I, 232), his stylistic development is conscious and determined. Despite the brevity of his writing career, the diversity of his experiments in versification is remarkable. His earliest surviving verses are in the Spenserian stanza, which he eventually brings to consummate perfection in "The Eve of St. Agnes." Keats's sonnets follow first the Petrarchan, then the Shakespearean rhyme scheme, but he express- es his dissatisfaction with both forms (*Letters*, II, 108) and tries out new ones (see especially "If by dull rhymes"). As H. W. Garrod first made clear, Keats's ode stanza is an outgrowth of experimentation with the sonnet form and consists basically (after the experiment in "Psyche") of a Shakespearean quatrain followed by a Petrarchan sestet.[8] Under Hunt's influence and probably in reaction to Pope, Keats uses the heroic couplet very loosely in the volume of 1817 and

Endymion with lines frequently running over from one couplet into the following.⁹ For his next narrative, "Isabella," he attempts *ottava rima*, and in *Hyperion* he employs stately Miltonic blank verse. (We have seen how he later objects to its "Miltonic inversions.") When he returns to the rhymed pentameter couplet in *Lamia*, now influenced by Dryden, he closes the couplet more often than in his early verse and uses it functionally for balance and antithesis, devices suitable to the poem's equilibrium between two worlds. The serpent-woman is a paradoxical creature who reconciles opposites:

> A virgin purest lipp'd, yet in the lore
> Of love deep learned to the red heart's core:
> Not one hour old, yet of sciential brain
> To unperplex bliss from its neighbour pain. (I.189–92)

Each of these two couplets pits innocence against experience, and the added opposition, in the last line, between bliss and pain reminds us of the contrast between the mystery of the human condition, in which these feelings are inextricably intertwined, and the supernatural power that can "unperplex" them.

Perhaps Keats repeatedly fixes upon particular poetic models and set patterns in order "to restrain the headlong impetuosity of my Muse," as he jokingly puts it in one of his letters (II, 97). In the *Poems* of 1817 he often fails to achieve effective integration of individual elements into an overall scheme, especially so in the longer pieces. He may be aware that the compact and demanding form of the Petrarchan sonnet tends to check his exuberant imagination from running off in one direction after another. (Eighteen out of the thirty-one poems in the 1817 volume are sonnets, all Petrarchan.) In the justly celebrated sonnet "On First Looking into Chapman's Homer" selected word pictures are skillfully grouped around a central exploration metaphor. Yet the focus on the object which inspired Keats and is announced in the title is somewhat blurred within the sonnet, where Chapman must compete for attention with Apollo and Cortez, with the realms of gold and the Darien peak. In subsequent sonnets such as "On Seeing the Elgin Marbles," "On Sitting Down to Read *King Lear* Once Again," or "To Homer" the poets or objects of art that inspire Keats occupy a more central position and are more characteristic of the unifying symbolism he will achieve through the nightingale or the Grecian urn. As they gain depth in the later work, such Keatsian motifs as the analogy between seasons and the life and

mind of man or between harvest and poetry contribute more and
more to structural unity and thematic coherence. For example, in "I
stood tip-toe," the long poem opening the 1817 volume, in the
description of the rudely torn bluebells "scattered thoughtlessly / By
infant hands, left on the path to die" (45–46), the change of the draft's
"Urchin's" to "infant" hints at the proximity of birth and death, but
this theme is not linked to the poem's concern with the inspirational
power of nature and a poet's birth. On the other hand in the sonnet
"After dark vapours," written slightly later, the collation of natural
and human cycles creates a more integral connection between "a
sleeping infant's breath" and "a poet's death." At the end of Keats's
career every detail adds to a poem's unity. In the ode "To Autumn,"
which personifies the season but mentions no man, woman, or infant,
images like the sweet hazel kernel and the ripe core of all fruit
enhance the poem's sense of a universal cyclical inevitability that also
comprises humanity.

The diction too aims at concentration from the beginning, although
with equally uneven success. Already in the *Poems* of 1817 we find
many compound epithets such as "deep-brow'd," "bright-eyed,"
"far-fam'd," and "sweet-lipp'd," some of which can be traced back to
Leigh Hunt. Although Keats's immediate adaptation of these
Huntian combinations is not always felicitous, his later compounds
serve admirably to compress and intensify sensation. A less promising device encouraged by Hunt was the use of abstractions to
communicate the sensuous, such as "dewiness," "silkiness," "fresh-
nesses," "flutterings," "smotherings." Keats may have thought that
such words fuse general concepts with actual observation of the
particular by conveying concrete impressions in abstract terms. Only
sentimentalism was lost and much sensuousness gained when he
later replaced these abstractions with physical objects. It is doubtful
whether Keats's poetry was enriched by the other verbal contriv-
ances which he took over from Hunt, such as the formation of
adjectives from nouns by adding the "y" suffix ("lawny," "leafy,"
"bowery," "pillowy"), adverbs from present participles ("trembling-
ly," "lingeringly," "staringly"), and nouns from verbs ("float," "trip,"
"incline," "amaze"), which certainly did little to tighten the texture of
his poetry. In a usage not owed to Hunt, he employed more effectively the opposite of the last-named device, namely, the formation of
verbs from nouns: even in his first poem, "Imitation of Spenser," we
meet the memorable phrase "the swan . . . oar'd himself along"
(14–15). But much of Keats's early verse remains vague and diffuse;
there are too many soft, gentle, milky, dewy, rosy, leafy, balmy,

windings, nestlings, flutterings, swoonings, and smotherings—and these often fail to muster into any unified structure.

It is Keats's failure, for the time being, to free himself from standard patterns and specific models and to " 'load every rift' " of his subject "with ore" (*Letters*, II, 323) that makes some of his early poetry sentimental and even vulgar rather than (as was long taken for granted) his use of words like "infant's gums" or "nipple" (*Endymion*, II.451, 869). When the apprentice poet speaks of woman, whose "Soft dimpled hands, white neck, and creamy breast, / Are things on which the dazzled senses rest," as "a milk-white lamb that bleats / For man's protection" ("Woman! when I behold thee flippant, vain," 16–17, 31–32), conventional epithets have betrayed him into merely referring to something that he will later be able to convey, namely, "dazzled senses." On the other hand the expression "a bunch of blooming plums / Ready to melt between an infant's gums" (*Endymion*, II.450–51), so often denigrated as sentimental or vulgar (presumably because of the repellence of toothlessness) is neither and splendidly reproduces in its unconventional implied comparison with a baby's mouth the softness of ripe fruit, the effect of the whole picture being enhanced by what Christopher Ricks has called "the potentiality for embarrassment, recognized and subsumed." [10] If we were to reject the image because of its distasteful associations we would be unable to embrace wholeheartedly the consummate artistry of a line from Keats's most perfect poem: "For summer has o'er-brimmed their clammy cells" ("To Autumn," 11). But even those who think it vulgar do not deny that the language depicting the soft plums is highly sensuous. The associations with touch, taste, and ingestion are particularly Keatsian and form part of a developing effort to convey an object through as many sensations as possible. The poet's famous and all-pervasive synaesthesia is only one aspect of this tendency, for example the "cool" purple of the wine a few lines earlier (II.444), which announces the complex mixture of sense perceptions compressed into the second stanza of the "Ode to a Nightingale," where the taste of the earth-cooled, purple-staining wine is combined with the smell of flowers, country sights, the movement of dance, the sound of song, the heat of the sun, and much more.

But perhaps the most characteristic Keatsian device is one that fuses poetry with painting and sculpture: the suspension of movement at a pregnant moment. His gift for reproducing real paintings and pieces of sculpture in language or inventing them is already remarkably demonstrated in the series of tableaux at the end of

"Sleep and Poetry," where Keats also tells us that pictures, statuary, and prints of them inspire his poetry. "The swift bound / Of Bacchus from his chariot, when his eye / Made Ariadne's cheek look blushing-ly" (334–36), for example, skillfully renders the significant moment of the mythological story which Titian's brush has caught.[11] It is not unlikely that the leg of Titian's Bacchus in mid-air and the startled sideway glance of Ariadne and the upward movement of her arm (or similar effects in another painting) have prompted not only the lines "Stepping like Homer at the trumpet's call" and "As Venus looking sideways in alarm" ("I stood tip-toe," 217, 220) but also all examples of arrested motion, dynamic poise, or motion about to begin, from the eagle stare of Cortez surrounded by the "wild surmise" of his men in "Chapman's Homer" to the gleaner with her "Steady . . . laden head across a brook" in the middle stanza of "To Autumn." The blush seems just to rise to Ariadne's cheek, since it is the "eye" of the god that has caused it, and the phrase "look blushingly" for once puts the Huntian participle-adverb to good use by introducing a linguistic equivocation, lacking in Titian's painting, about the spontaneity of Ariadne's blush. Nevertheless this phrase cannot compete with later figurative uses of the blushing of dawn (*Hyperion*, I.265) or evening (*Endymion*, III.357; *Lamia*, II.107), or with "Autumn's red-lipp'd fruitage too, / Blushing through the mist and dew" ("Fancy," 13–14), which briefly arrests the march of time in a striking manner, though not so magnificently as the "barred clouds" of "the soft-dying day" that "touch the stubble-plains with rosy hue" in the last stanza of "To Autumn."

Not far short of the latter ("Keats's greatest blush" according to Ricks)[12] is the personification of "the blushful Hippocrene" in the "Nightingale" (16), reinforcing sensations aroused by wine which have already been conveyed through all five senses, and the alexandrine crowning the splendid piece of architecture in one of the richest stanzas in "The Eve of St. Agnes": "A shielded scutcheon blush'd with blood of queens and kings" (216). What in these two instances contributes to the wonderful effect is Keats's ability to identify himself imaginatively with the object described. In the "Nightingale" the poet yearning "for a beaker full of the warm South" has briefly been replaced by a "winking" satyr (15–18), and in "St. Agnes" Madeline is temporarily neglected to bring the window to life. Sympathetic identification is even more remarkable in the first stanza of "St. Agnes" with its limping, trembling hare and Beadsman with numb fingers and "frosted breath," and in the second stanza, where Keats forgets his own identity by "filling some other Body"

(*Letters*, I, 387), the freezing "sculptur'd dead . . . / Emprison'd in black, purgatorial rails." Woodhouse reports Keats's assertion "that he can conceive of a billiard Ball that it may have a sense of delight from its own roundness, smoothness . . . " (*Letters*, I, 389). It is therefore not surprising that the poet's imaginative infeeling can animate the cold marble of a Grecian urn.

Finally, much of the fascination exercised by Keats's poetry is due to his sense of melody. "I well remember his telling me," Bailey writes to the poet's biographer, "that, had he studied music, he had some notions of the combinations of sounds, by which he thought he could have done something as original as his poetry"; and he also refers to a Keatsian theory according to which "the vowels should be so managed as not to clash one with another so as to mar the melody,—& yet that they should be interchanged, like differing notes of music to prevent monotony" (*Keats Circle*, II, 278, 277). Walter Jackson Bate has explicated this theory as involving assonance in addition to the alternation of long and short vowels.[13] Keats knows how to use onomatopoeia very effectively, for instance when he echoes the humming and buzzing of insects in "The murmurous haunt of flies on summer eves," in the "Nightingale" (50) or the sound of the wind in the line "Thy hair soft-lifted by the winnowing wind" ("To Autumn," 15), but most of his music is independent of the meaning of his words. Already in the verse epistle "To Charles Cowden Clarke" he shows his awareness of "Spenserian vowels that elope with ease" (56), and by January 1819 he has perfected his musical artistry. Stanza thirty of "St. Agnes," for example, renowned for the profusion of its exotic images, begins with the verse "And still she slept an azure-lidded sleep," in which the short "a" and "i" sounds are alternated with the long "e" of "she" and "sleep." The stanza ends with the alexandrine "From silken Samarcand to cedar'd Lebanon," and it is probable that the word "glutted," which is typical of Keats's fondness for expressions of ingestion and surfeit and which had superseded the earlier innocuous "wealthy" in the draft, was sacrificed to "silken" in order to reinforce the alliteration between the opening consonants of "Samarcand" and "cedar'd." Parts of the following two lines (69–70) from the "Ode to a Nightingale" are repeatedly quoted in this book for the themes they image:

> Charm'd magic casements, opening on the foam
> Of perilous seas, in faery lands forlorn.

"Love for Philosophy" (*Letters*, I, 271) there is increasingly in Keats's poetry, but to a large extent it is the music that produces the magic.

CHAPTER 2

The Letters

I General Characteristics

K EATS'S 251 surviving letters provide a detailed record of his three most creative years and of the last year, when he no longer wrote poetry. They give us a clear picture of his personality, trace his development as a poet, and are full of spontaneous pronouncements on the nature of poetry which have become starting points for countless discussions on aesthetics. We come across phrases like "negative capability," "truth of Imagination," and "Soulmaking" so often in criticism that we tend to forget the informal context in which such expressions first appeared.

Although, taken as a whole, Keats's letters may be seen as a fairly coherent body of thought, they consist of a series of insights scattered almost at random and interspersed with trivialities. Parts resemble lectures, others travelogues or pieces of journalism, and others again read almost like a diary. Four letters are verse epistles. Beside brief notes of four to six lines there are several lengthy journal-letters scribbled in installments; the longest, written to George and Georgiana from 14 February to 3 May 1819, extends over fifty pages (II, 58–109). The letters serve as a repository for puns and jokes as well as for aesthetic and ethical maxims, for slight verses as well as for magnificent poetry. They give us the circumstances under which many of Keats's poems were composed. Sometimes they are self-judgments, sometimes they judge the work of others. Often Keats copies finished poems into his letters, but at times he seems to be dashing off impromptu verses some of which he revises and publishes later. In at least one instance he consciously uses part of a letter (II, 93–94) as a rough draft: a passage consisting of a jocose critique of a friend's work (Reynolds's *Peter Bell*, a parody of Wordsworth) is later published as a review in Hunt's *Examiner*.

A lively sense of humor pervades the letters. In the midst of a serious discussion Keats may spring a jest upon his correspondents or else he may prepare them for a sustained piece of fun, as in the passage to his sister-in-law beginning "I want very very much a little of your wit my dear sister" and ending as follows: "While you are hovering with your dinner in p[r]ospect you may do a thousand things—put a hedgehog into Georges hat—pour a little water into his rifle—soak his boots in a pail of water—cut his jacket round into shreds like a roman kilt or the back of my grandmothers stays—sow *off* his buttons" (II, 92–93). Since poetry-writing is the central subject of Keats's serious discussions, it also repeatedly becomes the butt of his wit. Thus he can ridicule his friend's exertions: "Brown has been walking up and down the room a breeding—now at this moment he is being delivered of a couplet—and I dare say will be as well as can be expected—Gracious—he has twins!" (II, 66). More often he deflates his own poetic efforts. After copying the "Ode to Psyche," the first poem with which, he claims, he has "taken even moderate pains," he appends the comment "Here endethe ye Ode to Psyche" (II, 105, 108). The lines "And there I shut her wild wild eyes / With kisses four" from "La Belle Dame sans Merci" receive the following commentary:

Why four kisses—you will say—why four because I wish to restrain the headlong impetuosity of my Muse—she would have fain said "score" without hurting the rhyme—but we must temper the Imagination as the Critics say with Judgment. I was obliged to choose an even number that both eyes might have fair play: and to speak truly I think two a piece quite sufficient— Suppose I had said seven; there would have been three and a half a piece—a very awkward affair—and well got out of on my side—(II, 97)

Frequently the same letter combines the trivial with the momentous: all the above quotations are taken from the long journal-letter to George and Georgiana which culminates in the famous "vale of Soul-making" passage (II, 102). We depend chiefly on the letters and on poems first appearing in the letters for Keats's humor, there being almost none in the three volumes of poetry published in his lifetime.

No proof from the letters is needed for Keats's gift of conveying sense impressions in memorable language, but it is interesting to note how the prose of Keats's letters reminds us of particular sensations immortalized in his greatest poetry. The earth-cooled wine of the second stanza of "Ode to a Nightingale" appears, in a letter to Fanny Keats written about the same time, as "a little claret-wine cool out of a cellar a mile deep" (II, 56). The poet whose "palate fine" tastes a bursting grape at the end of the "Ode on Melancholy" would

give Dilke (in a letter he never sent) an unashamedly luscious description of swallowing a nectarine: "It went down soft pulpy, slushy,
oozy—all its delicious embonpoint melted down my throat like a
beatified Strawberry" (II, 179). Keats's talent for observing and
delighting in nature and his power of drawing a reader into his
experience are exhibited in his first letter from the Lake District: the
spectacle of the Ambleside waterfall is a pleasure which Keats,
characteristically, invites his brother to "taste" (I, 300–301). Vi-
gnettes such as the description of the old woman Keats and Brown
met on their return from Belfast (I, 321–22) or the imaginary conversation involving Hunt, Gattie, Hazlitt, Mrs. Novello, and Ollier
(II, 14) gives us an idea of what Keats might have accomplished had
time permitted him to fulfill his "greatest ambition," his promised
"revolution in modern dramatic writing," with "a few fine Plays" (II,
139, 234).

Yet Keats is always aware that he is writing a letter, not a dissertation, a travelogue, or a dramatic sketch, and he never forgets his
correspondent. The tone of his letters to friends differs markedly
from the tone he adopts toward his sister or toward Fanny Brawne
and changes abruptly within the same letter to George and Georgiana whenever he turns directly to his sister-in-law. There are more
subtle nuances in his attitude to different friends. Keats's letters to
Reynolds and Bailey, for example, include some of his most profound
reflections on art and life side by side with lighthearted banter, and
one letter to Bailey, who at that time was completing his clerical
studies, even contains sexual slang (I, 175),[1] but nevertheless we
detect a slightly more respectful tone in Keats's approach to the
latter. He knows that the written word, no matter how intimate, can
never capture the familiarity of oral communication: "Writing has
this disadvan[ta]ge of speaking. One cannot write a wink, or a nod, or
a grin, or a purse of the Lips, or a smile—O law! One can-[not] put
ones finger to one's nose, or yerk ye in the ribs, or lay hold of your
button in writing" (II, 205). More than once Keats would like to know
what "humour" the recipient of his letter is in (I, 303, 324). He
sometimes tries to guess his correspondent's mood by giving his own
or to catch the intimacy of conversation by depicting the exact
physical circumstances under which he is writing, as when he says:
"the fire is at its last click—I am sitting with my back to it with one
foot rather askew upon the rug and the other with the heel a little
elevated from the carpet" and requests that his brother and sister-in-
law give him a similar description of themselves (II, 73).

Evidently Keats must attach some importance to his letters, since he asks his sister to preserve them (I, 156). He suggests to George and Georgiana by way of a jest that he might print them one day (I, 305); and when two years later in a letter to Fanny Brawne, to whom he usually writes in a very different vein, he makes a similar joking comment (II, 282), we wonder whether he may not have been half aware of the intrinsic value of his letters. Today we accept Eliot's judgment that they are "the most important ever written by any English poet." [2]

II Keats's Personality as Reflected in the Letters

The warm humanity and charm for which the poet was remembered by family and friends show through his letters. Keats reveals himself as a generous, genial, and courageous man whose self-confident ambition is balanced by a healthy awareness of his own foibles and tolerance toward those of his fellows. He exhibits profound attachment whenever he writes to his sister Fanny, to Tom, or to George and Georgiana, who has become a second sister to him. At times he becomes unabashedly tender, as when he writes to his brother and sister-in-law: "embrace each other—thank heaven for what happiness you have" (I, 391), and later: "Your wants will be a fresh spur to me," or: "I will not omit any exertion to benefit you by some means or other" (II, 185, 210), a promise he faithfully keeps when in January 1820, in dire financial straits himself, he helps to fill George's needs from the family inheritance. Feeling acutely his sister's confined life under the guardianship of the Abbeys and his own enforced separation from her (I, 202, 214, 343; II, 33, 60), he tries to cheer her up by regaling her with accounts of his work and travels or amuse her with rhymed reminiscences of his childhood (I, 154, 310–15). Even when he undertakes to coach her for her confirmation, he avoids a patronizing tone and signs himself "Your affectionate Parson John" (II, 49–51).

The letters to Fanny Brawne, on the other hand, are characterized by an uncontrollable passion and self-contradiction. Keats tears himself away from his beloved in order to work and blames her for being able to bear their separation. Possessiveness and jealousy alternate with self-sacrifice; recriminations are followed by declarations of love. After writing Fanny an "excessively unloverlike and ungallant," indeed a "flint-worded Letter," he ends with: "O my love, your lips are growing sweet again to my fancy—I must forget them" (II,

141–42); he has been afraid of her "being a little inclined to the Cressid" and adds in the same breath: "but that suspicion I dismiss utterly and remain happy in the surety of your Love" (II, 256). His accusations show how unfounded his jealousy is: she has gone to town alone, perhaps she has smiled in the company of others (II, 290, 304). After demanding "You must be mine to die upon the rack if I want you," he attempts to recant but immediately reverses himself once more: "No—my sweet Fanny—I am wrong. I do not want you to be unhappy—and yet I do" (II, 291). Keats is of course aware of these inconsistencies and of his role as a mad and jealous lover. But his real feelings toward Fanny Brawne may be more complex than he realizes. Keats's sincerity allows us a momentary glimpse into his heart that should give us pause: "I look not forward with any pleasure to what is call'd being settled in the world; I tremble at domestic cares—yet for you I would meet them" (II, 133). His apprehension that they "should what people call, *settle*—turn into a pond, a stagnant Lethe—a vile crescent, row or buildings" (II, 138) seems to mask an anxiety that their relationship might stifle his poetic growth.

Geniality, generosity, devotion, passion, ambition, altruism, tolerance, courage—these traits almost complete the personality reflected in Keats's letters. But perhaps what is most characteristic about the emerging portrait is a unique blend of tact and straightforwardness. There are different nuances of apology to Bailey (I, 292, 340) and Reynolds (I, 325). Imaginative wit or a simple joke camouflages Keats's embarrassment at being obliged to acknowledge or ask for a loan (I, 145–46, 147–48; II, 154–55). The poet's resourcefulness and sense of humor usually extricate him also from the awkwardness of confessing that he should have written earlier (I, 226, 240, 289; II, 134), though when the victim is Fanny Brawne he refuses to take lightly even a delay of only four days (II, 140). His repeated admission that he is lazy and does not like letter-writing (II, 37, 51, 219) is best explained by the confession that he "cannot force [his] letters in a hot bed" (I, 288).

The four surviving letters from the last voyage and sojourn in Italy while Keats was dying of consumption still retain this remarkable fusion of discretion and frank spontaneity, at the same time bringing home to us both his tragic fate and his fortitude in bearing it. "Land and Sea, weakness and decline are great seperators [*sic*], but death is the great divorcer for ever," Keats writes to Brown from aboard ship (II, 345). Perhaps the most poignant words ever written to Fanny Brawne are from the letter which Keats, too broken to write to his fiancée directly, addressed to her mother. Throughout the letter he has restrained his feelings, and only in the postscript he turns directly to his beloved with the words: "Good bye Fanny! god bless you" (II, 350). The last letter was to Brown and ends: "I can scarcely bid you good bye even in a letter. I always made an awkward bow. God bless you!" (II, 360). Ricks justly calls this last farewell "the least awkward bow ever made," one that "brings tears to the eyes." [3]

III *The Truth of Imagination*

For all their wit, charm, and poignancy, the letters are of most interest to us for what they tell us about Keats's speculations on art and life. The thought expressed in the letters constitutes a set of developing ideas rather than a closed philosophical system, but there is a remarkable consistency in his approach. Always open to new experience, Keats leaves room for doubt, self-questioning, and ambiguity. He easily submerges his own point of view and casts himself into the role of another. He is not narrowly and aggressively intellectual: knowledge is to be acquired not by means of abstract analysis but through the senses, the heart, the imagination. Thus his speculations often drift toward aesthetics. In the letter on "the truth of Imagination" written to Bailey on 22 November 1817 (I, 183–87),[4] he begins by trying to smoothe over a quarrel between Bailey and Haydon and explaining that even when insulted he would not break off a friendship. This exhibition of tolerance at the expense of "principle" reminds him "in passing" of the nature of "Men of Genius," who, unlike "Men of Power," "are great as certain ethereal Chemicals operating on the Mass of neutral intellect—[but] they have not any individuality, any determined Character," any "proper self." From the later definitions of "negative capability" and "the poetical Character" (I, 193–94, 386–87) it becomes clear that Keats is here thinking of the mind which, impartially open to all new impressions, acts imaginatively yet imperceptibly, and effects its changes like a catalyst without imposing its own characteristics and preferences—a disinterested mind which does not seek to dominate others through dogma or rules of conduct.

Bailey's "momentary start about the authenticity of the Imagination" provokes Keats into a famous declaration of faith:

I am certain of nothing but of the holiness of the Heart's affections and the truth of Imagination—What the imagination seizes as Beauty must be truth—whether it existed before or not—for I have the same Idea of all our Passions as of Love they are all in their sublime, creative of essential Beauty. (I, 184)

Robert Ryan has shown that Bailey's doubts concerned the efficacy of the imagination, as distinct from reason, in comprehending life after death, and that "affections" and "passions" are used synonymously with "desire" in theological writings of the time. This explanation certainly clarifies the letter's subsequent excursion into the "here after"; and Ryan argues persuasively that for Keats anything the heart desires and the imagination conceives on earth may be fulfilled in heaven.[5] But Keats's reply to Bailey that "What the imagination seizes as Beauty must be truth" is no less relevant to art than to religion. Perhaps Bailey's "momentary start" about the imagination inspired Keats's affirmation of the "truth of Imagination" and of the creativity of passions, and he gradually adopted this theory in purely aesthetic contexts; but more probably he was already "certain" about the part of imagination and passion in artistic creation, and Bailey's theological point prompted him to apply this insight "as auxiliary to another favorite Speculation" of his concerning life in the beyond.

Keats states his belief that whatever is beautiful is as real as a fact known to be true; indeed, as he cryptically tells us in "Ode on a Grecian Urn," "Beauty is truth" (although in the letter he does not go on to claim that truth is beauty). Whereas beauty is perceived and created by the harmonizing imagination fed by "the Heart's affections," truth is independently apprehended by the analytical intellect; yet Keats thinks of the products of imaginative endeavor as truth. In the letter "truth" simply appears to mean "reality." Keats implies that a work of art on paper, on canvas, or in stone, whether still in the artist's brain or recreated in the mind of the audience, is as real as a natural phenomenon whose existence is an undeniable "truth." The composition of a passage of *Endymion* becomes "a regular stepping of the Imagination towards a Truth" (I, 218). "What the imagination seizes as Beauty" is never a mere fantasy divorced from actuality.

Nevertheless the imagination transcends everyday reality because of its power to create something "whether it existed before or not." By perceiving an existent object as beautiful the imagination announces a truth, by creating beauty where there was none before it establishes a new truth, a new reality. The expression "whether it

existed before or not" also presupposes a rejection of the mimetic
theory of art. The only criterion for the imagination's creation of truth
is beauty, not the imitation of existing models: the Grecian Urn Keats
creates in his ode is real even if not based on the reality of a particular
vase. The imagination is self-fulfilling and thus "may be compared to
Adam's dream—he awoke and found it truth." In Book Eight of
Paradise Lost Adam's dream becomes reality with the creation of
Eve, who has not existed before outside the dream itself. Rejecting
the step-by-step argumentation of philosophical inquiry, Keats exclaims: "O for a Life of Sensations rather than of Thoughts!" In his
account of the influence of Hartley and association psychology, James
Ralston Caldwell has demonstrated that "what Keats means by a life
of sensation, is the life of the imagination, a life solidly grounded in
bygone events of eye, ear, palate, etc., but modifying, refining, and
ramifying them into infinitely complex chains of [associations]." [6]
Based on his own experience, the fruit of the poet's imagination must
be truth.

Next Keats speculates on how the life of sensations provides the
raw materials for happiness in the "here after," where "we shall enjoy
ourselves . . . by having what we called happiness on Earth repeated
in a finer tone and so repeated." The wider the range of our sensations on earth, the more scope the imagination acquires to produce in
the beyond a happiness which is a more refined version of the
terrestrial variety. But since imagination, though rooted in experience, is not confined to experience, it may bring into being a happiness in heaven only desired but never attained on earth, just as it can
create worldly beauty which did not exist before. Keats contrasts his
"delight in sensation" with Bailey's "hunger . . . after Truth," his
own "simple imaginative Mind," which is self-sufficient in enhancing
any experience or memory thereof, with Bailey's "complex Mind—
one that is imaginative and at the same time careful of its fruits—who
would exist partly on sensation partly on thought." Bailey's life of
thought demands that he "increase in knowledge and know all
things" as part of his prospect for "eternal Happiness." On the other
hand the mind that lives on sensation alone lets no thought of future
bliss interfere with the momentary sensation: "I look not for it
[happiness] if it be not in the present hour," Keats writes, "nothing
startles me beyond the Moment. The setting sun will always set me to
rights—or if a Sparrow come before my Window I take part in its
existence and pick about the Gravel." This last sensation beautifully

illustrates Keats's power of empathy, of participating in the life of another being. It is the sympathetic imagination that allows him to project his feeling into the sparrow.

IV   Negative Capability

In his letter to Bailey Keats gives an early description of that tolerant, self-effacing, sympathetic, and imaginative attitude—that denial of the ego which modern criticism associates with "negative capability," [7] the term Keats coined a month later. At the same time, however, his own procedure illustrates the negatively capable approach. A man of imagination, who has no "determined Character," no "proper self," looks into the heart of a friend in order to forgive, and so completely forgets himself as to participate in the life of a sparrow before his window. Although the letter is obviously an attempt to reason, an argument answering Bailey, it substitutes what we call imaginative insight or a series of intuitive flashes for a chain of reasoning in which one point develops logically from the previous one, for what Keats calls "consequitive reasoning," of which he writes as follows: "I have never yet been able to perceive how any thing can be known for truth by consequitive reasoning—and yet it must be—Can it be that even the greatest Philosopher ever arrived at his goal without putting aside numerous objections." At this point Keats ironically tries to reason while questioning the soundness of the reasoning process and abandons this process while defending it. After admitting that he does not understand consecutive reasoning he postulates its validity: ". . . and yet it must be." This reversal is a blind assertion or an imaginative leap—it is not logical reasoning. Having questioned, then asserted consecutive reasoning as a valid method, Keats questions it once more and leaves the matter open ("However it may be"), but goes on to reject a life of "Thoughts" for himself. The incongruity, however, of invoking the nonrational faculty against consecutive reasoning in order to save the latter is more apparent than real. As a disputant in an intellectual argument with his friend Keats confesses his logical inconsistency; but his method of intuiting a conclusion contrary to his own analysis, by revealing his aversion to logical reasoning, reinforces his faith in "the Heart's affections and the truth of Imagination." Since he is "certain of nothing" but these two, or, as he says elsewhere, "never can feel certain of any truth but from a clear perception of its Beauty" (II, 19), he concedes immense latitude in philosophical inquiry and debate.

By emphasizing his own undecidedness and inconsistency, by acknowledging the powers of consecutive reasoning while claiming that he does not know how they work, and by accepting Bailey's rational approach which his own doubts undermine Keats gives proof of that tolerance which in this letter he calls "Humility and capability for submission" and later the capability "of being in uncertainties, Mysteries, doubts."

The formulation of this quality as "negative capability" occurs in the letter to George and Tom of 21 December 1817:

> . . . at once it struck me, what quality went to form a Man of Achievement especially in Literature & which Shakespeare posessed so enormously—I mean *Negative Capability*, that is when man is capable of being in uncertainties, Mysteries, doubts, without any irritable reaching after fact & reason—Coleridge, for instance, would let go by a fine isolated verisimilitude caught from the Penetralium of mystery, from being incapable of remaining content with half knowledge. This pursued through Volumes would perhaps take us no further than this, that with a great poet the sense of Beauty overcomes every other consideration, or rather obliterates all consideration. (I, 193–94)

Only the imaginative mind has negative capability. The acceptance of uncertainty and doubt merely implies recognition of an opponent's point of view, but the word "Mysteries" suggests, in addition, a state different from ordinary experience: it has associations with a higher mode of existence, with divine revelation, with what is shut to reason though accessible to the imagination. Keats condemns the quest for certainty as "irritable" because it encourages dogmatism and because ultimately it is doomed to failure. Since "fact & reason" can only take us up to a point and no further, we should be capable "of remaining content with half knowledge." By "a fine isolated verisimilitude" Keats seems to mean an imaginative insight or discovery as distinct from a conclusion reached by consecutive reasoning. The consecutive person is less interested in verisimilitudes than in proven facts, which present themselves not in isolation but in relation to other facts. Seeing all phenomena in their logical interrelationships, he will always attempt to verify his discovery, even one intuitively seized, and abandon it in his futile effort to fit everything into a perfect whole. The negatively capable person, on the other hand, accepts "a fine isolated verisimilitude" independently, without forcing it into a system by trying to answer all the questions it may raise. The great poet comes closest to negative capability, because his only criterion of truth is beauty and not, for example, logic or science which keeps "reaching after fact & reason." The last sentence of the passage, with its refusal to pursue the argument further by consecutive reasoning, with the carefully qualifying "perhaps," and with its appeal to an indeterminate "sense of Beauty," provides another example of the negatively capable attitude which Keats already exhibited in the letter to Bailey and which he is now defining; and yet he cannot be quite unaware of the irony of expressing his faith in the supremacy of beauty in a tone of certainty so incompatible with the spirit of negative capability which he is here trying to convey to George and Tom.

How "the sense of Beauty overcomes every other consideration" Keats illustrates earlier in the same letter where he establishes the criterion of intensity. He is commenting on Benjamin West's painting *Death on the Pale Horse* and apparently contrasting it with the same painter's *King Lear*:[8]

It is a wonderful picture, when West's age is considered; But there is nothing to be intense upon; no women one feels mad to kiss; no face swelling into reality. the excellence of every Art is its intensity, capable of making all disagreeables evaporate, from their being in close relationship with Beauty & Truth—Examine King Lear & you will find this examplified throughout; but in this picture we have unpleasantness without any momentous depth of speculation excited, in which to bury its repulsiveness—(I, 192)

As in the letter to Bailey, consecutive reasoning becomes irrelevant when imagination apprehends truth in terms of beauty; only in the earlier letter the focus was on creation and here it is on the effect of a work of art. To Bailey Keats wrote that passion is "creative of essential Beauty" and now he indicates how a beautiful painting or play arouses passion: through intensity. As Bate has shown, Keats's theories of imagination and negative capability were influenced by William Hazlitt, and the concept "intensity" by Hazlitt's expression "gusto" (although the similarity between the last two terms has been exaggerated).[9] For Keats the beauty in a work of art (its truth imaginatively conceived) harmonizes all discordant qualities by means of a process of concentration and refinement compelling us to submit to its full sensuous impact, which excites our imagination, and the imagination in turn causes sensations which enhance, enrich, and intensify experience. The expression "no women one feels mad to kiss" may refer to the female figures in *Death on the Pale Horse*, but Keats probably also means that a painting like West's *King Lear* (in which there are no women), unlike his less intense *Death on the Pale Horse*, arouses a feeling as overpowering as sexual passion. The expression "swelling into reality" may suggest that in a great painting a face seems to be taking on a third dimension. But for Keats the word "swelling," repeatedly associated with ripening (as in *Endymion*, I.836, II.59, III.799, and "To Autumn," 7), has undertones of fulfillment. The "reality" is that of the actual world of natural process, where flowers and human faces bloom and fade, but where they are alive. In a great work painted or sculptured objects like the dead and frozen figures on a Grecian urn *seem* to come to life under art's intensity.

While art enriches our experience by capturing reality in its most pregnant moments, it also creates a different reality, which transcends everyday actuality. By means of a process analogous to distillation in chemistry,[10] but imaginative and therefore ultimately inexplicable in terms of consecutive reasoning, an audience somehow experiences as pleasurable what would be painful in real life. Thus the work of art bypasses the problem of evil; or, more precisely, though it depicts evil, it refuses to treat evil as an issue, since "the sense of Beauty overcomes every other consideration."

Keats again and again invokes the patient, open, and imaginative approach of negative capability. Mental growth, like physical maturation, cannot be forced: in poetry, as in nature, everything will come to fruition in its own good time. If the "ripening of the intellectual powers" is gradual, all the better "for the purposes of great productions" (I, 214). It is one of Keats's axioms "That if poetry comes not as naturally as the Leaves to a tree it had better not come at all" (I, 238–39). In a letter to Reynolds of 19 February 1818 Keats suggests that once "a certain ripeness in intellect" has been attained, the mind's play upon "Poesy or distilled Prose" becomes a "delicious diligent Indolence," rather like the flower's receptivity than the honey-bee's impatient buzzing in pursuit of goals. Such freedom and openness to new impressions imply a tolerance toward the speculation of others and an eventual meeting between minds that have set out "in contrary directions" (I, 231–32).

In allowing things to come of themselves without irritably striving after them, the mood of diligent indolence is reminiscent of the "wise passiveness" of Wordsworth's 1798 poem "Expostulation and Reply."[11] Keats admires Wordsworth but condemns the latter's didactic manner:

. . . are we to be buillied into a certain Philosophy engendered in the whims of an Egotist. . . . We hate poetry that has a palpable design upon us. . . .

How beautiful are the retired flowers! how would they lose their beauty were
they to throng into the highway crying out, "admire me I am a violet! . . . (I,
223–24) [12]

Since Wordsworth feels he has "to put down his halfseeing" (I, 224) as
if it were an absolute rule to be followed, he apparently lacks Keats's
capability of remaining in uncertainty and of accepting his own ideas
as no more than half-knowledge; otherwise it would be all the more
presumptuous on his part trying to dictate them to others. Even in
"Expostulation and Reply," where he pleads for a wisely passive
attitude to nature, Wordsworth sounds quite certain about what he
advocates. Keats is less sure of himself; at least he does not tend to
impose his judgments as certainties to be dictated to others. After his
praise of indolence, receptivity, and intellectual tolerance, and after
writing a poem on the potential creativity of indolence ("O thou
whose face"), he concludes: "Now I am sensible all this is a mere
sophistication, however it may neighbour to any truths, to excuse my
own indolence. . . . It is [no] matter whether I am right or wrong
either one way or another . . ." (I, 233). Here he quite openly adopts
a negatively capable attitude toward his own theory of negative
capability. His philosophical noncommitment seems to know no
bounds. It is not surprising that he is self-effacing on the question of
religion in a letter to the future parson Bailey, but he can even
become "so very sceptical as to think Poetry itself a mere Jack a
lanthern to amuse whoever may chance to be struck with its brilliance." The discussion which follows contains affirmations as well as
skepticism, [13] but both are equally disowned by one more expression
of negative capability: "I have not one Idea of the truth of any of my
speculations—I shall never be a Reasoner because I care not to be in
the right . . ." (I, 242–43). Keats presses the acceptance of doubt to
the point of negating his opinions, leaving himself in uncertainty
about uncertainty.

In a letter to Woodhouse of 27 October 1818 this withholding of
final judgment has evolved into a denial of the poet's self-hood. Keats
is clarifying the earlier distinction between Wordsworth's writings,
which have the ulterior motive of drawing attention to the author and
his ideas, and "unobtrusive" poetry, "which enters into one's soul
and does not startle it or amaze it with itself but with its subject" (I,
224), that is, which has no purpose beyond itself. Now acknowledging the older poet's unique sublimity, Keats contrasts Wordsworth's
imposition of his identity upon readers with his own goal of what

elsewhere he calls "annulling self" (I, 323) by living in the subject described and thus bringing out its poetic nature:

> As to the poetical Character itself . . . the camelion Poet . . . is the most unpoetical of any thing in existence; because he has no Identity—he is continually in for—and filling some other Body—The Sun, the Moon, the Sea and Men and Women who are creatures of impulse are poetical and have about them an unchangeable attribute—the poet has none; no identity. . . .
> (I, 386–87)

The non-Wordsworthian poet resembles the chameleon, because he changes his identity with the subject he imagines or describes so that he is left with no identity of his own. But Keats ends the letter by asserting his self as appreciative friend and correspondent. He is usually aware of the irony and paradox involved in his negatively capable attitude: the relativism inherent in his insistence on uncertainty countered by his absolute faith in the truth of imagination and a poet's sense of beauty, his attack on consecutive reasoning by means of consecutive reasoning and his intuitive defense of it, the suggestion that his wise passiveness may be an excuse for laziness, his skepticism about skepticism, and now the necessity of emphasizing his identity as the grateful John Keats writing to the generous Richard Woodhouse even while insisting that he has no identity.

V *The Burden of the Mystery*

A basic paradox lies in Keats's insistence that for the great poet the sense of beauty overcomes all other considerations and his growing conviction that a life of sensations without thought is not enough if a poet is to become great. His assiduous quest for knowledge and philosophy (I, 271, 274; II, 116) jeopardizes his wise passiveness and seems more in line with the busy bee than the receptive flower. An individual no longer allows his mind to ripen naturally when he pursues knowledge into "the terra semi incognita of things unearthly; and cannot for his Life, keep in the check rein" (I, 255). Keats recognizes the irony of "reading Voltaire and Gibbon, although [he] wrote to Reynolds the other day to prove reading of no use" (I, 237). In his letter to Reynolds of 3 May 1818 he substitutes for the sensation-thought dichotomy of 1817 a "difference of high Sensation with and without knowledge," and clearly opts for the active acquisition of "extensive knowledge" (I, 277).

Later in the same letter occurs the famous parable of life as a "Mansion of Many Apartments." We first step into an "infant or thoughtless Chamber," and then, with "the awakening of the thinking principle," enter a "Chamber of Maiden-Thought." When we find "that the World is full of Misery and Heartbreak, Pain, Sickness and oppression," the second chamber "becomes gradually darken'd," a state in which "We see not the ballance of good and evil" and "feel the 'burden of the Mystery.' " Keats intends to follow Wordsworth in exploring the dark passages leading out of the second chamber (I, 280–81). The phrase "burden of the Mystery" refers, as in its source in "Tintern Abbey," to "the heavy and the weary weight / Of all this unintelligible world" (38–40). A negatively capable person should accept mystery without experiencing it as an oppressive weight. So long as Keats relied for certainties solely on the imagination, was content to be passive, allowed his intellect to ripen gradually, and accepted what he learnt as half-knowledge, he did not feel the need to explore mystery. The active pursuit of knowledge has made mystery into a burden, and, ironically, knowledge in various fields is now required to ease this burden (I, 277).

But the negatively capable attitude has been reaffirmed from another direction: in the feeling of uncertainty about all traditional moral values. Keats relates the burden of the mystery specifically to the moral chaos of a universe in which we can no longer see "the ballance of good and evil." The poet was always haunted by the idea of innocent suffering, exemplified for him in the suffering of women (I, 209, 292), and he recognized the inevitability of "Heart-vexations": "a man should have the fine point of his soul taken off to become fit for this world" (I, 188). In the negative capability letter Keats saw the sense of beauty overcoming all considerations of evil, mere disagreeables which evaporated in art's intensity, so that a poet's moral values became irrelevant to his work. Speculating further on Wordsworth's poetry, which he earlier condemned for its imposition of ideas, Keats now realizes that the sense of beauty need not obliterate consideration of "Misery and Heartbreak, Pain, Sickness and oppression." The evil of the amoral universe which we behold in the darkened Chamber of Maiden-Thought cannot simply be burned away by the poet's intense torch: it still weighs down upon him, and he admits his failure to cope with it. It is for this reason that Keats eventually bestows the highest rank upon "the human friend Philosopher" (II, 139).

VI *Soul-Making*

On 19 March 1819, near the middle of his long journal-letter to George and Georgiana, Keats tries to come to terms with the problem of evil by relating it once more to the aesthetic experience. Distinguishing now sharply between the moral detachment of aesthetic contemplation and the moral involvement of his philosophical inquiry, he places philosophical truth above the beauty of poetry. The starting point of his speculation is his own reaction to the misfortune of his friend Haslam. Keats's realization of how far he is "from any humble standard of disinterestedness" leads him to reflect that most people tend to act with the same purposive, instinctive self-interest as a hawk, a lion (or, for that matter, a robin) pursuing its prey. Instinctive, spontaneous, energetic conduct is beautiful even when morally reprehensible: "Though a quarrel in the streets is a thing to be hated, the energies displayed in it are fine; the commonest Man shows a grace in his quarrel." An action may be unjust yet entertaining, and an idea may be false yet amusing. Just as we derive pleasure from animal destructiveness or a street fight, so "a superior being" observing our mental activity may be amused by our reasoning though erroneous (II, 79–80). Such an attitude toward suffering and error in real life resembles the moral detachment with which we view a work of art. The philosopher within Keats hates the quarrel whereas the poet in him admires the energies displayed in it. As Keats wrote to Woodhouse six months earlier. "What shocks the virtuous philosop[h]er, delights the camelion Poet" (I, 387). Now Keats judges poetry, with its evasion of the moral aspect of an action and its refusal to distinguish between truth and error, to be "not so fine a thing as philosophy—For the same reason that an eagle is not so fine a thing as a truth" (II, 81). Yet the poet's amoral approach has its moral value: evil is an intrinsic part of the universe, and an appreciation of the beauty of instinctive life even in scenes of wrong and misery may help to reconcile us to the inevitable.

A month later Keats returns to the ineluctability of suffering: mortality would become unbearable if society were to improve till mankind achieved extreme happiness. "But in truth I do not at all believe in this sort of perfectibility," Keats confesses. Instead he proposes the perfectibility of the individual personality or what he calls the "soul" (taking immortality for granted for the purpose of his argument). Substituting the phrase "vale of Soul-making" for the traditional "vale of tears," Keats compares the world to a school, the intelligence or mind to an illiterate child learning to read, the heart to a hornbook or children's reading primer, and the soul to the child who has learned to read. Just as children learn to read at school from a hornbook, so intelligences, "sparks of the divinity," become souls when "they acquire identities . . . by the medium of a world like this" and through the agency of the human heart (II, 101–102). Thus suffering becomes an indispensable part of personality development or the soul-making process:

Do you not see how necessary a World of Pains and troubles is to school an Intelligence and make it a soul? A Place where the heart must feel and suffer in a thousand diverse ways! Not merely is the Heart a Hornbook, It is the Minds Bible, it is the Minds experience, it is the teat from which the Mind or intelligence sucks its identity—(II, 102–103)

"Intelligence" (for Keats the equivalent of "mind") and heart cooperate in soul-making.

Keats always felt that whatever is grasped intellectually must be submitted to emotional experience, but in the famous letter to Bailey of November 1817 he sees intelligence and heart in two opposing categories making conflicting demands upon him: on one side thought and consecutive reasoning and on the other sensation and the heart's affections which feed the imagination. In that letter he chooses sensation over thought and is certain of the heart's affections and the truth of imagination but puzzled about consecutive reasoning. He is, however, already aware of the paradox of rejecting consecutive reasoning by his own reasoning and acknowledges the compromise of Bailey's "complex Mind" which "would exist partly on sensation partly on thought" (I, 186). Philosophy is never merely abstract thought for a poet who judges everything "by larger experience," for whom philosophical axioms must be "proved upon our pulses" (I, 279), and who only a month earlier, immediately after ranking philosophy above poetry, writes that "Nothing ever becomes real till it is experienced" (II, 81). In the soul-making process the rival demands of heart and mind are fully reconciled. The mind or intelligence is essential as the embryo of the soul, and the heart, as Bible or nourisher of the mind, retains the importance it had in 1817. Intelligence depends on the heart to mediate experience; and as the intelligence proceeds to interpret this experience it acquires an identity.

This description of "identity" or the "identical soul" does not contradict Keats's earlier assertions that men of genius have no individuality and that the poet has no identity. Keats uses "identity" in two very distinct senses. In the letters to Bailey and Woodhouse identity is something fixed, a "determined Character" or "an unchangeable attribute," so that the poet has no identity because he temporarily takes on the qualities of each of his created characters by living in them for the moment (I, 184, 387). In soul-making, on the other hand, identity is formed in an ongoing process involving continual "provings and alterations and perfectionings" (II, 103). In this profounder sense identity is not a self-contained "unchangeable attribute," but the personality as it constantly transforms itself in the light of experience. It takes "a series of years" of adult life to form a character and create a sense of identity (II, 102; I, 392). This identity or soul is the total of the collaboration between heart and mind in their reactions to "a world of Circumstances" (II, 104), but it need never reach a final form: it is subject to development so long as the heart can suffer and the mind apprehend.

This difference between fixed and evolving identity is clarified in Keats's statement that his friend Dilke "cannot feel he has a personal identity unless he has made up his Mind about every thing." The incessantly unfolding personality emerging from the soul-making process does not depend on a consistent or clearly defined set of opinions for its sense of identity. Dilke, however, feels that he must take a stand on every question, so that other people and he himself may know once and for all who and what he is. His identity is fixed because defined by his intellectual positions, and there is little readiness on his part to submit these to the test of the heart in order to modify them. Dilke lacks negative capability: he cannot bear the uncertainty which results from the self-obliteration involved in casting himself into another's role and taking another's point of view. "The only means of strengthening one's intellect," Keats continues, "is to make up ones mind about nothing—to let the mind be a thoroughfare for all thoughts. Not a select party" (II, 213).

The doctrine of soul-making is therefore not a repudiation of negative capability as has sometimes been suggested,[14] but rather a reaffirmation of it. One could of course argue that Keats advances his conjectures with an air of conviction incompatible with the negatively capable attitude, for although at one point he describes his theory as a mere "faint sketch" (II, 103), he is less tentative in his manner than he was a month before when he admitted that he was "straining at particles of light in the midst of a great darkness" (II, 80). But he writes in a no less decisive tone about the truth of imagination and—we have seen that he was aware of the paradox—about negative capability itself. Negative capability is incompatible with the man of power's "proper self," with the irritable search for finalities by consecutive reasoning, with a didactic "egotistical sublime" (I, 387), and with the self-assertiveness of the made-up mind; it undermines the fixed identity but leaves the door open for the freely developing personality. In the vale of soul-making the intelligence abides in perpetual uncertainty awaiting instructions from its mentor, the heart. With negative capability intelligences never lapse into rigidity but remain open to new impressions, continually adjusting their positions "till they acquire identities, till each one is personally itself," till each one is a soul (II, 102).

Negative capability is the Shakespearean quality to which Keats aspires throughout his creative life. David Luke is right in pointing out that Keats does not really consider this quality "a negative condition," adding appropriately that it is "a state neither of ignorance nor of paralysis." [15] Negative capability frees a thinking man from the weary weight of the unintelligible world by raising mystery to the province of the imagination, and it permits a poet to submerge his identity in that of others whenever he composes or meditates on poetry. Keats's repeated suppressions of self in his works reinforce a native susceptibility to new experience and a capacity for growth; whereas, in turn, his evolving soul is the best guarantee for his talent to forget his own self in the subject of a new poem. On returning to actuality and selfhood he does not bask in any final certainty: neither as poet nor as man has Keats a fixed identity. He cannot afford one if he wants to remain creative.

CHAPTER 3

Unexplored Isles: Poems (1817)

I Apprenticeship

ALTHOUGH there is absolute agreement among critics that the volume of 1817 is inferior to the one published in 1820, less consensus is reached on the quality of the individual poems in the earlier collection. Granted, most critics admire the sonnets "On the Grasshopper and Cricket," "Keen, fitful gusts" and, in particular, "On First Looking into Chapman's Homer," as well as a number of passages from "I stood tip-toe" and "Sleep and Poetry," whereas few readers see much good in such occasional verse as "To Some Ladies" and "On Receiving a Curious Shell, and a Copy of Verses, from the Same Ladies," which Keats wrote in the summer of 1815 and felt were fit to include in the volume of 1817. But a number of poems, for instance the epistle "To George Felton Mathew" and the sonnet "On Leaving Some Friends at an Early Hour" ("Give me a golden pen . . ."), have been praised by some critics and condemned by others. John Middleton Murry describes the poetry in the epistle as "crude and naive, but spontaneous in feeling and unashamed in phrase," an estimate in which he includes even the extravagant couplet "Some flowery spot, sequester'd, wild, romantic, / That often must have seen a poet frantic" (37–38), which Douglas Bush (understandably) pronounces "execrable." [1] We are surprised to find Garrod including "Give me a golden pen" among the best of the early sonnets and Murry admiring its "ecstasy" and "splendid utterance," while the adverse judgment of Graham Hough ("concentrated vulgarity") may be exaggerated but not quite undeserved. [2] Yet with all the weaknesses (which critics tend to overemphasize and which Keats himself was one of the first to notice), beauties are scattered throughout the early work.

Keats's apprenticeship to poetry begins with "Imitation of Spenser," probably written in early 1814, in which, unlike Spenser in his "Bower of Bliss," he does not present his voluptuously reclining

figure (18) amidst a luxurious landscape with moral disapproval. In
1816, having fallen under the spell of Hunt's newly published *Story
of Rimini* (though he has not yet met Hunt in the flesh), Keats still
adheres to the Spenserian model in his "Specimen of an Induction to
a Poem," and the fragment "Calidore," both of which give evidence
of his early fascination with the medieval. Although the latter's
concluding passage contains the imagery of "Ode to a Nightingale" in
embryonic form (breeze, forest, nightingale, bower, incense, flower,
moon), the manner in which these images are presented is not
characteristic of the later Keats:

> Softly the breezes from the forest came,
> Softly they blew aside the taper's flame;
> Clear was the song from Philomel's far bower;
> Grateful the incense from the lime-tree flower;
> Mysterious, wild, the far heard tumpet's tone;
> Lovely the moon in ether, all alone:
> Sweet too the converse of these happy mortals,
> As that of busy spirits when the portals
> Are closing in the west; or that soft humming
> We hear around when Hesperus is coming.
> Sweet be their sleep.

These neatly listed, relatively conventional pictures lack the intensity, the incremental force and tumult, the closeness of texture en-
veloping the central symbols of the great odes. However notable this
passage might be as a subdued overture to adventure, the reader of
Keats expects his senses to be intoxicated by synaesthesia, his mind
challenged by ambiguity and oxymoron. These lines, which follow
the last event narrated—Calidore's spontaneous kiss of the hands of
two languorous ladies—decorate the story rather than propel it forward: it looks as if Keats did not know how to go on. The "green
leaves" which "The sweet-lipp'd ladies have already greeted" (135–
36) are purely ornamental. It would be absurd to suggest that these
descriptions are symptomatic of a Wordsworthian interchange between man and nature.

Nature is more alive in a sonnet of October or November 1816
describing the poet's walk home after a friendly literary evening at
Leigh Hunt's Hampstead cottage and beginning:

> Keen, fitful gusts are whisp'ring here and there
> Among the bushes half leafless, and dry;

> The stars look very cold about the sky,
> And I have many miles on foot to fare.

The fitful gusts are heard in the sibilants and the jolting rhythm of the first two lines, the homeward trudge in the alliteration of the fourth ("many miles on foot to fare"). In the sonnet's second quatrain the cold stars have become "silver lamps that burn on high" and serve as transition to the sestet with its warmth of "friendliness" and literary enthusiasm which the poet carries home within himself. Although Keats animates the nocturnal landscape and even kindles the stars, as it were, with his own fire, nature affects him but little in return: there is no Wordsworthian reciprocation between the two. Nevertheless this sonnet conveys a far more vital relationship between man and nature than, for example, "Calidore," in which the attempt at humanizing the landscape by letting the characters "greet" it is forced and artificial.

In the sonnet "On the Grasshopper and Cricket" (30 December 1816) Keats participates more completely in the life of the various phenomena perceived which together constitute "The poetry of earth." This poetry is heard in nature's voices throughout the year, in birds' and the grasshopper's song in summer and the cricket's in winter. Keats has previously associated the sounds of nature with poetry, in "The dying tones that fill the air" (45) of the "Ode to Apollo," for example, and more explicitly in "How many bards gild the lapses of time" when comparing the "pleasing chime" of poets with the "unnumber'd sounds" heard at evening out of doors. But the poetry of nature is not confined to her melodies. Sounds are supplemented not only by sights but also by organic, motor, thermal, and tactile sense impressions.[3] The predominance of nonvisual over visual imagery creates a unique impact, which is reinforced by the synaesthetic power of the synecdoche "a voice will run / From hedge to hedge," the "warmth" emanating from the cricket's song, and "the frost / Has wrought a silence," an expression over which Hunt grew ecstatic with some justification.[4] This interrelation of the senses suggests a unity in nature more profound than the harmony of music. There is no void in this perfectly ordered universe: the songs of grasshopper and cricket compensate for the loss of sounds silenced by summer heat and winter frost, and for each other's absence, thus creating a mutual balance, skillfully conveyed by the sonnet's structure. Keats's admiration for nature's perfect processes, and in particular for a seasonal cycle in which summer makes amends for winter and vice versa, foreshadows the later, more magnificent expressions of his acceptance of growth and decay, fulfillment and death culminating, at the end of his poetic career, in the ode "To Autumn."

The sonnet "On First Looking into Chapman's Homer" (October 1816) was already singled out for praise by the poet's contemporaries. Keats here evokes the sense of revelation we experience in the presence of any great work of art, but underlying this awe is a half-conscious pride at the discovery of his own poetic potential. Despite the sharp break in tone between octave and sestet, between patient exploration and the wonder of discovery, the basic voyage metaphor is sustained throughout. The "wide expanse" of the octave fuses the ocean, a part of Homer's "demesne," with the air above it, the bright, clear, and serene sky (a fusion reinforced by rhyme and the assonance of the long "e" sound) just as the "realms of gold" link earthly adventures with the bright rays of Apollo. With the "watcher of the skies" Keats moves imperceptibly from ship's pilot to astronomer while a planet "swims" into the field of his vision. The sea-voyage is now expanded into a quest through the entire universe to include whatever enters the discoverer's "ken," whatever pushes back the frontiers of knowledge. The excitement of discovery gathers momentum in the enjambments of the sestet until the poem is suddenly slowed down in the last line. Pauses are forced by the dash after "surmise" and the comma after the trochaic "Silent"; emphasis is added by the repeated "s" and the melody of the long "i" in the three consecutive words, twice in the combination "il"; and the sonnet comes to rest firmly "upon a peak in Darien." The calm self-confidence of Cortez, the conqueror of Mexico, staring at the sea "with eagle eyes" contrasts with the agitation of his men eagerly anticipating his fateful reply to their unasked questions. (Keats may have been impressed by a portrait of Cortez, but the substitution for Balboa, the discoverer of Panama, is justified because the name of Cortez conjures up gold and he rediscovered a continent as Keats rediscovers Homer.) The poet suddenly suspends the action as if, filming the scene and approaching for a climactic close-up, he had frozen the camera movement into a still picture, but one "swelling into reality" (*Letters*, I, 192), impatient to come to life again the next moment.

Having earlier read Pope's translation, with the discovery of the Chapman volume Keats has reached "a peak" which allows him to breathe Homer's serene air in all its purity. But the view of the boundless ocean unfolds infinite possibilities for discovering Homer's inexhaustible treasures, which explorers can only surmise. Cowden Clarke's record of the enthusiasm which accompanied Keats's immediate recognition of the poem's success (*Keats Circle*, II, 148) suggests that the poet may have sensed the achievement to be sufficient proof that one day he would be "among the English Poets" (*Letters*, I, 394). Thus the discoveries still to be made, which the present discovery makes possible but which lie as yet hidden in the endless expanse of the Pacific, are Keats's future poems. The climactic final arrest of motion in an archetypal seaward gaze reflects the balance between the attained and the yet-to-be-attained, between fulfillment and infinite aspiration. The sonnet's tone of bold, firm, and unhesitating self-confidence culminating in triumphant certitude precludes all speculation upon a possible threat from the unfathomable world symbolized by the Pacific Ocean, as there is in "the foam / Of perilous seas, in faery lands forlorn" in "Ode to a Nightingale" (69–70). As yet no ambiguity attaches to the artist: his imagination is no "deceiving elf," his art no "demon," his creation no "Cold Pastoral." [5] In the middle stanza of "To Autumn" motion is suspended at the moment of supreme beauty, ripeness, and fulfillment before the reaper's hook cuts down the next swath of grain and flowers, but only for an instant, till flux sets in again, and the film, moving once more, shows the migrating swallows flying over the harvested stubble plains. Since "Chapman's Homer" ends with an image of arrested motion, the slide remains projected on the screen. The picture perpetuates the poet's moment of triumph.

II *The Inspiration of Nature: "I Stood Tip-toe"*

Several concepts of Keats's poetic maturity are adumbrated also in "I stood tip-toe upon a little hill" (completed December 1816), the poem opening the 1817 volume, but the dominant theme is nature's inspiration of poets. Keats refers to this titleless poem as "Endymion" before beginning his romance on the same subject (*Letters*, I, 121). Following Wordsworth's example in the fourth book of *The Excursion*, he offers his conjectures on the origin of myths, elaborates on the story of Cynthia and Endymion, and speculates upon the healing effect of their love. The observation of natural phenomena is accurate and at the same time colored by the poet's imagination. Marjorie Norris rightly points out that with the inversion of the perspective caused by the reflection of the brook the clouds are seen lying "*On the blue fields of heaven*" (10),[6] but Keats's technique depends more

on empathy than on perspective: he does not so much display his
ability to look at things from different angles as to be them. After the
first line Keats is no longer standing tip-toe on a hill, but, as his
imagination begins to take over from his eye, he is inside the buds,
and then in the clouds. It is less important whether these clouds are
above or below him than that they have become newly shorn and
washed sheep with whose freshness the poet identifies, just as a
moment later he becomes one of the May flowers with roots "Moist,
cool and green" (33), that is, refreshed and revived. Keats participates both in the life of a landscape actually observed and in that of
objects seen only with the mind's eye. To describe what is beyond his
view he has to "picture out" (19) and "Guess" (22) or create his scenes:
"*let* long grass grow" (32), "*there* too *should be* . . . tree, . . . spring-
head . . . blue bells" (37–43). Most of the sights which make up
Keat's "posey / Of luxuries" (27–28) are defined by the line from
Hunt's *Story of Rimini* (1816) which serves as the poem's epigraph:
"Places of nestling green for Poets made," the bowers conducive to
poetic meditation. In "I stood tip-toe" refuge is offered "by the
bowery clefts, and leafy shelves" (21), in a "tasteful nook" overswept
by "a lush laburnum" (30–31), and even in the "bowery green" (84) of
a streamlet (for the "jaunty" streams in line 22 Keats had earlier
written "nestling" and for "refresh" "embower"). These retreats are
the poet's earthly sanctuaries.

How earth will no longer satisfy the poet's ceaseless aspirations is
here only hinted at in some of the images. Like the winged sweet
peas, Keats, though standing on the ground, is poised, as it were, "on
tip-toe for a flight" (57) into another world, so that finally his "wan-
d'ring spirit" must be checked from soaring too far (242). His yearning for a vision into the beyond always tends to blind him to his
human limitations, so that he says of the creator of the Endymion
myth: "Ah! surely he had burst our mortal bars" (190), an assumption
true only in the sense that imagination knows no bounds, for literally
he expresses a wish ("surely") rather than a fact. When, soothed by
the magic of poetry, "we feel uplifted from the world / Walking upon
the white clouds wreath'd and curl'd" (139–40), it is of course the
clouds that are "wreath'd and curl'd," but syntactically these two
participles may also belong to the antecedent "we." The wreathing
fits the ornamental shelter offered by several of the bowers described
earlier in the poem, while curling up like a foetus in self-protection or
concealment within the bower is a favorite Keatsian posture. The
syntactical ambiguity may conjure up a wreathed, curled up, cloud-

embowered poet, an image anticipating Keats's reluctance to abandon his womblike earthly sanctuary even as, paradoxically, he longs to detach himself from mother earth by seeking a higher order of reality.

In "I stood tip-toe" Keats remains bound to nature despite tentative and sporadic movements into another world. The first half of the poem is characterized throughout by a rich naturalistic sensuousness, not excluding the Apollo and Diana passages (47–56, 116–24); and the second half tells how even the immortals owe their immortality in verse to a poet's sensitive response to nature. The creators of Pan and of Narcissus stumbled upon their stories as they peeped through the boughs of a natural arbor (151, 166). The inventor of the Endymion legend drew his "Shapes from the invisible world" from the more airy bowers of "flowery nests" and the stars' "pillowy silkiness" (186–89) which, for all their distance and seeming abstraction, are actual natural objects. Standing indeed high "on Latmus' top" he still had his feet firmly planted on the ground, and though he wept over the piteous fate and desolate beauty of a goddess, it was the real moon that inspired him (193–204). Nature gives birth to myth and myth to poetry.

Although this poem is about nature's inspiration of poets, Keats has as yet hardly touched upon his favorite analogy, that between artistic composition and the ripening harvest, in the dual function of Apollo as god of poetry who strings harps and as sun-god who kisses dewy marigolds (52–53). Despite its various bowers the work has no overall imagistic pattern and symbolic structure. When we look back from the mature poetry to the bowers, the sweet peas on tip-toe, the mortal bars of the myth-maker, the writer borne aloft on curled clouds, Apollo commanding flower and song, or the thoughtless, murderous "infant hands" (46), we realize that the poem's lack of cohesion is due to a failure to unify the embryonic themes suggested by these different images even more than to the flimsy narrative or the splicing together of sections inspired and written on different occasions. An extreme case is the "noiseless noise" born of the sigh of motionless silence (11–13), which (unlike, for example, the unheard melodies of the "Grecian Urn") is in no way incorporated into the poem's theme. By combining an original personification and oxymoron with close observation of nature Keats creates a superb effect, but he makes no attempt to link the windless air to the poet awaiting inspiration, the Romantic metaphor[7] exploited in the Apollo passage (56). The exquisite picture of minnows which "taste the luxury of

sunny beams / Temper'd with coolness" (74–75) is more typical of
how far Keats at this stage integrates and fails to integrate individual
beauties into the whole. This scene combines warmth with coolness,
taste with touch, an accurate description of the elusiveness of the fish
as seen from the outside (78–82) with participation from the inside in
"their own sweet delight" (76), and freedom of movement with
retreat to a motherly refuge suggested by the word "nestle" (76). The
last image (the bower of the epigraph) is skillfully extended to the
"bowery green" of the watercresses giving cool protection to the
ripples of the stream (81–84), but, like many other passages in "I
stood tip-toe," this scene has really nothing to do with the theme of
inspiration and is certainly not an indispensable rung in a ladder
leading up to the poem's climactic question at the end: "Was there a
poet born?"

III   The Poetic Process: "Sleep and Poetry"

The concluding poem of the 1817 volume, "Sleep and Poetry"
(October-December 1816), is structured more tightly around a central theme: commitment to poetry. In the words of Michael G.
Cooke, "The poem proves an essay in the will as much as an exercise
of a budding art." [8] The "sleep" of the title provides the frame: the
poem opens with a comparison between sleep and something higher,
namely poetry (1–46), and ends with the description of a sleepless
night at "a poet's house" (354), most probably the library at Hunt's
Hampstead cottage, where Keats is inspired by the atmosphere
exuding from "sacred busts" (357) of old bards and from famous prints
and paintings, just as in "I stood tip-toe" he has been inspired by
nature. After mapping out the stages of his poetic development, he
realizes how presumptuous his vows of dedication are and yet refuses
to retract them (270–312).

The poem's different sections are all related to Keats's poetic
aspirations, but the structure is still far from perfect. The progression
of the argument is fairly arbitrary: Keats might, for example, have let
his attack on neo-classicism (181–206) or his assertion of the heroic
conception of his art, the "vast idea" that ever rolls before him
(290–91), precede his distinction between the separate stages of his
projected poetry (101–25). Nor is the title justified except in relation
to Keats's poems as a whole. For the embryonic theme of sleep, like
several others in the 1817 volume, acquires its full significance only
in retrospect. Gentle, soothing, cheery, tranquil, healthful, protec-

tive, serene sleep (1–9) will gradually become symbolic of the "diligent Indolence" (*Letters*, I, 231), preparatory to artistic creation, and sleep's "visions" (10) will develop into the waking dream, the benumbed, drowsy trance which, together with actual composition, constitutes the creative process itself. Within the poem "sleep" is mainly frame and foil to the "poetry" theme; in the context of Keats's total *oeuvre* "sleep" (preparation and vision) is the peer of "poetry" (composition).

And yet there are hints within the poem that "sleep" is already part of the poetic process:

> A drainless shower
> Of light is poesy; 'tis the supreme of power;
> 'Tis might half slumb'ring on its own right arm.
> The very archings of her eye-lids charm
> A thousand willing agents to obey,
> And still she governs with the mildest sway!
> But strength alone though of the Muses born
> Is like a fallen angel. . . . (235–42)

"Strength alone" is pitted against "might half slumb'ring," pure power against power combined with sleep. The blinded giants, "the poets Polyphemes / Disturbing the great sea" (234–35), probably include Byron, and it is conceivable that Keats (as Hunt testifies) [9] may also be thinking of Wordsworth, whose didacticism he will contrast in February 1818 with art that works by suggestion, the "unobtrusive" poetry which has no "palpable design upon us" (*Letters*, I, 223–24). After rejecting the "worms, and shrouds, and sepulchres" of the Graveyard School and the work that "feeds upon the burrs, / And thorns of life" Keats becomes very explicit about "the great end / Of poesy": "that it should be a friend / To sooth the cares, and lift the thoughts of man" (243–47). This idea recurs several times in the 1817 volume. [10] In "I stood tip-toe" we see Keats express it with some ambiguity, but in the vital language of sensation, as a charm that lifts us "upon the white clouds wreath'd and curl'd" (140), whereas here he is led by consecutive reasoning into the unpoetical language of thought. It is ironic that Keats ends his panegyric on unobtrusive, nondidactic poetry with a carefully worked out piece of Wordsworthian teaching, doubly ironic if Wordsworth is one object of his criticism.

But we cannot forget the magnificent figure representing poetry as "might half slumb'ring on its own right arm," a piece of statuary that

may come to life at any moment, perhaps the reclining figure of a god.
The arm is not raised to command, to strike, or to cast thunderbolts
(the preceding two lines might be reminiscent of Zeus visiting Danae
in a shower of gold), but power is unequivocally conveyed through
that latent drive of which we already caught a glimpse in eagle-eyed
Cortez and the "wild surmise" of his men on a peak in Darien. To
Murry "might half slumb'ring on its own right arm" conveys
"Strength, ease, majesty, naturalness, a softness as of sleep, a relaxa-
tion of all tensions, a passing-beyond all efforts, a sovereignty of
instinctive comprehension," and he carefully continues: "one could
go on trying to capture all the manifold implications of that line
forever." [11] Murry is right: the figure conjures up everything that
Keats associates with poetry and the poetic process. Slumber suggests the revitalization of the body, the refreshment of the senses on
which imagination depends, the restoration of the faculties in preparation for creative activity. Half-slumber is a state of perfect receptivity, an openness to all impressions unspoilt by the distractions of
waking activity. But the right arm symbolizes authority, direction,
command, discipline, power, energy, and potential action. The in-
domitable and dozing figure combines omnipotence with an attitude
of indeterminateness, of acquiescence in half-knowledge and mysteries which precludes all irritable reaching after fact and reason.
Among many other things the image is an embodiment of negative
capability, just as negative capability is required to appreciate its
inexhaustible implications. Poetry arrests the "might" of life and thus
immortalizes it.

Sleep is also associated with the first stage of Keats's projected
poetic development, "the realm . . . / Of Flora, and old Pan" (101–
102), another delightfully vague and suggestive image. The informa-
tion that the phrase, like several other details in the poem, seems to
have been inspired by a print of Poussin's *L'Empire de Flore* [The
Realm of Flora] [12] does not enable us to pin down precisely what kind
of poetry Keats is here contrasting with the later work which is to deal
with "the agonies, the strife / Of human hearts" (124–25). Keats may
have had in mind pastoral as distinct from epic poetry, or his planned
romance *Endymion* as opposed to the dramas that he intended and
never lived to write. Too much has sometimes been made of the
parallel between the development described in "Sleep and Poetry"
and the progression from "the infant and thoughtless Chamber"
through "the Chamber of Maiden Thought" in the letter to Reynolds
(I, 280–81), and of the resemblance of these two passages to the lines

describing the movement through three successive stages in Wordsworth's attitude to nature in "Tintern Abbey" (66–102); but, as
J. Burke Severs has shown, the only similarity lies in the evolution
from an initial sensuous stage.[13] Perhaps Keats implies here that the
sensuous nature descriptions of the 1817 volume are to be superseded by attacks upon sublime human themes, and we can only be
grateful that he did not abandon the language of sensation when (as in
the odes, *Lamia*, and the two *Hyperions*) he engaged "the agonies,
the strife / Of human hearts."

The realm of Flora and Pan is a world of unlimited physical delights
in which the poet can freely indulge his appetites for food and erotic
play. The description begins with the familiar Keatsian pose of "sleep
in the grass" (102) and ends with the equally characteristic "rest" "in
the bosom of a leafy word" (119–20), our old acquaintance the protective bower. As Morris Dickstein reminds us, "Sleep, which shelters
and refreshes, is itself a bower 'more healthful than the leafiness of
dales' " (7).[14] Sleep is interrupted and the shelter momentarily abandoned by the poet's pursuit of nymphs one of whom, says Keats, "will
entice me on, and on . . ." (117). At this point the chase promises to
become endless, and readers of Keats may remember Pan frustrated
by Syrinx and Alpheus by Arethusa or the lover who will never kiss
his beloved "Though winning near the goal." [15] But in the bower
realm of Flora and Pan desire is gratified and conflict resolved.
Enticement and pursuit are followed by rest and fulfillment within
the bower, with the lovers "like two gems upcurl'd / In the recesses of
a pearly shell" (120–21). Though the poet has never left his imaginary
realm, it seems as if he had briefly ventured into the real world of
strife and unsatisfied desire and had then undone his birth by fleeing
back to the protected sleep within the womb. The realm of Flora and
Pan is fictitious, because in it enjoyment is unvexed by pain, and the
consummation of pleasure neither causes surfeit nor is followed by
decay, whereas for Keats life is more paradoxical (85–95). He must
therefore "bid these joys farewell" (122) and come to grips with
reality by depicting the actual world of unresolved conflicts and
dissatisfied human hearts, of fulfillment that cloys and beauty that
dies.

This projected poetry of real life, however, is as yet no more than
an idealized vision for the Keats of 1816. The poetic ideal, symbolized
by the charioteer (the Apollo in Poussin's *L'Empire de Flore*), is
threatened by "A sense of real things" (157), the everyday actuality of
natural process encompassing the self-doubting poet. The vision is

dispelled, but only temporarily, for Keats vows to preserve the
memory of the fled chariot. Several times he pledges himself pas-
sionately to his art (47, 53, 58–61, 81–84, 96–97, 290–93, 301–304),
and despite repeated hesitations he remains finally undeterred
(311–12).

At the end of "I stood tip-toe" we can only guess the answer to the
question "Was there a poet born?" In "Sleep and Poetry" Keats still
vacillates between self-doubt and self-assertion, but his overall confidence and final determination are undeniable. Henceforth Keats
"will strive / Against all doubtings" (159–60). His commitment to
poetry is here already made in absolute terms, at the price of his life,
a sacrifice to Apollo (58–61), a commitment transcending the limitations of space and time. In "I stood tip-toe" the poet confines his
aspirations within human bounds, and the halfhearted assertion that
some myth-maker "had burst our mortal bars" is undermined by the
wing-clipping final line: "My wand'ring spirit must no further soar."
There is no such compromise in "Sleep and Poetry." Earth is left
behind as the poet's wings either "find out an immortality" (84) or
melt and destroy him by bearing him, Icarus-like, too near the sun
(302–304). For the surmise as he gazed with Cortez at the unexplored
Pacific has now become certainty: he has recognized his poetic goal as
infinite, "An ocean dim, sprinkled with many an isle" (306).

CHAPTER 4

The Poet "Ensky'd": Endymion

I   *Ripening, Mortality, and Eternity: Three Sonnets*

WITH the decision to write a work of four thousand lines on the Endymion myth as "a trial" or "a test of Invention" (*Letters*, I, 169–70), Keats's commitment to poetry becomes irrevocable. In poems written in the first four months of 1817, which saw the publication of his first volume (March 3), Keats continued to seek out "A bower for his spirit" ("On *The Story of Rimini*") in nature and in works of art. In *Endymion* the "thing of beauty" that "will keep / A bower quiet for us" may be any piece of natural scenery or "all lovely tales that we have heard or read" (I. 1–22). As if the composition of his poem were part of the seasonal growth, he is confident that it will come to fruition: begun in spring, it should be complete by autumn (lines 39–57 are an accurate forecast).

In the sonnet "After dark vapours" (31 January 1817) the gradual ripening progress from buds to harvested sheaves is analogous to the passage of a human lifespan through an hourglass. The poem associates the buds of spring with autumn suns, thus the sleeping infant with the dying poet. The labor pains of spring give birth to "calmest thoughts" about the later season of death. In the picture of "fruit ripening in stillness," holding on to a present halfway between spring's budding and autumn's harvest, and in the sand trickling through the hourglass, we foretaste "To Autumn," which more remarkably arrests motion at the point of fulfillment and death and then resumes nature's gradual but inexorable process.

As the elliptical imagery of "After dark vapours" will be expanded into an ode "To Autumn," so in the sonnet "On Seeing the Elgin Marbles" (1 or 2 March 1817) the equally compressed juxtaposition of "Grecian grandeur" and "old time" foreshadows the "Ode on a Grecian Urn." But whereas the urn is a symbol of perfection fostered by time, the marbles brought by Lord Elgin from the Athenian Parthenon are wasted by time, and, as Benjamin Griffith has shown,

possibly by shipwreck.[1] Mortality and immortality cause "an inde-
scribable feud" in the poet's heart. The conflict is not only between
the sense of impotence of a mortal poet, "a sick eagle looking at the
sky," and his longing for immortal achievement; it also reflects the
earthly limitations of both the poet and the time-ravaged statuary
vis-à-vis an aesthetic ideal. The imagination, however, is boundless,
and Keats's imaginative recreation of the Endymion legend and of a
marble urn in rhyme will counter the notion that a work of art is
mortal: the loveliness of "A thing of beauty" increases ever, immune
to the "Wasting of old time" such as the ravages of "a billowy main."[2]

The element of destructiveness is submerged in the ocean's pri-
mordial power in the sonnet "On the Sea" (17 April 1817). This power
is expressed as "eternal whisperings," unobtrusive like the might of
poesy "half slumb'ring on its own right arm" in "Sleep and Poetry"
(237). It seems as if Keats were waiting for inspiration, for the next
day he promises Reynolds to begin Endymion (Letters, I, 134). The
letter makes it clear that the sonnet itself was inspired by the scene
near Dover in King Lear as well as by the view on the Isle of Wight
(I, 130–32). Keats combines visual, auditory, tactile, motor, and
organic (hunger and surfeit) imagery in order to convey the ocean's
ebb and tide, its overwhelming turmoil alternating with extended
periods of calm, and its infinite potential for refreshing, enchanting,
and inspiring mankind. Perhaps under the shock of Gloucester's
blinding, Keats hints at the eye's sensitivity: "O ye who have your
eyeballs vexed and tir'd. . . ." Surfeited eyes and overfed ears may,
ironically, still their hunger by feasting "upon the wideness of the
sea," uncloying, mysterious, infinite. The universal harmony heard
in the "mighty swell" of the tide into caverns drowns out man's
"cloying melody," just as an ideal grandeur seized by the imagination
dwarfs all mortal achievement; and human ephemerality is brought
home to us no less by the timelessness of the ocean than by time's
relentless hourglass. Whether inspired by the observation of nature,
by works of art, or by a combination of the seascape outside the poet's
window and a Shakespeare play, the poems written just before
Endymion convey a growing awareness of the earthly limitations
against which Keats's unbounded aspirations rebelled in "Sleep and
Poetry."

II Keats's Version of the Endymion Legend

Earthly reality and heavenly ideal, mortality and immortality
Keats finds reconciled in the myth of Endymion. He probably first

became acquainted with the fable in his school days through John Lempriere's *Classical Dictionary*, which was still among his books at his death, and Joseph Spence's *Polymetis* (see *Keats Circle*, I, 256; II, 148). In a letter to his sister (I, 154) Keats summarized the classical tale about the love of the moon-goddess (variously known as Cynthia, Diana, Phoebe, and Selene) for the shepherd Endymion, whom she carried away while he was dreaming. The poem develops the myth's basic motifs of love between mortal and immortal and the passiveness of a sleeping hero into Keats's version of "love immortal" (I.849) and "a sleep / Full of sweet dreams" (I.4–5), adding the theme of joy and infinite glory in "A thing of beauty." Although Keats leads his hero to the ideal by way of the actual, he adheres to his model by allowing the final union between man and goddess. On the other hand he repeatedly betrays a typically Romantic awareness of the ultimate futility of all human endeavor.

The story begins with a celebration in honor of the Greek nature deity Pan. The despondence of the shepherd prince Endymion during the festivities is observed by his sister Peona, to whom he confides his dream of a heavenly lady. Peona's attack on the idleness of dreams provides the stimulus for Endymion's argument beginning "Wherein lies happiness?" (I.777), which Keats in a letter to his publisher revised and described as "a kind of Pleasure Thermometer" measuring "the gradations of Happiness" (I, 218). Endymion traces a pleasure scale from the touch of a rose leaf through music, friendship, and immortalizing human love to the immortal love of an immortal being. In the name of such doubly immortal love he claims reality for a dream (I.850–57), a claim reinforced by the subsequent waking encounters with his dream apparition in a well (I.896) and her voice in a cave (I.965–69). Endymion's disillusioned awakening into a world where nature no longer has any joys for him (I.691–705) might be taken as a Blakean loss of innocence and the birth of a craving for a higher form of existence which makes him dissatisfied with his human limitations. The return to a frustrating actuality, which often ends the poems of Keats's maturity, occurs at the beginning of *Endymion* and forms the starting-point for the hero's quest. For once this quest will end in reunion with an immortal being.

An active seeker, Keats's Endymion is not borne to the moon by Cynthia in his sleep; rather, like the hero in Michael Drayton's *The Man in the Moone* (1606), which Keats had evidently read (though probably not Drayton's earlier *Endimion and Phoebe*), the shepherd prince sets out in pursuit of the goddess. Possibly because in Book

One he has encountered her in a cave, in a well, and in his dream as
coming from the sky, Endymion will try to find her in the bowels of
the earth (Book Two), in the waters of the ocean (Book Three), and in
the air (Book Four). In Book Two Endymion comes upon the sleeping
Adonis (II.393) and encounters the disembodied lady of his dream
vision in a "jasmine bower" (II.670). The sensuality of these descriptions has frequently been condemned as vulgar, in particular the
expression "Those lips, O slippery blisses" (II.758), but perhaps
Christopher Ricks's eloquent defense may be heralding a change in
taste: Keats intentionally disconcerts us by letting us recognize the
saliva so as to widen our response to ecstatic love which should
overcome all embarrassment.[3] Endymion lights upon two springs
(II.918–19) from which he overhears a dialogue between the river-
god Alpheus and Arethusa, a fountain nymph pursued by the god.
Endymion's prayer for their happiness (II.1017) is the first indication
of his sympathy for the suffering of others, a theme developed in his
undersea adventure in Book Three. There he meets Glaucus (a
fisherman transformed into a sea-god in classical myth), who immediately recognizes him as his deliverer (III.234) and tells him the
story of his love for the sea nymph Scylla, his enchantment by Circe,
and a prophecy of redemption after ten centuries through the intervention of an elect youth. Endymion performs the appropriate
magic ritual, rejuvenates Glaucus, revives Scylla, whom Circe had
slain (not, as in Ovid, transformed into a monster), and also reani-
mates many drowned lovers (III.775–90). During the ensuing
celebration in the palace of the sea-god Neptune, Venus, who has
guessed Cynthia's love, exhorts Endymion to "A little patience"
(III.908).

In Book Four Endymion is torn between two loves. Having gone in
search of a golden-haired dream goddess he now falls in love with a
dark-haired Indian maiden. He is borne aloft on winged steeds with
his human paramour, encounters "Sleep slow journeying with head
on pillow" (IV.370), and dreams of Diana, whom he now recognizes
as the heavenly figure he has been seeking. Opening his eyes he
"Beheld awake his very dream" (IV.436). When he kisses the Indian
maiden Diana disappears, and as he turns to the beauty of the moon
the maiden beside him "melted from his grasp" (IV.509). Endymion
recovers in the "Happy gloom" of a "Cave of Quietude" (IV.537, 548)
which resolves man's most perplexing contraries, a state "beyond
sorrow and joy" after unbearable grief, of "ripe peace and consummation . . . Yet also . . . deathly void," of "especially profound

sleep . . . the entry to final mysteries." [4] Keats's poetry here strikingly conveys hushed, macabre solemnity and feverish effort followed by unforeseen release: ". . . as when on curtain'd bier / The deathwatch tick is stifled. Enter none / Who strive therefore: on the sudden it is won" (IV.530–32). The rhythm of the last line echoes the contrast between strain and instantaneous relief further developed in the following image of the ice-cold drink which alleviates burning suffering (IV.533–35). Back on earth Endymion finds the lost Indian again. Recognizing that he has been "Presumptuous against love, . . . against the tie / Of mortals each to each" (IV.639–41), he chooses the maiden over the goddess. But now the maiden reveals that their love is forbidden. As Endymion bids her and his sister Peona a final farewell, the Indian is suddenly transformed into the goddess Cynthia and the two lovers disappear so abruptly (rather abruptly ending Keats's romance) that we cannot blame Peona for going "Home through the gloomy wood in wonderment" (IV.1003).

III   *Love Immortal*

Whatever else Keats may make of the Endymion myth, his poem remains an exquisite tale of love. Like "The Eve of St. Agnes," the story may have appealed to Keats because of its erotic wish-fulfillment. As E. C. Pettet suggests, a dream goddess who makes the first overtures to her lover is a common fantasy-compensation for men who feel constrained in the presence of attractive women. The heavenly Cynthia may stand for our erotic dream fantasies and the Indian maiden for the woman we actually meet when awake. The latter closely resembles but clearly falls short of the perfection of our dream figure, for whom we secretly still long. While Endymion inevitably "must and will surrender himself to the Indian Maid, at the same time he is still somehow faithful to the memory of Cynthia." [5] On the other hand if we read the love quest as an expression of Keats's yearning for a return to infancy and oneness with the mother prior to individuation and the sense of death, then Endymion's marriage with Cynthia becomes a fantasy fulfillment of the frustrated cravings for immortality and union with the ideal other which pervades Keats's poetry and finds its supreme statement in "Ode to a Nightingale."

Endymion seems to be speaking for Keats when he places love at the pinnacle of his scale of happiness (I.807) and thinks that it "might bless / The world with benefits unknowingly" (I.826–27). Apparently

nothing but "The mere commingling of passionate breath," love may
really produce "more than our searching witnesseth," though the
poet claims not to know what this "more" is (I.832–35). But the
examples of swelling green fruit, the bright mail of fish, runnels in the
meadows, seed, and harvest (I.835–40) intimate that all fruition and
renewal in nature depends on procreative love. Moreover, love gives
the lute its tones (I.840), for music-playing, like the nightingale's
song (I.828–30), is an act of love, and the sound of music would lack
ravishment if there were no communion between loving souls (I.841–
42). Keats may also be referring to the spirit with which "human
souls . . . greet" (I.842) the tones of the lute, that is, listen to music:
in the words of one of his letters, the tones would be "semireal" or
"Nothings" without "an ardent pursuit" or at least "a greeting of the
Spirit to make them wholly exist" (I, 243).

The tentative thought about some vague "benefits" bestowed "unknowingly" by love suddenly becomes explicit statement expressed
with firm conviction: "this earthly love has power to make / Men's
being mortal, immortal" (I.843–44). Endymion may have reached
this conclusion because love renews human generations just as it
revives nature and because it creates permanence in art. Perhaps,
like many lovers, Endymion simply asserts love's immortality. If
earthly love can conquer death, then Endymion, who has been
wooed by a goddess, has hopes of a double immortality (I.849):
eternal life and a happiness in that life so far surpassing anything
known on earth that it can only be termed "immortal." Later Cynthia
indeed promises him such "an immortality of passion" (II.808), and
the goddess herself (who is of course immortal already) wins "Immortal bliss" through Endymion (III.1024).

Endymion's immortalization through love is foreshadowed by
Adonis, whose yearly resurrection by Venus symbolizes the renewal
of nature in spring. The poem's central love union has a similar
beneficial influence: Cynthia's wedding is to bring "health perpetual
/ To shepherds and their flocks" (IV.831–32), a hint of the healing
effect more fully described at the end of "I stood tip-toe." Keats also
emphasizes the sovereignty of love in the reviving and ripening
process of nature by extending powers usually associated with Ceres
or with Phoebus-Apollo to his sister Phoebe-Cynthia:[6] "Thou dost
bless every where, with silver lip / Kissing dead things to life"
(III.38–43, 56–57). Resurrection "unknowingly" granted by love is
best illustrated in the Glaucus episode. Endymion not only matures
into sympathy for the suffering of others (as has generally been noted)

but, more accurately, in the course of the pursuit of his beloved he is
humanized; indeed he stumbles upon Glaucus at the precise moment
when "he lifted up his eyes to swear / How his own goddess was past
all things fair" (III.189–90), and he is immediately recognized as
liberator (III.234) because he is a lover, having "lov'd an unknown
power" (III.301). Endymion's deliverance of Glaucus, Scylla, and the
drowned lovers is not, as has been suggested,[7] particularly magnani-
mous, since he has virtually no choice (III.710–11): the love quest has
thrust a redemptive role upon an unsuspecting hero. Lovers deserve
immortality, and the drowned lovers, ostensibly resuscitated by
magic, have really been ransomed by love, by their own and by
Endymion's love for his goddess. With love as guarantee of immortality the erotic wish-fulfillment of the Endymion legend acquires
religious overtones.

By immortalizing his hero through love for a human being, that is,
by having him finally choose the Indian maiden and then transforming her into the goddess Cynthia, Keats may have wished to suggest
that the ideal is attained by means of a real person, a trancendental
joy through the life of the senses. On 22 November 1817, about the
time he was composing this passage, the poet wrote in his famous
letter to his friend Bailey (discussed in chapter 2) that happiness in
the hereafter is "happiness on Earth repeated in a finer tone," which
is secured by "delight in sensation" (I, 185). Endymion's union with
Cynthia is the epitome of that "self-destroying" entanglement with
the other for which Keats coined the term "fellowship with essence"
(I. 779, 798–99) in the revised passage he sent his publisher, a more
precise formulation than the "blending pleasureable" which it replaced, because it implies both "fellowship divine, / . . . till we shine,
/ Full alchemiz'd and free of space" and a fusion with concrete things
such as a rose leaf touching finger and lips (I. 778–83). We may, with
Earl Wasserman, call this kind of empathy "mystic absorption into
the essence of outward forms" so long as we remember that "essences, / Once spiritual" (II.905–906) may become mere physical
objects.[8]

A figure embodying the combination of physicality and spirituality
is the nature-god Pan. As the power presiding over the natural
process of maturation (described in language anticipating "To Autumn") Pan is a "forester divine" who partakes of the earthly
(I.247–62) yet "gives it a touch ethereal" (I.298). Pan is the playful
satyr king who delights in watching nymphs (I.236–37, 272–76) and at
the same time a mysterious being, "the unimaginable lodge / For

solitary thinkings; such as dodge / Conception to the very bourne of heaven, / . . . a symbol of immensity" (I.288–99). Here Pan represents the utmost point reached by the imagination. The passage has been read by a Jungian as "a precise description of the experience of the archetypal," but a sentence from a philosophical dialogue included in Shaftesbury's *Characteristics* (1711), "The Moralists," which probably influenced the hymn to Pan, gives Keats's meaning more simply: "In thy immensity all thought is lost . . . and wearied imagination spends itself in vain." [9] Warren U. Ober and W. K. Thomas have recently elucidated Keats's evolving idea of Pan, though perhaps they claim too much for the poet's final conception of this deity: "Pan, god of nature-as-process; eternal, universal, and all-inclusive Pan; a god outlasting and finally incorporating all other gods." [10]

Although imagination is powerless to define ultimate immensities, it can express them symbolically. The marriage between Endymion and Cynthia represents the fulfillment of our aspirations to cast off human shackles. On the other hand, at the beginning of his search in Book Two Endymion's condition symbolizes the reality of the human predicament: the pattern of disenchantment following upon the apparent attainment of an ideal, the typical Romantic craving for infinitude. Keats-Endymion rationalizes his frustrated yearnings in a comparison with a conquerer who has captured a city, is disappointed with the prize, consoles himself by seeing endeavor as its own reward, and attacks another city. The poet recognizes in this alternation between accomplishment and discontent the essence of human existence, a continuous battle highlighted by the contrasting quiet of death (II.142–59). As he stands on a "jutting head of land" or "misty peak" (II.163, 166) and gazes into the unknown (in a posture reminiscent of Cortez staring at the Pacific from a peak in Darien), Endymion searching for his "thrice-seen love" (II.168) becomes the ever-dissatisfied Romantic aspirer restlessly looking ahead for new experience; but the Keatsian image suggests that the heroic seeker soars into the beyond in spirit even while his feet are still firmly planted on the ground. Endymion's inner tension, due to the inadequacy of his mortal state to his conceptions of immortality, is reflected in his prayer to Cynthia (whom, ironically, he does not recognize as his heavenly apparition). His entreaty for release from the "tyranny of love," for the respite from an erotic pursuit which symbolizes all human striving, is immediately countermanded: "rather tie / Large wings upon my shoulders, and point out / My love's far dwelling"

(II.174–79). Like Icarus he deems to "burst" the confining "bars" of the human condition by "sailing . . . through the dizzy sky" (II.185–87), when, as so often in Keats, the illusion of having left earth behind is suddenly shattered: "my spirit fails" (II.193). For a moment Keats suspends time. He compares Endymion, still a mortal, to two figures immortalized in literature and painting, "old Deucalion mountain'd o'er the flood" and "blind Orion hungry for the morn" (II.197–98),[11] thus once more perpetuating them through his art. But Endymion is not yet ready for deification, and escape from the world of time would mean freezing "to senseless stone" (II.200). For Endymion is still subject to the growth and decay, aspiration and disappointment, delight and melancholy of a world in which only senseless stone is immutable, be it a barren cliff or a Grecian urn. But for supernatural intervention his Faustian overreaching would cost him his life. And yet, paradoxically, Endymion will be "crown'd / With immortality" because he loves a goddess, follows "airy voices" (II.211–13), and trusts his dream.

IV *A Sleep Full of Sweet Dreams*

Nothing seems to be further removed from the inertia of the mythological Endymion courted by Diana and eventually borne in his sleep to her heavenly home than the Faustian striving to transcend human limitations and the indefatigable quest of immortal love which characterize Keats's hero. Yet the latter, too, is passive to a great extent, "led on . . . by circumstance," as Keats says, and "overshadowed by a Supernatural Power" (*Letters*, I, 207, 213). For although Endymion appears to initiate action by going in search of his goddess, it is she who woos, gratifies, and finally immortalizes him. He is variously guided, aided, or saved by a butterfly-nymph, a subterranean voice, cupids, a Jovian eagle, the scroll of Glaucus, Neptune's nereids, and Mercury's steeds. We may see the encounter with Adonis, Alpheus, Arethusa, Glaucus, and the Indian maiden as a series of successful trials in an educational process which has sometimes been called "spiritualization–through–humanization";[12] but Endymion never seeks out these trials, and in the Glaucus episode we see his humanitarian role virtually imposed upon him by supernatural powers. Although in Book Four Endymion makes real choices, he is still under divine rule as much as ever. When he finally fixes upon the Indian maiden, he seems to gain control over his actions, but Diana immediately frustrates his decision by claiming, in the person of the Indian, to be "forbidden" (IV.752).

If, as we have suggested, Keats wishes to show how ideal love is attained through love for a real person, why is Endymion not deified the moment he chooses the Indian maiden? Keats anticipates the question:

> Endymion! unhappy! it nigh grieves
> Me to behold thee thus in last extreme:
> Ensky'd ere this, but truly that I deem
> Truth the best music in a first-born song. (IV. 770–73)

Some readers still believe that Keats's determination to "make 4000 Lines of one bare circumstance and fill them with Poetry" (*Letters*, I, 170) is his only reason for postponing the apotheosis of Endymion, although Murry has persuasively argued that in that case Keats would not appeal to "Truth" to justify his delay.[13] Several critics, among them Glen Allen, Clarice Godfrey, Ward, Evert, Dickstein, Chatterjee, Sperry, and Ende, claim that Keats changed his attitude to the myth in the course of composition, so that vacillation or spiritual crisis may account for the delay of the conclusion. Sperry, for example, follows Glen Allen by contending that the poet's " 'ensky'ing' of his hero had lost much of its climactic importance"; and Ende goes further by claiming that through his reading of Milton and Wordsworth Keats has so acutely become aware of the inevitability of separation and loss as to have come to feel at variance with a myth in which a mortal is eternally united with a goddess. "The narrator's 'truth' in *Endymion*," writes Ende, ". . . refutes Cynthia's promise of union in the skies." [14]

The letters and poems Keats wrote during and shortly after the revision of *Endymion* for the press certainly exhibit a growing awareness of suffering and inner conflict which quite possibly might already have found its way into Book Four. Nevertheless Keats's delay of the hero's apotheosis and his invocation of "truth" to justify this delay can be explained without imputing to the poet an inability to manage his subject and without converting his romance of wish-fulfillment into a crisis poem. The narrator tells us that Endymion succumbs to "fancies vain and crude" (IV. 722), rejects his dream as "a nothing," renounces those "airy voices" which lead to immortality, and artificially resolves the conflict between earthly and divine love by deferring the latter to some future "pure elysium" (IV. 636–59). He is not yet ready to be "Ensky'd." But then the "golden eve" of summer shows Endymion the beauty of the things that must die, and he becomes prepared for his own death, though not without a protest that he "did wed / [Him]self to things of light from infancy" (IV.927, 957–58). His last words represent him as ready to fulfill his destiny, whatever it may be: " '. . . I would have command, / If it were heaven's will, on our sad fate' " (IV.975–76). By submitting to heaven's will he renounces neither earthly love nor dreams and airy voices beckoning toward a higher mode of existence. Like a knight-errant he is asking, as it were, for a heavenly sign, prepared to act upon it. If this is a final test he passes it. As the maiden's "long black hair swell'd ampler, in display / Full golden; in her eyes a brighter day . . ." (984–85), Endymion does not see heavenly supplanting earthly beauty but rather heavenly beauty in the earthly, the same beauty "repeated in a finer tone" (*Letters*, I, 185), in the "ampler" proportions and "brighter" intensity of the divine.

Endymion's apotheosis, however, has ultimately been decided in heaven and its timing is not the hero's. Glaucus had to wait a thousand years for his redemption, " '. . . *until / Time's creeping shall the dreary space fulfil* . . .' " (III.705–706); and Endymion has not been "Ensky'd ere this" because the time for his final union with Cynthia is not yet ripe. Like Adonis under the spell of sleep not broken by the kiss of Venus before spring, Endymion must await his appointed hour, and this hour is determined by "decrees of fate" (IV.990). Endymion, too, becomes associated with the natural cycle when the glorious death of a summer day signals the consummation of his destiny.

Keats's hero, therefore, though no longer the personification of sleep he appears to have been in classical myth,[15] retains much of the passiveness of his prototype. He, too, is lying, as it were, in sleep's protective bower: not only does he repeatedly sleep and dream and once behold "awake his very dream" (IV.436), but the romance itself is like one long "sleep / Full of sweet dreams" (I.4–5), in which Endymion's fate gradually ripens and culminates when Cynthia finally reveals herself and he is about to be "Ensky'd," embowered by heaven. At that point his sleep is over (though the reader's dream of wish-fulfillment continues for a few more lines till the poem ends). If we use Northrop Frye's scheme of the four realms of "heaven, the innocent world, the ordinary world, and hell," Endymion is elevated from the second to the uppermost level.[16] For despite his modern consciousness he never leaves a world of enchantment and thus remains little more than a pawn of Diana.

At the symbolic level, however, Endymion's passive dreaming is

the actively creative imagination. "What the imagination seizes as
Beauty must be truth—whether it existed before or not. . . . The
Imagination may be compared to Adam's dream—he awoke and
found it truth," Keats says in his letter to Bailey of 22 November 1817
(I, 184–85), six days before completing the first draft of his poem.
Since Endymion's fulfilled dream stands for the truth created by the
imagination, the pursuit of the dream vision seems to symbolize the
aspiration to become a poet or a poet's faith in his imagination and in
his quest of beauty. Endymion's dream gradually ripening toward
fulfillment under Cynthia's guidance, "like a flower . . . passive and
receptive—budding patiently under the eye of Apollo" (*Letters*, I,
232), represents the imaginative openness and wise passiveness
associated with negative capability. Circe withering Glaucus to old
age caricatures the rejuvenating and resuscitating loves of Venus and
Cynthia. If Glaucus' experience with Circe, "this arbitrary queen of
sense" (III.459), is also seen as parody of dream-fulfillment, then the
imagination acquires some of the ambivalence of "La Belle Dame
sans Merci"—and yet in *Endymion* imagination ultimately keeps
faith.

In the same passage of his letter to Bailey Keats writes: "I have the
same Idea of all our Passions as of love they are all in their sublime,
creative of essential Beauty," and he refers to the first book of
Endymion and the Indian maiden's song "O Sorrow" in Book Four for
illustration (I, 184–85). In Book One Keats-Endymion conjectures
that love is the basis of all beauty, as for example the nightingale's
love produces melody (I.826–42). The Indian maiden's song also
shows sorrow creating beauty: sorrow transfers the red of lips to rose
bushes, the eye's light to the glow worm, and the mourning of a
tongue to the nightingale (IV.146–63), which is a representation from
the fancy "of the probable mode of operating in these Matters"
(I, 185) rather than a copy of the facts as observed. The beautiful song
of the nightingale, for instance, is fancied to have originated in
Philomela's sorrows. Nevertheless beautiful pictures, verses, tones,
and, for that matter, stories like those of Philomela or of Endymion
express intuited truths. The various interpretations of *Endymion*,
including the present one and in particular those which treat the
romance as narrowly allegoric,[17] are attempts to translate the truth
that Keats has imaginatively represented as a thing of beauty into
terms to be grasped by the analytical intellect. The song "O Sorrow"
has rightly been admired as an English lyric and thus, Keats would
say, represents truth. We instinctively concede that somehow the

"natural hue of health" from lips mysteriously reappears in the tips of the daisies (IV.148–51). Slightly less fanciful, the song's fourth stanza claims that if there were no sorrow, there would also be no "merriment of May" for a lover, because "Heart's lightness" must be paid for by the "drooping flower" trodden on by dancing feet (IV.164–72). Like the "droop-headed flowers" of "Ode on Melancholy" (13), the flower of this song is sacred to the bower of sorrow (IV.171): the drooping of the flowers in both poems indicates their destiny. In stanza five the maiden sings about the constancy of sorrow and then, in illustration, tells of her futile attempt to elude grief by plunging into a Bacchanal, concluding her "roundelay" (IV.145) with two stanzas reaffirming the inescapability of a sorrow which she now fully accepts. The flower crushed by the dancing foot has best demonstrated this inescapability and has made the poetic truth of the first three stanzas accessible to abstract thought. The beautiful fiction of sorrow transferring color, brightness, and sound according to some capricious principle of compensation has yielded doctrine: there can be no joy without sorrow, and the sorrow of death is no less "creative of essential Beauty" than life-giving love. In Book One the picture of arrested motion, in which "tiptoe Night holds back her dark-grey hood" (I.831) to hear the song the nightingale unknowingly bestows upon all listeners, symbolizes the power of procreative love as mainspring of all natural fruition and all "ravishment" (I.841) in art. In the maiden's song the pallor of lips offset by the color of rose bush and daisy is another beautiful picture in which Keats's imagination has seized upon a truth, this time about joy and sorrow.[18] *Endymion* vindicates the imagination and the passions on which imagination feeds; it vindicates the creation of things of beauty.

V   A Thing of Beauty

Endymion begins by justifying beauty in the name of joy:

> A thing of beauty is a joy for ever:
> Its loveliness increases; it will never
> Pass into nothingness; but still will keep
> A bower quiet for us, and a sleep
> Full of sweet dreams. . . . (I.1–5)

A stable element in a world of change, a thing of beauty is enhanced by time while all other things decay: it is a bastion against mortality. Beauty is imagination's supreme refuge from the struggles of exis-

tence. The first line, justly famous and often quoted out of context for
the basic Keatsian principle it embodies, relates directly to the
project on which the poet is now embarking. A tale like Keats's
favorite Endymion myth grows lovelier every time it is told and
charms us away from the consecutive reasoning associated with
everyday realities into imagination's "sweet dreams." Keats "will
trace the story of Endymion" (I.35), because things of beauty are
indispensable to our survival. They provide health-restoring sanctuaries amidst the "despondence," "the gloomy days," "the un-
healthy and o'er-darkened ways / Made for our searching" (I.8–11).
Our questing spirit cannot help exploring the darkening "Chamber of
Maiden-Thought," but we can escape at least temporarily from our
world of unfulfilled dreams and ceaselessly disillusioned endeavor in
face of the " 'burden of the Mystery' " (*Letters*, I, 281) into bowers of
beauty such as the dream world of romance. In *Endymion* we share
vicariously in the hero's apotheosis, which releases him from the
human plight of frustrated aspirations.

Things of beauty combine spirit and matter. "Heaven's brink" is
the source of all beautiful things, "essences" which become per-
manently "bound to us" (I.24–31). On the other hand, although they
derive from heaven and bear us from actuality into imagination's
bower, things of beauty, paradoxically, "bind us to the earth" (I.7).
(The last expression is difficult to reconcile with certain Platonic
interpretations of the poem that would see Endymion's journey as a
quest for a body-denying spirituality.) The moon, mentioned with
"glories infinite" after beauty has been traced to the "endless fountain of immortal drink," is earlier listed among other natural objects
(I.29; I.23; I.13). Just as Endymion attains the moon-goddess Cynthia through an earthly maiden, so we apprehend an infinite glory by
means of sensuous perception of the beauties of moonlight. For Keats
the Romantic yearning for infinitude manifests itself as love of "the
principle of beauty in all things" (*Letters*, II, 263).

Keats's comment that "the Lovers of Poetry like to have a little
Region to wander in where they may pick and choose" (I, 170) and his
later recollection that in *Endymion* his "mind was like a pack of
scattered cards" (II, 323) have encouraged critics to exaggerate the
poem's lack of coherence. They have sometimes refused to see the
relevance of the inductions or how the four books are inter-related.
After invoking, in the induction to Book One, the theme of beauty
and using it to justify his poem, Keats hails love in Book Two, Cynthia
in Book Three, and the muse in Book Four. The object of these four

invocations is one and the same: Cynthia is the inspiration and model in Endymion's quest of immortal love and beauty. The induction to Book Two champions love against heroic deeds. Love is the theme of the Adonis episode, the encounter in the jasmine bower, and Alpheus' pursuit of Arethusa. In the induction to Book Three Keats opposes patience and constancy to tyranny and hypocrisy, "ethereal things" (III.25) to the crass materialism of politicians, and, by implication, negative capability to selfishness, the unobtrusive operation of "Men of Genius . . . on the Mass of neutral intellect" to the importunate activity of "Men of Power" (*Letters*, I, 184). Among the benevolent supernatural powers invoked Cynthia is the "gentlier-mightiest" (III.43), a coinage reminiscent of the definition of poesy as "might half slumb'ring on its own right arm." Cynthia's imperceptible influence is felt in the part she plays, as the object of Endymion's search and redemptive love, in the deliverance of Glaucus. In Book Four, in which we saw Endymion's destiny fulfilled after his submission to heaven, Keats apostrophizes a muse who was "patient" (IV.11) till the time ripened for the flowering of poetry in England. Though Keats occasionally strives too hard to accomplish his self-imposed task of completing four thousand lines and takes joy in luxurious descriptions for their own sake, he always keeps his theme in sight.

For example, at the beginning of his story it seems as if Keats had lost himself in one of his characteristic descriptions of lush vegetation:

> Upon the sides of Latmos was outspread
> A mighty forest; for the moist earth fed
> So plenteously all weed-hidden roots
> Into o'er-hanging boughs, and precious fruits. (I.63-66)

Enticed by fruit, cooled by the shade of a natural bower, brushed by densely grown weeds, perhaps slightly discomforted or even repelled by contact with projecting roots and damp earth, we have no doubt that we are in a real forest. But from this actuality of moist earth and roots the supernatural world of Keats's romance emerges imperceptibly. As we move into less tangible, more distant, and slightly mysterious "gloomy shades, sequestered deep" (I.67) and unconsciously stray with the real lambs, miraculously preserved, to the "herds of Pan" (I.78), we leave an observed landscape for a legend (" 'twas believed ever" [I.73]). Then we return to the natural world of a lawn with the "marble altar" (I.90) of Pan, the nature deity we saw earlier as symbolic of man's link with the beyond. Keats more explicitly relates the dawn scene with its "silvery pyre" of eastern clouds (I.96) to the theme of self-annihilation. The contrast between the "pleasantness" (I.89) of a real altar on a real sunlit lawn and the "gloomy shades" leading to a landscape of fantasy may reveal more than the poet himself recognizes by anticipating his later ambivalence toward the imagination. On the one hand the pleasant lawn and altar, where we find refuge after losing our way in the forest's gloom, may symbolize the beautiful sanctuaries seized by the imagination, which "bind us to the earth / Spite of . . . the gloomy days, / . . . and o'er-darkened ways" (I.7–10). On the other hand it is the imagination that has teased us out of the daylight of nature into the dangerous gloom of romance, from which we are rescued by the pleasant environment of a real landscape. This "sense of real things," which in "Sleep and Poetry" (157) unsuccessfully opposed an ideal vision, will eventually undermine the heroes' dreams in "La Belle Dame" and *Lamia* and the fairyland song of "Ode to a Nightingale."

The fairy world of *Endymion*, however, still holds out against the onslaught of reality. While retaining the motif of the classical story of immortality and eternal love won under the protection of sleep, Keats's poem becomes a myth of self-fulfilling dreams, redemptive love, reunion with the ideal other, entrance into a higher order of existence through fellowship with essence, the joy-giving, restorative, and transcendent power of beauty, the creative omnipotence of the imagination, and infinite cravings on earth satisfied in heaven. In *Endymion* the imagination still wins a final victory: Keats still allows us to dream through a romance of wish-fulfillment without rudely awaking us at the end. Taking up the self-stricture of "mawkishness" in the Preface, critics have condemned the poem's escapism and its profusion of lush descriptions and incidents. Indeed some readers, accustomed to Keats's standard pattern of return from the excessive joys of his world of imagination to the pain of actuality, may be disconcerted by the pleasure bowers of *Endymion* because of the poem's romantic ending. But the boundless luxuriance, though sometimes self-indulgent, can basically be justified: it is functional to the theme of a life of sensations as stepping-stone to eternal happiness. Throughout his *Keats and Embarrassment* Christopher Ricks redeems passages of *Endymion* attacked by his critical predecessors. Nevertheless there is a danger that the super-abundance of florid bowers begins to pall as we lose sight of Keats's goal in the mazes of the plot. On the other hand the condemnation of the romance for its unabashed escapism should be rejected outright. Although Keats has not yet developed the dialectic between vision and actuality which pervades the great odes, there underlies the poem's unearthly flight and wish-fulfillment a poignant awareness of the actual world of inevitable sorrow, of frustrated yearnings and flowers crushed by lovers' feet. What Paul Sherwin has said of *Hyperion* is also true of *Endymion*: "Keats remains a self-conscious modern despite his embrace of old-style myth." [19] Speaking through Endymion in a sober mood, the poet emphasizes the vanity of all human aspiration, and yet, paradoxically, he appeases his hero's infinite hunger by letting the quest come to fruition. Romantic aspirers start out on a journey into a world of absolutes conscious of the futility of their enterprise. Only in a fairyland like Endymion's can it lead to fulfillment.

CHAPTER 5

On the Shore: Winter to Spring 1818

I   The Winter's Wind

A number of lyrics Keats wrote after the completion of the first
draft of *Endymion* (28 November 1817) and while he was
revising and copying his romance (January-March 1818) exhibit a
markedly firmer grip on reality and bring to the fore the frustrating
consciousness of human ephemerality. Thus "In drear nighted December" (December 1817) opposes man's excruciating knowledge to
the blissful ignorance of a leafless tree and frozen brook oblivious of
the pleasures of spring and summer. Man's consciousness of his
failure to recapture bygone happiness causes a desperate sense of
loss, which Keats calls "The feel of not to feel it" (21). The line was
changed by another hand to read: "To know the change and feel it," [1]
presumably in order to clarify the contrast between mankind's painful memory and nature's "sweet forgetting" (13). But Keats's version
has a wider significance. As John Jones comments, the poet "has put
his finger on that bereft self-enfolded state, the pressure of something missing, definite yet featureless, precise but unutterable, perfectly known and conceptually void." [2] There may also be a hint of
poetic impotence resulting from a deficiency of emotional response. [3]
Perhaps Keats thinks of the unhappiness of lovers who feel that they
no longer feel the way they once felt. In another sense, however,
"The feel of not to feel it" refers to nature, not man: "not to feel" is
precisely what the first two stanzas are about (the phrase perfectly
summarizes the present destitution of all sensation characterizing the
wintry landscape) and in stanza three the poet contrasts this
"numbed sense" of nature with the poignancy of human awareness.
The revision "To know the change and feel it" reinforces the idea that
the "change" from past happiness to present gloom breeds agonizing
reminiscences, whereas "The feel of not to feel it" intimates that the
poet envies tree and brook because they are free from both the pains
of memory and the pains of consciousness. The editor's line tends to
reduce the poem to a sentimental lament for vanished bliss; Keats's

words emphasize the theme of consciousness. They also explain why the experience "Was never said in rhyme" (24). Bards had always dealt with the painful memory of past joy, and although recently some (Goethe, Wordsworth, Byron) had become equally concerned with the idea of consciousness as an agonizing burden, Keats, who more than any other artist longed for "a Life of Sensations rather than of Thoughts" (*Letters*, I, 185), who was master of the sensuous object, of the "feel" of things, here becomes the first poet whose imagination seizes this truth as beauty, the first to translate the abstract notion of unconsciousness into imaginative rhyme by means of vividly sensuous pictures. The expression "feel," which epitomizes sensation, is most appropriate to that absence of all reflection and conceptualizing which thinking man begrudges nature. Even the present insentience of the tree and brook can, paradoxically, be expressed in the vocabulary of sensation as "The feel of not to feel it," because sensation, not thought, is proper to tree and brook: in spring the branches must have *felt* their "green felicity" (4), in summer the waves must have *felt* the rays of Apollo (12). "Green felicity" humanizes the dreary rural scene despite its contrast with humanity and suggests that although nature knows nothing of the distress of man's maturity it shares the happiness of his childhood. Keats calls tree and brook happy, because, numbed as they are now by December frost, when they do feel they are happy. They are "too happy" (2, 10) not only because their happiness is too great for December, but because it is greater than man's, in fact greater than anything man can conceive, since lack of consciousness is nature's alone. And mortality, the chief burden of consciousness, belongs to man and not nature. No winter frost can prevent branches "From budding at the prime" (8), and the "happy, happy tree," like the "happy, happy brook," enjoys a perpetuity pointing forward to the "happy, happy boughs" of the "Ode on a Grecian Urn" (21). But whereas the cold, lifeless eternity of the urn's sculptured boughs is counter-balanced by the heat of human passion, here the living indestructibility of nature seasonally renewing herself leaves Keats without compensation for his loss.

"On Sitting Down to Read *King Lear* Once Again" (22 January 1818), on the other hand, holds promise for the poet's rebirth. In this sonnet Keats turns away from the seductions of "golden-tongued Romance," such as the fairy power of Spenser and of his own *Endymion*, to Shakespeare's tragic paradigm of suffering in the hope of spiritual regeneration as man and poet. Keats prepares to "burn through" the "fierce dispute / Betwixt damnation and impassion'd clay," to contemplate the spectacle of an adverse fate and hostile

82

JOHN KEATS

world in conflict with a passionate individual weakened by age, and expects to widen his consciousness by exposing himself to the "Hell torment" as captured in "the old oak forest" where Lear's distiny is played out.[4] The drama is "bitter-sweet" because poignant yet intensely beautiful, with the bitterness of the struggle leaving behind the sweetness of enhanced insight, a learning through suffering and catharsis anticipating Keats's theory of soul-making. Keats here emphasizes the redeeming power of consciousness, which is not so much pain as the final outcome of a painful struggle. He believes that by confronting misery he will be able to pass on from the world of Flora and old Pan which he has been describing so far to the more agonizing strife of human hearts with which he will deal from now on in preparation for play-writing, his "greatest ambition" (*Letters*, II, 234). The self-doubting notion of wandering "in a barren dream" arises only to be dispelled at once. In the sonnet's climactic ending (which is given special emphasis by an alexandrine and the substitution of the Shakespearean couplet for the Petrarchan rhyme) Keats calls for the fire of conflict and suffering to burn him pure, so that, in his infinite aspiration, he may die to be reborn like the mythical phoenix.

This confident tone of poetic promise is challenged by a more sustained undertone of self-doubt in "When I have fears that I may cease to be" (January 1818). The mood which inspired the poem may have been nostalgia caused by a chance meeting with a particular woman or a premonition, arising out of Tom's disease, of the poet's own early death, but these and other even conflicting moods are organized into a harmonious whole, probably as a result of conscious imitation of the Shakespearean sonnet. In "When I have fears," Keats's first sonnet with the Shakespearean rhyme scheme, he uses both theme and structure of Shakespeare's sonnets for his own purpose. In Shakespeare the menacing clock, "Time's scythe" or "Time's fell hand," is balanced by the bard's immortal "poor rhyme," [5] but Keats fears that he may die before he has fulfilled his poetic potential. The first quatrain conveys this apprehension in Keats's characteristic harvest imagery ("glean'd," "Hold like rich garners the full-ripen'd grain") and the second in terms of the night sky as the source of poetic inspiration. The third quatrain expresses human ephemerality through the anticipated loss of a lovable "fair creature of an hour" (according to Woodhouse the same lady to whom Keats's next Shakespearean sonnet, "Time's Sea," is addressed).[6] So far Keats has strictly heeded the Shakespearean sonnet structure, giving us three parallel quatrains, introduced by "When," "When," and "And when," each reflecting some aspect of the poet's confrontation of his own mortality; and Keats also follows Shakespeare in balancing these three quatrains against the concluding lines, beginning with "then," in which he pits his personal experience against "the wide world." But the sonnet structure is loosened with the attachment of the final couplet to the previous line. The enjambment and the hurried rhythm caused by the unstressed syllables "on the" and "Of the" create an effect of onrushing waves about to overwhelm the lone poet on the shore and immerse him in an all-embracing ocean in which the insignificant individual's "love and fame" are absorbed like water drops. Keats's fear that time may cut him off before he has fulfilled his artistic promise has been expanded to include a lament for the transience of love and beauty and has finally given way to a recognition of universal mutability.

But the declared dread of premature death seems to hide a more complex spiritual crisis, perhaps even comprising a fear of failing as a poet, unusual for the Keats of 1818. Despite the self-confident assertion of his "teeming" fecundity, he may shy away from the immense task of converting into written words mere "cloudy symbols," indistinct and fleeting images, however "huge." A life of thought has encroached upon his life of sensations. So long as love was "unreflecting," he refused to see that the beloved was ephemeral, but from enraptured lover he has now become a thinker isolated by the weight of consciousness he bears. The "magic" moment of inspiration, the "fairy power" of love's ecstasy, and the "high romance" conceived by inspired poet and felt by impassioned lover have given way to a reality hostile to wish-fulfillment. The sonnet reads like a dirge for the departure of the poet's instinctively assured, blindly trusting, unthinking former self.

In "O thou whose face" ("What the Thrush Said") the poet seeks to return to the life of sensations by rejecting a fretful pursuit of book-knowledge in favor of a Wordsworthian "wise passiveness." The thrush, extreme in its antagonism to the temper of Icarus and the Faustian overreacher met elsewhere in Keats, promises a rich spiritual harvest to those who are receptive to nature's influence, and concludes, paradoxically, that there is something creative in the poet's attitude to his own indolence:

> He who saddens
> At thought of idleness cannot be idle,
> And he's awake who thinks himself asleep.

The plea for seeming idleness and the repeated admonition "O fret not after knowledge" is best explained in the letter to Reynolds of 19 February 1818 (which contains the poem) with its injunctions of susceptibility to new ideas and flowerlike growth (I, 231–32). The sonnet "Four seasons fill the measure of the year," in spirit not unlike the thrush's wise passiveness, traces the receptive mind from its vigorous springtime when it "Takes in all beauty with an easy span" through the more leisurely ruminations of its summer to the inertia of its autumn. The closing couplet reminds us that the mind "hath his winter too of pale misfeature, / Or else he would forget his mortal nature." What the thrush may have hinted at when it referred to the "winter's wind" is here made as explicit as in "In drear nighted December": the human individual does not share that cyclical renewal in nature which makes branches bud in spring and the thrush's song come "native with the warmth."

II Overbrimming Wine: Light Verse

Side by side with lyrics lamenting ephemerality, Keats composed or improvised almost half of his thirty-or-so humorous poems in the first three months of 1818. A letter to Haydon of March 21 contains the playful enumeration of the place-names in "For there's Bishop's Teign," the folksy "Where be ye going, you Devon maid" with its sexual innuendo, and the more openly bawdy "Over the hill and over the dale." Keats produces a delightful parody of the opening apostrophes of Milton's sonnets to great men, as in "Fairfax, whose name . . ." or "Cromwell, our chief of men, who . . ." or "Vane . . . whom . . ." with the heroic beginning of a sonnet entitled "To Mrs. Reynolds's Cat" (January 16):

> Cat! who hast passed thy grand climacteric,
> How many mice and rats hast in thy days
> Destroy'd?—How many tit bits stolen?

In this period Keats probably also wrote the six short pieces collected under the title "Extracts from an Opera," one beginning:

> O, I am frighten'd with most hateful thoughts!
> Perhaps her voice is not a nightingale's,
> Perhaps her teeth are not the fairest pearl.

These lines not only imitate Shakespeare's satire of Petrarchan similes in the sonnet "My Mistress' Eyes Are Nothing Like the Sun" but also mock Keats's own preoccupation with nightingales. (The nightingale has already been mentioned ten times in Keats's poetry, twice as "Philomel"; further allusions and the great ode are yet to come.) Another piece from this group, "The stranger lighted from his steed," anticipates "La Belle Dame sans Merci" as Keats's first poem in the ballad style and, furthermore, perhaps as a frivolous counterpart to the theme of the fatal woman, which may well have been in the poet's mind already. In "O blush not so!" (January 31), an amusing extemporization on "maidenheads . . . going" considered too obscene for publication by the Victorians, Keats becomes "a good-humoured discriminator of blushes," [7] fully aware of his own embarrassment, which—so he hints to his correspondent Reynolds—the writing of this ditty is intended to cover up (I, 219). These cynical poems might be regarded as Keats's unconscious reaction to his picture of the divine Cynthia, to a "Boyish imagination" which in his school days used to make him think "a fair Woman a pure Goddess" (*Letters*, I, 341), and we may surmise that he has not quite outgrown this notion.

Whereas we can only guess at what prompted him to write bawdy verses, Keats gives us the background to the composition of two other basically lighthearted poems, "Robin Hood" and "Lines on the Mermaid Tavern." These were sent to Reynolds on February 3 "In answer to his Robin Hood Sonnets." Despite an undertone of transience, with the rollicking rhythm of their heptasyllabic couplets they give more playful than nostalgic pictures of carefree revelry and independence from a bygone age and recapture the "unobtrusive" tone Keats admires in the Elizabethans, whose poetry, unlike Wordsworth's, has no "palpable design upon us" (*Letters* I, 223–25). In a less jovial poem Keats would not so irreverently praise the earthly canary wine at the Mermaid Tavern above an Elysian beverage. A more typical Keatsian preference for wine overbrimming with Apollo's "golden sunshine" is expressed in "Hence burgundy, claret, and port," apparently improvised in the letter of January 31 to Reynolds (I, 220–21). The poem is lighthearted enough, but at the mere mention of Apollo Keats seems to be reminded of the tragic conflict between the real and the imaginary world. In "God of the meridian" (which immediately follows in the letter and is often printed as the final twenty-five lines of "Hence burgundy, claret, and port") the poet suffers "A terrible division" between soul and body, a "madness" from which only Apollo can grant release.

III   *The Epistle to Reynolds ("Dear Reynolds . . .")*

On March 25, 1818, Keats gave poignant expression to a crisis of excessive self-consciousness in a verse epistle in rhymed couplets to Reynolds, in which he fathoms the insufficiencies of reason and imagination. Most readers have agreed with Keats that the verse is "careless" (I, 263); but even if the poem was improvised, it is more coherent than appears at a first reading. The light tone of the opening is consonant with the enumeration of "all disjointed" (5) dream-land figures of incongruity. Pious pagans, rare godlike creatures who live the harmonious lives depicted in some paintings by Titian and Claude Lorrain,[8] may perhaps enjoy nothing but beautiful dreams (13–25). The poet's own dreams, however, not only "please" but also "vex" (4), since they are bound to his "daytime" world (70) of joy mixed with pain, of undue conceptualization that tends to spoil delight in mere sensation by exposing the inherently ruthless struggle for existence (86–105).

In this poem Keats's theory of negative capability undergoes a severe strain. Ignoring the Thrush's admonition, he frets after "High reason" (75), which can only lead to frustration, for the probing intelligence fails to resolve the issues it raises. The self-consciousness resulting from overreaching ourselves "forces us in summer skies to mourn" summer's imperfections and the approach of winter, and "spoils the singing of the nightingale"; and looking "too far into the sea" brings to light the "eternal fierce destruction" beneath nature's calm exterior (84–85, 94–97). It is not only "High reason" but also the imagination that thus overextends itself:

> Or is it that imagination brought
> Beyond its proper bound, yet still confined,—
> Lost in a sort of purgatory blind,
> Cannot refer to any standard law
> Of either earth or heaven?— (78–82)

If Keats is here thinking of that imagination whose visions are confined to heaven, then he implies that humans will call in vain for its aid in their struggle with earthly ills. More probably, however, he means that the scope of our imagination is limited by our temporal condition. The verse epistle itself illustrates how, within its proper bound, imagination transforms nightmares into poetry by using other products of the imagination (paintings by Titian and Claude) as catalysts. Within imagination's sphere lies also the promised "new romance" which will provide refuge from "horrid moods, / Moods of one's mind!" (105–106, 111). Only when it presses for final answers to life's riddles does imagination, like reason, overreach itself, so that it remains suspended between its terrestrial raw material and metaphysical aspirations. In Keats's post-*Endymion* phase imagination is as helpless as reason before a mystery which has become a burden. Henceforth the poet recognizes imagination's limits. Unable to come to terms with the struggle for existence, he tries to dismiss his vision of destruction. Nevertheless the present crisis has taken Keats a tremendous step forward toward acceptance of reality; and even the final escape into romance, paradoxically, serves reality by restoring imagination to its proper bound and sharpening the distinction between life and art.

IV *"Isabella"*

The romance Keats has in mind at the end of the epistle to Reynolds is "Isabella; or, the Pot of Basil" (February-April 1818). The story, taken from Boccaccio's *Decameron*, tells how Lorenzo, Isabella's lover, is murdered by her brothers and then visits her in a nightly vision, and how Isabella disinters Lorenzo's head, places it in a pot of basil plant, and dies after her brothers steal the plant.

The poem has had its ups and downs. It had a mixed reception from the first reviewers, was accorded the highest praises by Sidney Colvin in 1887, was severely downgraded by Amy Lowell and John Middleton Murry in 1925, and was held in relatively low esteem until the 1960s and 1970s, when a number of critics showed that despite its fantastic story it confronts reality.[9] Keats so hinted himself, even as he foresaw the attacks of the reviewers, when he wrote to Woodhouse: "There are very few would look to the reality" (II, 174). The poet's invocations to Boccaccio and to Melancholy create aesthetic distance, which should encourage us to look beyond a sentimental fairy tale about "simple Isabel" (1, 446). The black-white contrast between the villainous brothers and the innocent lovers might appear mawkish and be taken as evidence of Keats's avoidance of moral dilemmas after the dubious morality depicted in the epistle to Reynolds if it were not for the incisive realism in the characterization of the brothers which led Bernard Shaw to think of Keats as a social reformer.[10] The poet further tempers the romance by means of realistic details of disease and decay, and despite his protests he does not flinch from the "wormy circumstance" (385) of the digging, the

buried corpse, and the severing of the head. Perhaps Keats is trying
to test the power of his art, "its intensity, capable of making all
disagreeables evaporate, from their being in close relationship with
Beauty & Truth" (*Letters*, I, 192), for example when he makes us
share Isabella's arduous task as she stops "to throw back at times her
veiling hair" (376). Such an intensity of empathic feeling charac-
terizes much of the poem. The echo from *Romeo and Juliet* ("a young
palmer") in the opening stanza may appeal to some readers, but more
distinctively Keatsian is the line "But her full shape would all his
seeing fill" (12). Although any figure of speech may be ridiculed if
taken literally, some of Keats's have made him a favorite target, and
this is one of them. Nevertheless in its context this image is remarkably powerful. Keats conveys the mutual feeling between the lovers,
the idea that Isabella was all to Lorenzo and he to her. As Lorenzo
identifies himself with Isabella, so we identify with Lorenzo's sensation; as Isabella is cast into Lorenzo, so are we, until "her full shape"
fills our seeing, too. The image not merely converts the visual into
the tactile but suggests contact, roundness, contentedness, ripeness,
completion—in short, fulfillment.

Indeed the poem is about fulfillment and nonfulfillment. The
heroine seeks to accomplish her destiny by means of union with the
basil plant. Keats takes over Boccaccio's concept of love, the "immortal Lord" (397), outlasting death,[11] but, possibly under the influence
of the Wordsworthian theme of humanity's communion and fusion
with nature, he sees in the fable of the lifeless head grown into a living
plant the universal process of ripening, change, death, and rebirth
comprising nature and mankind. This process of fruition of which
death is the consummation will find its supreme expression in "To
Autumn," but in "Isabella" it is perverted when fulfillment is twice
denied. The poem repeatedly associates human life with plant life by
describing Lorenzo while still alive or when he appears in the vision
in terms which anticipate the mute plant growing in the flower pot.
His voice is "Stifled" (45), his forehead "waxing very pale and dead"
(53), and his happiness grows "like a lusty flower" (72). (The much-
admired prolepsis "So the two brothers and their murder'd man /
Rode past fair Florence" [209–10] [12] is the poem's most conspicuous
instance of this technique of anticipation.) When in the vision Lorenzo describes himself as surrounded by vegetation (298–301), he
seems to prophesy his rebirth as a basil plant. The beautiful line "And
thou art distant in Humanity" (312) not only reflects the contrast
between a living woman and the ghost of her dead lover but also the

movement of Lorenzo, now "Upon the skirts of human-nature dwelling" (306), toward plant life. In his brilliant discussion of the typical
Keatsian "feel" John Jones aptly points to the line "At last they felt the
kernel of the grave" (383) as "blazing inspiration," [13] but Keats's
felicity in this instance is easier to account for than Jones assumes, for
surely it has something to do with Lorenzo's head later becoming the
life-giving kernel of the basil plant. Even Isabella's tears, which the
human lover is prepared to drink (39), acquire a new significance as
they later fertilize the plant, keeping it "ever wet" (416), moistening
it "unto the core" (424), and feeding it (425) by showering it continually (452). Isabella's humanity is also linked to Lorenzo's vege-
table existence by means of expressions such as "Thy beauty grows
upon me" (319), "Upon the murderous spot she seem'd to grow"
(365), or "she sat drooping by the basil green" (458). The metaphor of
love leading Lorenzo "from wintry cold . . . to summer clime" (65–
66) [14] looks forward to Isabella's restoration of her lover. With special
emphasis Keats devotes the poem's middle stanza (stanza thirty-two)
to a luscious comparison between Isabella's "gradual decay from
beauty" and the encroachment of "The breath of Winter . . . / And
the sick west" on autumn's "gold tinge" (249–56), an analogy less
serving conventional embellishment than to identify the fate of the
lovers with the inevitability of the natural process.

The love between Isabella and Lorenzo, which is cut short by
murder, seeks fruition on another level between the woman and the
basil plant. Completion would be achieved if Isabella were allowed to
die with her basil. As he will tell us in "Ode on Melancholy," "Beauty
that must die" (21) summons in Keats the feeling of melancholy; and
so now, in anticipation of Isabella's self-fulfilling death, the poet
prays: "O Melancholy, linger here awhile!" (433). [15] This melancholy
implies an acceptance of the inevitable which sees in death the
necessary fulfillment of life. When the treacherous brothers steal the
garden pot they again forestall fulfillment, this time the sad fulfillment of a union in death. Keats must therefore retract his invocation
to Melancholy:

> O Melancholy, turn thine eyes away!
> ....
>
>   For Isabel, sweet Isabel, will die;
> Will die a death too lone and incomplete,
> Now they have ta'en away her basil sweet. (481–88)

The melancholy process of completion is truncated. Fulfillment, however, is finally achieved when the fate of Isabella and Lorenzo is eternalized in a song "born" (501) of their story, so that if not in death they are reunited in legend. As in the "Grecian Urn," a perfection withheld in the world of nature is vouchsafed in the realm of art.

V Budding Morrow

The flowering basil plant symbolizes that continuity and renewal which Keats earlier represented as "leaves / Budding—fruit ripening in stillness" ("After dark vapours"). In "Mother of Hermes! and still youthful Maia" (the Ode to Maia, written 1 May 1818) and the sonnet "To Homer" (probably April or May 1818), which reflect Keats's affinity with the poets of antiquity, he expresses hopes for spiritual rebirth, in the former by direct appeal to a deity and in the latter through a most beautiful and original figure: "There is a budding morrow in midnight." Keats never finished the Ode to Maia as he had promised (*Letters*, I, 278), but its one fourteen-line stanza is a self-contained unit. Singing a hymn to Maia (one of the Pleiades, sometimes worshiped as an earth goddess), the poet prays for the simple-heartedness and "old vigour" of Greek bards and disclaims the need for a wider audience than "the quiet primrose, and the span / Of heaven and few ears." The simplicity of the poem prompted Colvin to assert that it is "in a more truly Greek manner than anything else" Keats wrote,[16] but this claim requires qualification. The poet's analytical nostalgia, his consciousness of the discrepancy between the world of antiquity and his own, make the Ode to Maia modern rather than ancient, or "sentimental" according to Friedrich Schiller's treatise *On Naive and Sentimental Poetry* (1795), Romantic rather than Classical. Keats may have abandoned the fragment because he realized that his prayer to achieve the contentment of ancient poets "Rich in the simple worship of a day" could not be granted. Two days after composing the Maia stanza Keats describes to Reynolds his passage from "the infant or thoughtless Chamber" of life into the gradually darkening "Chamber of Maiden-Thought" (I, 280–81). Henceforth he recognizes the futility of trying to recapture the unconscious felicity of an Edenic past. In *Hyperion* even the "infant world" (I.26) of the early gods is pervaded by suffering and awareness of change and loss.

In "To Homer" the blind bard to whom the gods gave inner light focuses Keats's aspirations. Ignorant of the Greek original, Keats depends on accounts he *hears* from the translators who have actually visited Homer's "dolphin-coral." Blind Homer achieves the "triple sight" of imagination which encompasses infinity: Pan's forest, Jove's sky, and Neptune's ocean, or the spheres of "Earth and Heaven and Hell." Like Apollo's "aching ignorance" in *Hyperion* (III.107) just before his enlightenment and apotheosis, Keats's "giant ignorance" symbolizes all human limitations. In the sonnet Keats compares his own ignorance to Homer's blindness ("So wast thou blind") and implies an analogy between himself sitting "ashore" longing for "deep seas" and Homer "on the shores of darkness" about to be visited by light: as Homer was inspired when "Jove uncurtain'd Heaven," so Keats, too, may receive a sudden illumination which will revive him as a poet and grant him a vision transcending mortal bounds. The shore-sea dichotomy represents the gap between reality and aspiration which the poet here still hopes to bridge.

CHAPTER 6

Dying into Life: The First Hyperion and "The Eve of St. Agnes"

I Hyperion: A Fragment

IN July and August 1818 Keats went on a walking tour through the Lake District and Scotland with his friend Charles Brown. He regarded the trip as a kind of pilgrimage during which he would enrich his impressions and gather material for poetry. The first and perhaps the best of the poems written on this tour [1] was "On Visiting the Tomb of Burns" (1 July 1818), a sonnet reflecting the discrepancy between a scene imagined and its reality and haunting the reader with the line "All is cold beauty; pain is never done." Burns's country, Keats felt, was conducive to the composition of an epic (*Letters*, I, 331). Fingal's Cave on the Isle of Staffa, which prompted the verses "Not Aladdin magian," conjured up a vision of "the Giants who rebelled against Jove" (I, 348) and thus inevitably of a battle between the Olympians and Titans in the projected *Hyperion* epic, where this cave would reappear as "cathedral cavern" (I.86).

Whereas in *Endymion* Keats simply described beauty as "a joy forever," in his first *Hyperion* fragment (Books One and Two, autumn 1818; Book Three, spring 1819) he emphasizes the relation of beauty to change, loss, and suffering. For Endymion the problems arising from the confining predicament of mankind were presumably solved with his final apotheosis by a *dea ex machina*, but Apollo, the parallel poet-figure of *Hyperion*, continues to bear the sufferings of humanity after his deification, and indeed undergoes agony even as he "Die[s] into life" (III.130). (The expression "dying into life," reminiscent of the Christian concept of physical death as the gateway to eternal life in Heaven, is often applied in Keats criticism to the process of passing from one of two worlds, the temporal and the atemporal, to the other.) The idea of progress formulated by Oceanus is frequently held to be the poem's central topic, [2] but it is in fact subordinate to the theme of the timelessness of poetry. Keats may have found the material for his projected epic about the Titans, the barbarous deities who reigned till Zeus the Olympian overcame his father Saturn, in *The Pantheon* (1806) by "Edward Baldwin" (a pseudonym for the philosopher William Godwin).[3] *Hyperion: A Fragment* humanizes these deities. In epic fashion the poem begins *in medias res* with all the Titans except Hyperion already vanquished. Book One describes the dejection of the fallen leader Saturn, who cannot grasp his defeat at the hands of the younger generation of gods, and the ill forebodings of Hyperion, who suffers, in Harold Bloom's words, "a failure of nerve, or even a nervous breakdown." [4] In the war council of the second book (modeled on the council in Book Two of *Paradise Lost*) Oceanus and Clymene accept the new order, while Enceladus advocates rebellion. The fragmentary third book depicts the deification of Apollo, who is to supersede Hyperion as the sun-god. Hyperion was sufficiently vague in Greek myth to have permitted Keats to treat him freely if he had completed his fragment. The poet had probably planned a more important role for his titular hero, who seems indeed to be the only figure in the fragment to allow of development in the direction of a tragic inner conflict.[5]

Having lost his kingdom (I.90) Saturn cannot adapt to the new situation. "I have left / My strong identity, my real self . . ." (I.113–14), he cries. Saturn found his identity in kingship and the order that accompanied his rule. With this order gone he has lost his bearings and no longer recognizes himself. His personality is fixed so that he must learn to adjust to novelty, and he is as yet incapable of seeing himself in his new subordinate position. He would rather "fashion forth / Another world" (I.142–43) in the image of the old to find himself again. The new Olympian order represents an unaccustomed set of values by which Saturn feels threatened, because he lacks the negative capability which would allow him to absorb them.

If the Titan Saturn stands for what Keats in his letter to Bailey called "Men of Power," Olympian Apollo, god of the sun, of poetry, music, and medicine, is the representative of men of genius, of the poet who has no fixed identity, who lets "the mind be a thoroughfare for all thoughts" (*Letters*, I, 184, 387; II, 213). The young Apollo feels the "green turf" of his native isle, indeed the whole face of the earth, to be too confining, so long as there are sun, moon, and stars to explore (III.93–102). His "aching ignorance" (III.107) reveals a painful longing, an openness to new experience which allows his per-

94 JOHN KEATS

sonality to evolve. In Apollo's growth into godhead we see the soul-making process at work.

While Apollo is deified, the Titans, formerly supreme divinities, are repeatedly compared to frail mankind (I.43, 169–70, 332–35; II.101–106). We are not intended to imagine that, poisoned by "mortal oil" (II.97), Saturn will die one day, for we have been assured that the Titans remain "immortal" (I.44). Rather Saturn, still a god, has lost his former placidity and acquired the "frailty" (II.93) of earthly passions, including the futile hope of reinstatement, the human refusal to confront inevitable loss. Since at one time "Fate seem'd strangled" in his grasp (I.105), he now finds it difficult to accept that, like man, he is ruled by destiny. Furthermore, although the fall of the Titans seems to be modeled on the defeat of the rebel angels in *Paradise Lost* (with the difference that the Titans are the former established power and the victims of rebellion), we are also reminded of the Fall of man. The overthrow of the Titans may symbolize that stage in man's development at which he was overwhelmed by the consciousness of his mortality, the knowledge gained with the eating of forbidden fruit in Eden. Unlike Adam and Eve, the Titans cannot learn of their own future death (since they are immortal); but now experiencing themselves for the first time the pernicious effect of change all around them, they gain new insight into the nature of mortality. The immediate change they discern is their loss of power.

The defeated Titans become dimly aware that, like humans, they are enslaved by "aching time" (I.64). Even if we assume that Adam and Eve were created mortal and did not fall into mortality but into consciousness of mortality, we can construe their earlier childlike immunity to the sense of transience as a kind of immortality. Similarly, so long as Saturn was unaware of the passage of time, time seemed to stand still for him; he seemed to be time's master. Keats would have found in Godwin's *Pantheon* that Saturn and Time "may indeed be considered as the same deity, the Greek names for each differing only in a single letter; Κρόνος [Kronos] being Greek for Saturn, and Χρόνος [Chronos] for Time." [6] With his fall into consciousness Keats's Saturn has lost his identity as god of Time. Even unfallen Hyperion, who has yet to awake to the sense of transience, experiences a new subjection to temporality. Having overreacted to ill premonitions by commanding dawn to rise before the appointed hour, he has failed and "bent / His spirit to the sorrow of the time" (I.300–301).

Alone among his brethren Oceanus comes to terms with Time by seeing it as progress. Like Asia in Shelley's *Prometheus Unbound* (act 2, scene 4), Oceanus enumerates the overthrow of successive genera- tions of mythological deities, but his hierarchy is one of beauty: " 'tis the eternal law / That first in beauty should be first in might" (II.228–29). His genealogy begins with "Chaos and blank Darkness," who were replaced by Heaven and Earth, then by his own genera- tion, the Titans, and now by the Olympians (II.206–15). For Oceanus the dispossession of the old race by the new is not the result of revolution or conquest (II.215–17) but the "course of Nature's law" (II.181), a process like the ripening of fruit (II.192–94). Saturn, who still labors under the delusion that time can repeat itself, ironically imagines his old kingdom ripening for his repossession (I.121–25). Oceanus' theory of evolution, on the other hand, combines the cyclical pattern of nature with the linear progress of history: things ripen and decay, but each generation is more beautiful than the previous one. As the most adaptable of the Titans he can give a resigned and dispassionate account of the surrender of his empire before the superior beauty of Neptune (II.232–39). Recognition of transience leads Saturn to baffled despair, Enceladus to (doubtless futile) rebellion, Clymene to a sentimental elegy that "joy is gone" (II.253), and Oceanus to positive acceptance. Oceanus has lost his status as a ruling god of the sea yet gains a new identity seeing himself as a link in the chain of progress.

Oceanus is right in recognizing the defeat of the Titans as the triumph of beauty. But his perspective is still the perspective of time, whereas Keats depicts the change of power from the point of view of eternity. Oceanus goes on to conjecture: ". . . another race may drive / Our conquerors to mourn as we do now" (II.230–31). In- asmuch as we can judge by the evidence of the fragment, which only allows us to guess at the ending, and in the absence of a clear authorial voice, we may assume that here Oceanus is wrong. There is no evidence in either of the two *Hyperion* fragments[7] or anywhere else in Keats's poetry of the future defeat of the Olympians (as Shelley's Jupiter is cast down in *Prometheus Unbound*); on the contrary, Keats repeatedly portrays the Olympian gods, and especially Apollo, as symbols of permanence. Most important, even though Apollo is represented as evolving, he seems to be evolving into a Keatsian ideal of eternal supremacy. To what extent, then, is Oceanus speak- ing for Keats? *Hyperion* neither endorses (as is often taken for granted) nor does it necessarily refute Oceanus' theory of a progres-

96 JOHN KEATS

sively improving world, or, to be more precise, of a world growing progressively more beautiful. Blinded by the beauty of the Olympians and their victory over the Titans, Oceanus may be confusing nature's law of change with the law of the timelessness of beauty. The Titans' overthrow of the previous generation of gods may have been due to nature's law of the young displacing the old rather than the Titans' greater beauty, or beauty in unaging gods may merely symbolize the youth of mortals. Whether the genealogy of the earlier gods represents the progress Oceanus has in mind or only the history of cosmic change, the advent of the Olympians does not symbolize just one more stage in an endlessly evolving universe. The previous victories were changes that took place in the course of time; the recent one is the victory of timelessness. *Hyperion* is concerned with the contrast between change and permanence, between the historical process and the domain of art, between the inevitable surrender of the old to the new and an eternally youthful perfection.

This perfection is represented by Apollo. Unlike Saturn and Hyperion, who are being forced into a recognition of their bondage to a mutable cosmos, Apollo struggles for his new awareness of a world of transience and suffering and thus, paradoxically, enters the realm of eternity:

> Knowledge enormous makes a God of me.
> Names, deeds, gray legends, dire events, rebellions,
> Majesties, sovran voices, agonies,
> Creations and destroyings, all at once
> Pour into the wide hollows of my brain,
> And deify me. . . . (III.113–18)

Apollo's deifying "Knowledge enormous," which includes the tribulations of Titans and men, raises him to the vantage point of timelessness. The parallel expression in *The Fall of Hyperion*, "A power within me of enormous ken, / To see as a God sees" (i.303–304), makes it clear that Keats is thinking of the imaginative knowledge of the poet. The poet has the power of a god over the scenes and characters he has invented or recreated and is not subject to an imagined temporality of his own making. Standing outside the "deeds," the "dire events," and the "rebellions" he has created, he can visualize them "all at once." Apollo's prophetic dream of Mnemosyne, goddess of memory and mother of the muses, prefigures his future role as god of poetry, "the Father of all verse" (III.13), a prophecy which is partially fulfilled when he awakes to find a golden lyre by his side (III.59–63). Like the "happy melodist" of the "Grecian Urn," "unwearied, / For ever piping songs for ever new" (23–24), the "ear of the whole universe" remains "Unwearied" by Apollo's "new tuneful wonder," a music reproducing the mixture of "pain and pleasure" of a mutable world yet not subject to time (III.65–67). "Sick / Of joy and grief at once," Clymene hears this unearthly "golden melody" which combines life and death, progression and simultaneity: "A living death was in each gush of sounds, / . . . / That fell, one after one, yet all at once" (II.280–89). Apollo's dream is fully realized with his deification under the tutelage of Mnemosyne (Memory), who bridges the Titans' temporal world and the Olympians' timelessness by forsaking "old and sacred thrones" for Apollo's "loveliness new born" (III.77–79). [8] The birth of the god of poetry seems to have heralded the triumph of art's eternal perfection over a world of natural process in which events follow upon each other in a series of successive moments, in which powers rise and fall, and in which men are born and die. The birth of timeless beauty has caused the fall of the Titans and their leader Saturn-Kronos-Time.

The apotheosis of Apollo, which consummates this victory of eternity over time, presents Keats with a more formidable difficulty than the humanization of the Titans. Though no human being, Apollo is described as if he were ascending from humanity into godhood in stages: his prophesied birth, his dream of the "eternal calm" (III.60) of Mnemosyne's eyes, his creation of divine music, his dream of Mnemosyne come true, his infinite aspiration, his superhuman struggle against "aching ignorance" (III.107), and finally his assumption of immortalizing knowledge. If this process symbolizes the growth of the poet to maturity and immortal fame, then Apollo's native isle, the Endymion-like world of "bower" and "green recess" pervaded by the inspiring sounds of nature (III.31–41), may stand for the realm of Flora and old Pan, whereas the seizure of "agonies / Creations and destroyings" (III.115–16) may represent the strife of human hearts. *Hyperion* develops the theme, suggested by the song "O Sorrow" in *Endymion*, that suffering is "creative of essential Beauty" (*Letters*, I, 184). Apollo, now standing with the poet beyond the temporal world depicted in the narrative, recognizes that beauty inheres in suffering and in the ephemeral nature of all things (an insight which Oceanus, who is fettered to time, fails to achieve though he justifies his own suffering in the name of beauty). The world of change and sorrow confronted by Apollo remains to be proved upon his pulses and so he reenters it. This experience is depicted by means of the "wild commotions" Apollo undergoes to "Die into life" (III.124, 130). Christ-like, he seems to be taking upon himself the agonies he sees in Mnemosyne's silent face. In order to emphasize that Apollo's entry into the realm of immortality is accompanied by an initiation into the suffering of mortals, that he becomes man when he becomes god, his transformation is compared with a birth pang, sexual orgasm, and death, with the world of generation as distinct from the deathless world of Eden, a Heaven, or a Grecian urn.

The Fall of Hyperion makes it clear that Apollo's vision of agonies comprises those of the fallen Titans, but the first version breaks off before we are told what the vision is. Keats may have ended the poem in the middle of a line with "from all his limbs / Celestial . . ." in order to bring out the ineffability of divine nature. Murry claims that the poem is "finished" because with Apollo's deification Keats had achieved his purpose, "to reveal the secret of the poetic nature," and "had told all that he knew of that nature." [9] But if we regard the poem as a fragment we should not assume that Keats failed to go on only because in Book Three he had no further guidance from mythology. More probably, as Pierre Vitoux argues, the poet "had the conception, however dim, of a fairly elaborate narrative" but foresaw difficulties in the execution of his epic design. [10] Perhaps Keats found his increasing involvement with Apollo (to whom we have seen him attracted from his earliest works) incompatible with the sympathy he had already aroused for the Titans. This problem might have been solved by letting Apollo merge with Hyperion rather than displace him (as the omnipotence of the Aeschylean Zeus seems eventually to have fused with the omniscience of Prometheus). Keats probably had greater difficulty in reconciling the role of Apollo as participant in the epic with his evolving conception of the god as a poet-figure who envisions the action, so that he took up the fragment again only after he had decided to relinquish the objective epic for a subjective dream-vision. But even then he possibly discovered (or rediscovered) that he could not live up to his promise to Haydon that "Apollo in Hyperion being a fore-seeing God will shape his actions like one" (I, 207), because Apollo was unfit for action. Tom's death on the first of December had probably something to do with Keats's decision to put the poem aside; Keats may have added the climactic deification of Apollo, as Bate suggests, merely to get this central episode "off his chest" and "to provide . . . some hint of what lay ahead." [11]

We must also consider Keats's own remarks to Reynolds (quoted in chapter 1) and the almost identical words to George and Georgiana on "Miltonic verse" and on devoting himself to "another sensation" (II, 167, 212). He made these comments when he abandoned the second *Hyperion* but they are equally relevant to the first version, since he asked Reynolds to mark passages indicating "the true voice of feeling," and Reynolds could only have had the text of the first version before him. Perhaps, as Brian Wilkie thinks, by September 1819 Keats simply wanted to relax from his large Miltonic project.[12] "Sensation," however, reminds us of the famous letter to Bailey of November 1817 where this word was associated with youth and eternity: "O for a Life of Sensations rather than of Thoughts! It is 'a Vision in the form of Youth' a Shadow of reality to come" (I, 185).[13] Keats may have felt that both *Hyperions* too often lacked the language of sensation ("the true voice of feeling") to be consistent with his vision of the triumphant, perpetually youthful god of poetry.

Critics long ago commented upon Keats's attempt to overcome the Miltonic influence in a poem that uses Milton as epic model. Recently, following Bate's biography of Keats and his study on *The Burden of the Past and the English Poet*, scholars have pointed more persistently to what Stuart Sperry calls Keats's "strong sense of the oppressive weight of poetic tradition, the difficulty of saying something new."[14] The "revisionary" criticism of Harold Bloom and his followers, which regards poets as ephebes "misreading" their precursors, makes much of Keats's struggle with the shadow of Milton (and Wordsworth).[15] Thus Paul Sherwin adds a vital dimension to our understanding of *Hyperion* when he shows how Keats, "affirming his own truth as opposed to Milton's error" by bold "misrepresentation," conveys the "dim sense of . . . a mysterious force whose ways cannot be justified." But Sherwin goes on to see in Hyperion's serpentine spasms and impotence (I.259–301), as well as in Apollo's convulsions with which the fragment breaks off, Keats's failure to free himself from Milton's bonds: "Falling away from Milton, he nevertheless keeps falling back into, or holding on to, Milton." Still, Sherwin describes the work as "a poem about the progress of poetry."[16] Similarly Sperry, who also sees Keats in both Hyperion and Apollo but tends to identify Saturn with Wordsworth and Enceladus with Byron, finds in the poem an expression of decline and rebirth of poetic energy.[17] "The relation between the new god and the old is the relation between the new poet and Milton" for Leslie Brisman, and also for Stuart Ende, whose revisionary reading, like Sherwin's, makes Milton "the sovereign who rules the poem."[18]

Keats's rebellion against Milton is beyond doubt: "I have but lately stood on my guard against Milton. Life to him would be death to me," he writes to George (II, 212). Nevertheless our analysis has tried to show that the poem is not so much about different ages of poetry and different poets as about the birth of poetry whose timeless beauty conquers a beauty subject to time. Keats rejects Milton because it is Milton's epic and Milton's theme of man's rise to the dual challenge of mortality and consciousness that the younger poet has been trying to transform into a proposition of his own which he now can accept less and less. Increasing doubts about the unqualified triumph of poetry and timelessness make Keats put aside his project in or before April and abandon it in September 1819.

Yet *Hyperion* is not the failure it is so often held to be. This is not to say that the work is anything but a poetic fragment—events and characters, notably Hyperion himself, are left dangling, and of the plot development and eventual outcome nothing is certain except the triumph of Apollo—but it does mean that Keats's recurrent preoccupation with the immortality of beauty has been rendered consistently as a successful thematic whole. By the time the poem breaks off, the theme has been essentially conveyed, and until then Keats has succeeded in keeping his doubts under control. Although the evolution of his ideas over an extended period of time must have affected *Hyperion*, the repeated claim that the poet fails to reconcile different concepts within his work is no more warranted than in the case of the completed *Endymion*. The theme of progress, for example, already appears in the letter to Reynolds of 3 May 1818 containing the parable of life as a "Mansion of Many Apartments," where Keats writes of "a grand march of intellect" (I, 280, 282). We have seen how this theme, enunciated by Oceanus, is dramatically integrated into the poem's contrast between the mutability of nature and the permanence of art, which also subsumes Keats's gradually unfolding concept of ephemerality enhancing beauty, a thought not fully developed till the great odes of 1819. Nor is the work's coherence impaired by Keats's return from the sublime Miltonic diction of the first two books to the style and even the imagery of *Endymion*. This "regression" (the word is used by Gittings) has disturbed some eminent Keatsians: Bate, for example, feels that Keats "fell back numbly . . . upon familiar stances and habitual idiom." [19] Yet the atmosphere of *Endymion* perfectly suits Keats's purpose: the portrayal of Apollo's fulfilled dream, his aspiration to leave the protective but confining bowers of his native isle for the stars, a craving which

makes him "Spurn the green turf as hateful" (III.94), and his growth
toward immortality. Even the three lines from the "dying into life"
passage (III.124–32) omitted from the manuscript, "a hue more
roseate than sweet-pain / Gives to a ravish'd Nymph when her warm
tears / Gush luscious with no sob," which M. R. Ridley denounces as
"a disastrous spasm of the old fatal Leigh Hunt influence," an "unfor-
tunate and incongruous interlude," [20] appropriately present an explicit image of the sexual stage completing the generative cycle of
birth, procreation, and death; and "sweet-pain" and sobless weeping
are characteristic Keatsian evocations of the paradoxes of the human
predicament unperplexed only in higher realms. Although Keats
apparently singled out "white melodious throat" (III.81) as an instance of unconsciously seized beauty at which he himself later
wondered, the expression has been queried and attacked. [21] But is
the magic hand of chance here at work not the same as that which will
paint the "silken flanks" of the "heifer lowing at the skies" in "Ode on
a Grecian Urn" (33–34)? By combining the whiteness of an Apollo
statue with throbbing melody Keats telescopes the effect of motion,
sound, and passion encrusted upon frozen marble which juxtaposes
time and timelessness in the ode.

There are, however, numerous expressions and whole passages in
Hyperion in which even those who regard the poem as a failure see a
new level of achievement. In the universally admired opening, for
example, Keats attains unsurpassed intensity in uniting cold, silence,
motionlessness, hardness, and lifelessness by means of an incremental repetition of ideas, words, and sounds. Withdrawal into
silent inertia following a fall from power is suggested from the outset:

> Deep in the shady sadness of a vale
> Far sunken from the healthy breath of morn,
> Far from the fiery noon, and eve's one star,
> Sat gray-hair'd Saturn, quiet as a stone. . . . (I.1–4)

Deprived of his rule over the temporal order, Saturn sits in gloomy,
statuesque silence as if the march of time could be arrested by his
own immobility and by his concealment from the moving heavenly
bodies which announce day and night. The Titan's petrified posture
is reinforced by the alliteration of the "t" and "st" and the repetition
of the syllable "sat" in "Saturn," contrasting with the softer surround-
ings echoed in the "d's" of the first line and the melodious assonance
of "shady" with "vale," a word whose very sound conveyed "cool
pleasure" to Keats. [22] His friend Bailey quoted the first six and

one-half lines of *Hyperion* to illustrate the poet's vowel theory,
which, we saw, probably involved the alternation of long and short
vowels and also assonance.[23] Pettet calls attention to Keats's rejection
of the word "thundrous" from line 7 of the draft and his choice, after
revision, of the expression "summer's day" in line 8 in order to show
how the poet repeats a sound (here that in the "sunken," "one," and
"hung" of the preceding lines) not mechanically but in a calculated
attempt at creating the desired melodic pattern.[24] The absence of
light and "breath" in the poem's first three lines modulates into more
insistent negations with "No stir . . . Not so much life . . . not one
light seed" (I.7–9). The finality of the fall is reflected in the cadence of
the line "But where the dead leaf fell, there did it rest" (I.10) with its
Miltonic pause after the sixth syllable; and when the ten monosyl-
lables have come to a full stop, we believe that even the lightest leaf
remains on the ground for lack of wind, held down, as it were, by
spondaic stress, and the weight of a masculine caesura (the break
after an accented foot).[25] The Spenserian melody and Miltonic tone
restore some dignity to the stupefied Titan and help to raise the poem
to epic level.

No doubt thinking of Meyer Abrams's seminal essay on the breeze
as the Romantic metaphor for inspiration, Geoffrey Hartman draws
attention to the strange windlessness in "verses which normally
contain a call for *in-spiration*."[26] But of course the mother of the
muses has deserted Saturn for Apollo's isle, where no spot is "Un-
haunted by the murmurous noise of waves" (III.40), whereas in this
vale of "fallen divinity" water is "voiceless" (I.11–12). This adjective
prepares us for the culminating epithets of benumbed defeat in the
description of the Titan's "old right hand" as "nerveless, listless, dead
/Unsceptered," with the loss of sovereignty epitomized in the felicitous expression "realmless eyes" (I.18–19). The feet of this sluggish
colossus succumb to sleep as if unable to carry a ponderous trunk and
a head bowed in surrender (I.16–17, 20). How unlike that earlier
Keatsian sculpture which expressed vigorous, creative potentiality as
"might half slumb'ring on its own right arm"! The might was that of
Zeus, who visited Danae in "A drainless shower of light" and whose
"supreme of power," despite its airiness, commanded, even charmed
obedience in "The very archings of . . . eye-lids" ("Sleep and Poetry," 235–38). That sculpture was of course poesy. In *Hyperion*
Kronos-Saturn, the god of time, has been dethroned by Zeus-
Jupiter. Inevitably the Titan Hyperion, who is already being com-

pelled to bow to time, will be overcome by another Olympian, the
god who represents the timeless might of poetry.

II *"Fancy"*

Written in playful trochaic heptasyllabic couplets, "Fancy" (which
Keats copied out in his journal-letter to America on 2 January 1819) is
probably the poet's most explicit statement of how the timeless
imagination transcends the limitations of our wearying everyday
existence. The "winged Fancy" (5) is compared to a caged bird which,
freed from its "prison-string" (91), will grant us uncloying pleasure
known only to immortals. By seeing spring, summer, and autumn
simultaneously on a winter night and interchanging them at random
before the novelty of each wears off, fancy can idealize reality, soaring
beyond the disenchantment through surfeit which prevails in this
phenomenal world:

> Every thing is spoilt by use:
> Where's the cheek that doth not fade,
> Too much gaz'd at? Where's the maid
> Whose lip mature is ever new?
> Where's the eye, however blue,
> Doth not weary? (68–73)

The craving for the "ever new" is one aspect of that infinite Romantic
aspiration which we met in Endymion's Faustian longing. Keats now
faces the paradox that the only manner of preserving the freshness of
a maiden's "lip mature" is not to enjoy it, for every consummation
involves a death. Desire satisfied dissolves "Like to bubbles" (4, 78),
so that the natural beauties of cheek, lip, and eye all too soon lose
their attractions. On the other hand the imagined heroes of timeless
myths do not "weary" (they neither cloy nor are cloyed) any more
than the "ever new" melodies of the "ever young" figures in the
"Grecian Urn" (24, 27). In the companion piece to "Fancy" in
the journal-letter, "Bards of passion," which, Keats says, "is on the
double immortality of Poets" (II, 25), he imagines dead poets in a
heaven "never cloying" (28), where the nightingale sings "divine
melodious truth" (19), of which we shall hear more in the great ode.
   While "Fancy" repeatedly emphasizes how nothing in our mutable
world survives the curse of tedium, it introduces another motif,
which seems to undermine this sense of weariness. When Keats

copied the poem into his letter in January 1819 the meaning of "Whe[e]re's the cheek that doth not fade / Too much gaz'd at?" (II, 23) was unambiguous: as the lover's hunger is stilled by his gaze, he gradually drains the beloved's cheek of its charm. But the comma after "fade" in the version published in 1820 briefly creates the impression that the poet laments the ephemerality of beauty, and only when we read on do we return to the theme of satiation. Since in most of the poems of the 1820 volume Keats is concerned with the transience-permanence dichotomy, he may have wished to inject an ambivalence by hinting that every mortal cheek, lip, or eye not only cloys but grows weary and wastes away with age. The theme of transience comes out more explicitly side by side with the theme of weariness when we are told that "the enjoying of the spring / Fades as doth its blossoming" (11–12). But can the poet consistently mourn both ephemerality and tedium? Does the very ephemerality of beautiful things not save us from having to bear their cloying weight indefinitely since they will die eventually? And, conversely, since joys are transient, is it not just as well that they should cloy because otherwise the thought of their transience would be unbearable? For Keats the tragic human predicament which precludes the attainment of full pleasure on earth explains both the implied lament over the transitoriness of all things and the inevitable weariness experienced after beauty has been enjoyed. Either the cheek fades and dies while we still desire it or else our satiated gaze will ultimately destroy enjoyment. A mind thus oppressed by the double burden of tedium and a sense of transience anticipates the sipping bee-mouth which turns honey to poison in "Ode on Melancholy" (24). Harassed by consciousness of the inadequacy of pleasure and therefore unable to rest content in the present moment, such a mind solves its self-provoked dilemma by creating a world of fancy.

III   *"The Eve of St. Agnes"*

"The Eve of St. Agnes" (January 1819) takes us from the real world into the timeless realm of fancy and back again. St. Agnes' eve, the twentieth of January, supposedly the coldest night of the year, commemorates a thirteen-year-old martyr whose virginity was miraculously preserved, and the celebration the following day involves two white "lambs unshorn" (71) whose wool will be woven by nuns (115–17). According to popular superstition a virgin who observes certain "ceremonies due" on St. Agnes' eve, including fasting and not

looking around her while undressing, will have a vision of her lover
(46–54). Madeline, the heroine of Keats's poem, follows the pre-
scribed ceremony, and while she dreams of her lover Porphyro, the
latter, having gained admittance to her chamber with the aid of the
aged nurse Angela, appears in the flesh, makes love to Madeline, and
elopes with her. Like Endymion, the hero of Keats's other romance
of wish-fulfillment, Madeline, at the moment of awakening from her
dream to find it truth, undergoes an experience transcending ordinary human love: in the arms of a lover who is now "Beyond a mortal
man impassion'd far" (316). But whereas Endymion is to stay "Ensky'd," Madeline and Porphyro return to earthly reality. And even
less than in *Endymion* can we here remain indifferent to the affirmation of a human sexual love (now inspired by Fanny Brawne though
the poem's topic was suggested by Isabella Jones).

Many readers will agree with Douglas Bush (an authority on more
than one period of English literature) that *"The Eve of St. Agnes* is by
far the most beautiful short narrative of its age, or perhaps of any age
of English poetry."* [27] Keats creates a highly artistic structure and
uses his magnificent Spenserian stanzas to produce a combination of
life and death, sensuality and abstinence, a haunting medieval atmosphere and a palpable present, a hint of supernatural magic and stark
realism. The first and last stanzas, sometimes regarded as the outer of
a series of concentric circles, [28] frame the living warmth of the lovers
in Madeline's chilly chamber with benumbing coldness, self-denial,
and death. The opening introduces a pious old Beadsman, who dies
at the end, as does old Angela. "The joys of all his life were said and
sung" may hint ironically that the Beadsman has wasted his life in
barren asceticism, but the line should probably be taken literally to
mean that since his deathbell has rung already his joys are over now,
though he is still as susceptible to "Music's golden tongue" as he was
in his youth (20–23). Perhaps his penitence is treated ironically. In
hope of a Christian heaven he prays to Jesus and Mary with "frosted
breath" which "Seem'd taking flight for heaven, without a death"
(6–8). A deathless transition from earth to heaven would imply that
the Beadsman stands outside the natural process in which death
consummates the ripening movement of life, so that the prayer
would miss its mark and go "past" the Virgin's picture. Ironic or not,
the Beadsman's abnegation is in glaring contrast to Keats's plea for a
"Life of Sensations," his speculation "that we shall enjoy ourselves
here after by having what we called happiness on Earth repeated in a
finer tone," and his rejection of the "little circumscribe[d] straight-

ened notion" that "we are to be redeemed by a certain arbitrary interposition of God and taken to Heaven" (*Letters*, I, 185; II, 101–102). The Beadsman is a foil to Madeline with her initial superstition and saintly piety followed by acceptance of physicality, and he is balanced at the other extreme by the gross revelers in the hall, while the superstitious yet slightly cynical old nurse may represent a kind of human norm in contrast to the two lovers' immortal passion and rude awakening into a menacing reality. Deathly cold is conveyed by the sculptured figures of knights and ladies buried in the chapel, although, paradoxically, Keats's verse seems to bring them to life as they ache in the chilliness instead of the heat of "purgatorial rails" (14–18), reflecting, as Stuart Sperry notes, "the harsh repression of human warmth and feeling." [29] The last stanza's "large coffin-worm" (which Keats must have remembered from an engraving by Carlo Lasinio seen the previous month at Haydon's) [30] and the concluding "ashes cold" contribute to the poem's insistence on the ephemerality of all mankind which includes the two lovers who "ages long ago . . . fled away into the storm."

Like its structural contrasts, the poem's finely wrought imagery, which (anticipating the great odes) appeals to each of the senses and usually to more than one at a time, brings out the intensity of the lovers' experience in a basically cold and hostile universe, reflects the seizure of a magic moment of fulfillment before the inevitable lapse into a world of process, decay, and time, and gives the characters a spiritual aura only to bring them back to earth. In stanza twenty-six, for example, the highly erotic description of Madeline undressing introduces an element of physicality essential at this stage in the plot. Comparison with the draft shows Keats enhancing sense impressions by adding warmth to Madeline's jewels, fragrance to her bodice, and a rustling sound to her attire, and by replacing an elusive "Syren of the Sea" with the tangible seaweed of a mermaid. Although like the siren the mermaid simile introduces a supernatural element, Madeline not only has become less dangerous but, with the concrete seaweed, appears to be (however slightly) more accessible to Porphyro. A moment ago (in stanza twenty-five), kneeling like a saint in a religious picture with a halo round her head, she was an unapproachable "angel, newly drest, / . . . for heaven," protected by a supernatural purity and "so free from mortal taint" that her mortal suitor "grew faint" watching her. If the narrative is to proceed, Keats must now focus on Madeline's attractions as a desirable and attainable woman. The sense-intoxicating stanza showing Madeline disrobing (like the sumptuous feast of stanza thirty) restores the poem's delicate balance between the spiritual and the physical.

Stanza twenty-seven depicts Madeline's fall into sleep as a transition from the condition of human frailty to a transcendental immunity from earthly vicissitudes. At first Madeline is "trembling in her soft and chilly nest" with the vulnerability of a bird but all too human in her "perplex'd" expectations from the superstition. Her "sort of wakeful swoon," characteristic of the Keatsian trance that precedes vision, is sufficiently paradoxical to suggest that her perplexity derives from her human predicament which fails "To unperplex bliss from its neighbour pain" (*Lamia*, I.192). But as soon as "the poppied warmth of sleep oppress'd / Her soothed limbs," she leaves earth behind, "Blissfully haven'd both from joy and pain." Her transcendence is now expressed in the earlier religious imagery ("Clasp'd like a missal") and also in a simile which reverses the typical Keatsian figure of natural process toward fruition and death: "As though a rose should shut, and be a bud again." This image, reinforced by melodious assonance and alliteration (Keats's hesitation in the draft between "shut" and "close" shows his concern for the sound effect), conveys the beauties of childhood innocence, but no doubt it symbolizes more. Madeline has escaped from a world where flowers never revert to buds and "a rose . . . cannot destroy its annoyances" in "a cold wind" (*Letters*, II, 101). She is now, in Wasserman's words, "an emblem of Becoming eternally captured, and therefore perfect and immutable." [31] On the other hand, so long as Madeline is protected by sleep and the enchantment of St. Agnes' eve from the natural world of time, of happiness and suffering, growth and decay ("Blinded alike from sunshine and from rain"), she remains in a sense as lifeless as the similarly immortal lovers sculptured on the Grecian urn. Yet we should also remember that in the case of Madeline life has only been temporarily held off. For John Bayley already "the words *clasp'd* and *blinded* promise the struggle and tears, the necessary onset of life, promise it, as it were, without speaking." [32]

Madeline's return from timelessness to time proceeds in stages. Whereas in "La Belle Dame sans Merci" and "Ode to a Nightingale" harsh reality dispels vision as soon as the dreamer awakes, Madeline's dream of Porphyro, like Adam's of Eve, comes true. The fulfillment of the rapturous dream, however, is not perfect as in Endymion's final apotheosis and union with his goddess, because Madeline reenters the "eternal woe" of perplexing human temporality, where Porphyro has undergone "a painful change" by reverting from "spiritual" clarity and "looks immortal" to the "pallid, chill, and drear" appearance of mortals (300, 310–14). Stanza thirty-six depicts a momentary return to the transcendental:

> Beyond a mortal man impassion'd far
> At these voluptuous accents, he arose,
> Ethereal, flush'd, and like a throbbing star
> Seen mid the sapphire heaven's deep repose;
> Into her dream he melted, as the rose
> Blendeth its odour with the violet,—
> Solution sweet: meantime the frost-wind blows
> Like Love's alarum pattering the sharp sleet
> Against the window-panes; St. Agnes' moon hath set.

The sexual consummation intimated by the fusion of star with heaven and of rose with violet was made more explicit in the revised version rejected by Keats's publisher.[33] Since Porphyro has remained awed by Madeline until her present appeal demands his response, the "stratagem" that shocked Angela could hardly have been a conscious plot to seduce Madeline but rather came as a not fully worked-out thought which was nevertheless compared to "a full-blown rose" (136–39). Though Porphyro had probably not considered the outcome of his scheme (would he merely watch her, talk to her, surprise her with a feast, or abduct and marry her?) the meeting itself was already an accomplished fact for him. Now the imagined scene has been translated into actuality: Porphyro's dream has also come true. When he takes up Madeline's challenge to restore her lost dream vision, they die together into the higher life of immortal passion. As Endymion tells Peona, "earthly love has power to make / Men's being mortal, immortal" (*Endymion*, I.843–44), and in "The Eve of St. Agnes" two mortals immortalize each other. Porphyro's renewed spiritualization lasts only for one ecstatic moment but, like Endymion's, it is attained through the life of the senses. The physical experience reaches such a degree of intensity as to transcend actuality. Thus Porphyro's ambivalent attitude toward Madeline as object of desire and worship culminates in a "voluptuous" yet "Ethereal" act, which symbolizes the fusion of the physical and the spiritual, actuality and dream, time and timelessness. The "throbbing star" simile not only has sexual overtones, but perfectly combines steadfast eternity with warm pulsating life which appear separately in the octave and the sestet of the "Bright star" sonnet. Rose and violet do not revert to the state of budding as Madeline seemed to in her sleep, but, "full-blown" as in Porphyro's imagination sometime earlier, they will soon fade: they expose themselves to the inevitability of a natural process in which fulfillment involves death. Abruptly Keats reminds us of the "frost-wind" which will eventually send the lovers the way old Angela and the Beadsman go before dawn. Repetition and onomatopeia reinforce our impression that the frost-wind "pattering the sharp sleet" which "quick pattereth" (323–25) calls the transfigured lovers back to reality. Having haunted Porphyro throughout the night (77, 112, 127, 200, 217, 253, 284) the setting "St. Agnes' moon" (more chaste than chaste Diana's) not only suggests Madeline's loss of virginity but also that the magic of St. Agnes' eve is over and that Madeline's dream world is broken for the second time, this time forever—as she realizes a moment later: " 'No dream, alas! alas! . . . ' " (328).

Keatsians from Woodhouse to Stillinger have often assumed that Madeline has been dreaming up to this point.[34] Indeed "she look'd so dreamingly" (306) and Porphyro melts into her dream (320) and later tells her, " 'This is no dream . . .' " (326), yet surely as she addresses her lover with "eyes . . . open, . . . / . . . wide awake" (298–99), she may still be in a visionary trance but is no longer asleep. It is only in the wider sense in which Endymion is sleep-embowered throughout his poem, and only as far as the lovers have not yet relapsed into the actual world symbolized by the frost-wind, that an unbroken spell guards them both. In this sense their dream is not quite over yet. The charm lasts as long as they remain indoors, where, "like phantoms," they are immune from the potential danger posed by porter, bloodhound, and groaning hinges (stanza forty-one). The frost-wind outside sounds like "an elfin-storm from faery land," because in stanza thirty-nine we are still in the world of enchantment; and for this reason Keats may have sacrificed the beautifully realistic touch "put on warm clothing" of his draft for an echo from the Song of Solomon ("Awake! arise! my love") and exchanged the specific "Dartmoor" for the vaguer "southern moors." Once outdoors (in the last stanza) the lovers must confront "the storm" of real life. The story, however, breaks off shortly after the moment of greatest intensity, so that we do not know whether Porphyro and Madeline would have died like Romeo and Juliet (evoked by the family hostility and by the old nurse) or whether they would have survived until their love cloyed—only that "they are gone." But although their death-defying passion may have destroyed them "ages long ago," they have now died into the higher realm of art.

The works of Keats repeatedly suggest the immortalizing power of art. And yet, as much as any poet, Keats is aware of art's limitations, here the limitations of romance. Keats preserves a neat balance between realistic details and the supernatural atmosphere which reflects the lovers' dreamlike state. The vague medieval setting haunted by ancestral superstitions and animations such as the threatening "dragons," the spectral arras, and the carpets rising from the floor as if in pursuit (stanza forty) make us forget that there is no incident in the poem that might not occur in the most realistic story; even the "elfin-storm" is nothing but the frost-wind blowing against the windowpanes. On the one hand Keats manipulates his narrative as if it were a fairy tale in which he can "wish away" (41) characters at random and on the other he dismisses an almost incredible coincidence as a mere "happy chance" (91). But in both cases he is simply drawing attention to the legitimate control every creator exercises over his material. He claimed this authorial autonomy when he defended to Woodhouse the change in the last stanza with which he intended to enhance a shift in sentiment (*Letters*, II, 162–63). The deaths of Angela and the Beadsman, which irrevocably jolt us back to the world of time (a transition also reflected in the abandonment of the present tense), are portrayed with an unsentimental realism. Michael Ragussis, who shows that the narrator, like Madeline, seems to fall into a dream and to reawaken, sees in the reference to Merlin's doom (171) "a suggestion of the danger every magician-poet faces, namely, that of falling victim to his own spell." [35] As in *Endymion*, Keats's imagination has seized the truth that passionate love has the power to overcome all obstacles, but here the poet's distancing effects remind us that imagination is ultimately what in "Ode to a Nightingale" he will call a "deceiving elf" (74). Keats's poem about Madeline and Porphyro remains a romance of wish-fulfillment, but we are warned that it is nothing more. Both *Endymion* and "The Eve of St. Agnes" are stories of dreams come true, but in "The Eve of St. Agnes" Keats suggests that the story itself is only a poet's dream.

IV   "The Eve of St. Mark"

Like "The Eve of St. Agnes," the fragment in iambic octosyllabic couplets entitled "The Eve of St. Mark" (13–17 February 1819) is based on an opposition between actuality and a visionary experience reflected in the contrasts between cold and warmth and between a crowd scene and a scene of secluded withdrawal. The fragment shows us Bertha on the eve of St. Mark, after everyone has gone to church, poring over an illuminated medieval manuscript which describes the martyrdom of the saint commemorated that night (the twenty-fourth of April). Scholars are not agreed whether the passage of sixteen lines in Middle English beginning " 'Gif ye wol stonden . . . ,' " which appears as an additional fragment in a transcript by Woodhouse and is often inserted after the words "from time to time" (98), was intended to form part of the finished poem. This passage describes the legend that on the eve of St. Mark one may behold the ghosts of those who are destined to die during the following year entering the church.

The precision of details in the individual pictures, which later so appealed to the Pre-Raphaelites, may obscure Keats's supreme artistry in integrating unobtrusively, almost imperceptibly (and perhaps unconsciously), his most original images into his evolving thematic pattern. The word "unmatur'd," for example, in the "unmatur'd green vallies cold" (8) of the opening after-rain April landscape renders the process of completion by strikingly calling attention to incompletion. Critics have commented upon the seasonal opposition between this representation of spring and the scene in "To Autumn." [36] But judging from "Isabella" and "The Eve of St. Agnes" we can also ask ourselves what clue this ripening image might provide for the development of the poem's theme and its truncated narrative.

Commentators often quote Dante Gabriel Rossetti's conjecture (in a letter to Harry Buxton Forman) of how Keats might have continued the story: "I judge that the heroine—remorseful after trifling with a sick and now absent lover—might make her way to the minster porch to learn his fate by the spell, and perhaps see his figure enter but not return." [37] Others have supposed that the fragment would have gone on to treat "the love theme with some emphasis on the psychology of frustration," that it is only the prologue to Bertha's projected dream vision, that Keats shifted his attention from the superstition associated with the eve of St. Mark to St. Mark's martyrdom, that he gradually gave up the idea of writing a narrative, and even that he perhaps "did not quite know where he was going either when he began or when he stopped." [38] David Luke sees the poem simultaneously affirming and denying the power of the imagination and the heroine growing in awareness until the book has fulfilled its promise to Bertha and she is "obviously no longer a 'poor cheated soul' " (69), whereas Jack Stillinger again (as he did in connection with "The Eve of St. Agnes") finds Keats satirizing a young girl's foolish dreams, and, by implication, those questers for impossible ideals who fall victim to the deceiving elf fancy.[39] One might push Stillinger's analogy between Bertha and Madeline further. The sheltered "sycamores and elm trees tall," as distinct from the more natural, wild-growing forest, are "By no sharp north-wind ever nipt" (44–46), and thus, as it were, immune from the destructiveness of nature. If sycamores and elms symbolize Bertha withdrawn from the chilliness outside, then she is seemingly beyond the natural process of maturing green valleys and resembles Madeline returning in sleep from flowering rose to bud, a figure in which Stillinger saw a reflection of Madeline's self-deception. But Keats does not always describe a state beyond nature as delusion. Endymion's apotheosis is the supreme example. We have found "The Eve of St. Agnes" to be far from the unconditional vindication of dreams in *Endymion*, but nevertheless a legitimate romance of wish-fulfillment. Unlike Stillinger, we have seen Madeline not as a self-hoodwinked dreamer, but as a heroine whose dreams come true and who, courageously accepting a flawed reality and her own womanhood, regains a momentary transcendence. Similarly, Bertha's escape into the visions of St. Mark's martyrdom is a self-deception only to the skeptic: to the visionary the person of consecutive reasoning is the "poor cheated soul" (69). As in "The Eve of St. Agnes," Keats here holds a delicate balance between disillusion and fulfillment, between the ominous gigantic shadow threatening like a mocking queen of spades (the death card) and joyful sainthood. Bertha's solitariness, like Madeline's fast, is a small price to pay for the fulfillment of a dream wish. The fragment does not clarify whether Bertha is a cheated soul because she has fallen a prey to superstition or because she has been temporarily frustrated by the darkness from dying into the life of the heavenly kingdom described in her illuminated manuscript.

V   "*La Belle Dame sans Merci*"

With an inimitable magic Keats depicts another cheated soul in "La Belle Dame sans Merci." Flight into visionary experience and back again is expressed by means of the well-known motif (to be used once more in *Lamia*) of a mortal's ruinous love for a supernatural lady: a knight encounters and falls in love with a beautiful "fairy's child" (14), dreams in her "elfin grot" (29) of "pale kings, and princes" and

"Pale warriors" (37–38), and wastes away "On the cold hill's side" (44). The poet may have dashed off this masterpiece of the literary-ballad genre straight into the journal-letter on 21 April 1819, which gives us the version usually preferred to the one printed in Hunt's *Indicator* in May 1820. (The latter, among other things, substituted "wretched wight" for the "knight at arms" of the first line, and in stanza eight omitted "kisses four," the expression Keats singled out for the banter quoted in chapter 2.) Whether Keats was most inspired by Spenser, the popular ballad "Thomas Rhymer," Dante, vampire literature, Celtic lore, Wordsworth and Coleridge, his own earlier poems, a painting by William Hilton, or his relationship with Fanny Brawne[40] is less important than the skill with which he conjures the most diverse elements into a unified impression of spellbinding mystery.

The poem comprises three concentric dream circles. The outer frame (dream 1) consists of a weird encounter between the poem's first speaker and a haggard knight on whose cheek the rose is fading, while the knight's ride through the mead and the kisses in the grotto form an inner frame (dream 2) to the dream about the pale kings with the starved lips (dream 3). The aura of a transcendental experience which pervades the meeting with the fairy lady (dream 2) is undermined by the knight's dream of the death-pale kings and warriors (dream 3) with its suggestion of mortality and betrayal. This dream within the knight's dream in the dream poem—this third dream of the starved lips and horrid warning—comes true when the knight awakes on the cold hillside pale and enthralled as the dream prophesied. The realization of this dream of deathly pallor and starvation has moved in the opposite direction from Endymion's and Madeline's dreams, where fulfillment signified a shift from the actual to some ecstatic transcendental realm. Within the overall dream frame of the first speaker's words to the fantastic knight-at-arms and the latter's reply, the transition from the dream within a dream in the supermortal elfin world to the world of the withering sedge (from dream 3 to dream 1) has a touch of harsh reality. On the other hand the entry into, journey through, and sojourn in the elfin world itself remains pure dream throughout (dream 2). This dream comprises the poem's six central stanzas from the knight's encounter with the fairy's child till she lulls him to sleep; and the encroaching domination of the fairy world is reflected in the transfer of the initiative from the knight's "I" in stanzas four to six to the lady's "she" in stanzas seven to nine. The lady's ambiguity (does "as she did love" in stanza five mean that her love is true or sham? is she a flirtatious seductress or a caressing mother-figure?) and eccentricity (her sidelong bending, unusual food, strange language, and sore sighing), though explicable in a supernatural and perhaps even a natural context, yet create an atmosphere of dreamlike vagueness. The knight has evidently never entered a grotto and never left "the cold hill's side," for here, we are told, he dreams "The latest dream" (35–36), so that instead of awaking in the grot he finds himself in the setting of the outer frame.

In the final stanza the knight tries to explain his sorry condition to the questioner. A folk ballad such as "Lord Randall," structured on question and reply, solves its mystery in the last stanza. In "La Belle Dame," however, the explanation ("And this is why . . .") raises more questions than it answers. The knight explains his haggard appearance and why he does not go home in the inclement season: he is "in thrall" (40). But this explanation merely confuses the questioner, who sees that the knight is under a spell and wonders what the nature of this spell is. It is unclear whether the knight himself knows exactly how, why, and what things have happened to him. The dream in the grotto (dream 3), which is supposed to provide the key to the riddle, tells the questioner at the most what the knight himself has learned but what the reader has known all along from the title: the knight is entranced by a cruel lady. By only pretending to provide a solution to the enigma, this ballad calls attention to the indeterminacy and frequent mystery of its genre just as "St. Agnes" showed how the author of romance manipulates his reader. But whereas in "St. Agnes" the last stanza cast us abruptly back from romance to reality, the last six lines of "La Belle Dame," though apparently returning us to a realistic level, leave us in fact still within the dream world of the outer frame, which makes rational explanation of what has happened impossible and superfluous. The solution that does not solve anything merely confirms our initial impression that we have here the presentation of something felt on the pulses, of a beauty seized as a truth by the imagination and expressed in a language of sensation inaccessible to consecutive reasoning.

The poem pushes negative capability to a new extreme. Since we have to guess even at what has happened, it is not surprising that readers fail to agree upon what the lady, the knight, his journey, and his dream might symbolize. In this "most mysterious and evasive of all Keats's poems," we cannot know whether the fairy's child is a Cynthia who has failed to "make / Men's being mortal, immortal"

(*Endymion*, I.843–44), a vampire, a Circe, "a fairy mistress from hell," or "neutral as to good and evil." [41] If we conjecture that she stands for the poetic imagination, we still do not know whether the knight's lapse from vision is due to her refusal to keep up the deception or to the knight's own failure to sustain the transcendental experience; and in the latter case, whether this failure is, as Wasserman suggests, the inevitable concomitant of his mortal condition or the result of some particular deficiency on his part—for instance, as Richard Benvenuto argues, his fear of facing death. [42] The lady may stand for any of the four intensities that attract Keats in "Why did I laugh tonight?": verse, fame, beauty, and death. She may represent the fatality of beauty or of what in "Ode on Indolence" the poet sees as "a fair maid, and Love her name" (25), no less than the allurements of what in the ode he calls "my demon Poesy" (30), especially since the perils of love have repeatedly appeared in Keats's poetry, notably in "Isabella" and in the Romeo and Juliet motif of "St. Agnes." But Murry's assertion that behind the poem lies "the anguish of an impossible love" (of Fanny Brawne) is only one more conjecture and his assumption that the joking comment on the four kisses in the letter (II, 97) "is the detachment of a man who has uttered his heart and must turn away from what he has said" can be proved no more than Jane Rabb Cohen's contrary (and more extravagant) suggestion that the comment indicates the humorous mood in which the ballad itself was written. [43] The supposition that the knight's journey symbolizes the tragedy of Faustian rejection of human limitations is appealing, because the "starv'd lips" (41) echo a passage in *Endymion*: "There never liv'd a mortal man, who bent / His appetite beyond his natural sphere, / But starv'd and died" (IV.646–48).

We only know for certain, however, that the knight is a victim of his supernatural adventure and no longer finds his bearings in the natural world of birdsong, harvest, and decay. While he was journeying through the fairy kingdom, birds sang and the squirrel filled the granary; now the harvest is over and the knight is left unprovided for. (In the first two quatrains the truncated stanzaic close echoes the finality of this loss.) Those who boldly confront this world of growth and decline (as Keats does in "To Autumn") not only see the withered sedge but also experience the joys and fulfillment of harvest-time. In his vain attempt to die into the life of fairyland the knight separates himself from the natural order and thus becomes a double loser: cheated of both the wonders of elfin land and of nature, he suffers a

kind of death-in-life. The Romantic journey into vision vindicated in
Endymion and still depicted as a worthwhile risk in "St. Agnes" here
proves disastrous.

VI *From Sonnet to Ode*

The themes of the great odes (like their stanzaic form) [44] are
prepared by a number of sonnets Keats copied into his journal-letter
to George and Georgiana in spring 1819. The epigraph of one of the
two sonnets "On Fame" ("How fever'd . . ."), "You cannot eat your
cake and have it too," might serve as a motto for the great odes, in
which the poet is torn between present enjoyment and feverish
aspiration, between nature and self-consciousness, and between his
ties to his mortal condition and his craving for something more. The
sonnet is not so much about the pursuit of fame in particular as about
spoiling the joy of the present moment by looking before and after,
whatever the reason, be it the desire for fame or for immortality. The
"Nightingale" will explain: "but to think is to be full of sorrow" (27).
In antithesis to the unnatural self-plucking, self-fingering, and med-
dling described in the sonnet's second quatrain, Keats advocates that
patient submission to nature's processes of completion which is
expressed with consummate artistry in the images of "To Autumn."
Both sonnets "On Fame" take up the theme of wise passiveness of "O
thou whose face" ("What the Thrush Said") and "Four seasons" and
look forward to the "Ode on Indolence." The "Sonnet to Sleep" is
more overtly concerned with the curse of consciousness with which
Keats contrasts the bird in the "Nightingale" and anticipates the
"embalming" image of the fifth stanza while half concealing the
equivocal death-wish openly acknowledged in the sixth stanza of the
ode. "As Hermes once" ("On a Dream") is more closely linked with
"La Belle Dame" than with any of the odes; but the "feathers light,"
which symbolically rescue the poet's "idle spright" (an expression
recurring in "Ode on Indolence," 59) from the watchful Argus eyes of
everyday reality, are reminiscent of "the viewless wings of Poesy" in
the "Nightingale" (33).

"Why did I laugh tonight?" (copied into the letter March 19)
touches upon several of Keats's favorite themes more fully developed
in the odes. We can only guess at the experiential beginning of the
sonnet: the poet may have laughed at some trivial circumstance, for
example the black eye received from a cricket bat the previous day
which he jokingly connects with his "langour" [languor] (II, 78). Then

suddenly he seems to have been reminded of a sad event, perhaps Tom's recent death, and asked himself how he could have laughed. Or his reverie may have been interrupted by the intrusion of the brutal fact of a friend's grief, which led him to muse that "While we are laughing the seed of some trouble is put into the wide arable land of events" (II, 79). Here we have again a case of "but to think is to be full of sorrow," only the sonnet describes the end of an experience which the "Nightingale" expresses as flight into a transcendental realm and return to the feverish and fretting world of actuality. "Why did I laugh tonight?" reflects the poet's perplexity at the human situation, which undermines the slightest pleasure with awareness of pain, a predicament he will define and fully accept in the "Ode on Melancholy." The sonnet, Keats tells George, "was written with no Agony but that of ignorance" (II, 81). In "To Homer" we saw that Keats still hoped to overcome his "giant ignorance" of the human situation, and in *Hyperion* he showed the enlightenment of Apollo's "aching ignorance" (III.107). The "darkness" he experiences upon failing to receive an answer, more frightening than the blinding mist of Ben Nevis which taught him his ignorance in "Read me a lesson, Muse," now converts laughter to "mortal pain."

Whereas the mind's "irritable reaching after fact & reason" (*Letters*, I, 193) has only led to despair in the face of the burden of the mystery, the sonnet's concluding tone of self-assurance reflects a faith which satisfies the questioner. As in "Ode to Psyche" he strives for an ultimate stage of consciousness and turns from traditional beliefs to himself; but with a Faustian all-or-nothing approach he chooses the experience of death over the "utmost blisses" attained by the imagination. Like the "Ode on Indolence," "Why did I laugh tonight?" dismisses the three intensities of "Verse, fame, and beauty" for a greater one, although the sonnet is not pervaded by the ode's wise passiveness. The suggestion that death makes life worth living will be developed in the paradoxical contrast between the lifeless coldness of an immortal artifact, the Grecian urn, and the living warmth of mortals, and will culminate in the images of ripe beauty ready for harvest in "To Autumn." In retrospect laughter becomes an intuitive affirmation of the human condition despite its paradoxes and death becomes the dying-into-life which will resolve those paradoxes.

"Sane I went to bed and sane I rose," Keats writes to George (II, 82) after composing the sonnet. The balance will not last, however. In the "Nightingale" Keats reminds us that he has been "half in

love with easeful Death" (52) on occasions like the present, but he
will show that such escapism solves nothing; instead of dying into a
higher life he will be driven back to reality from his voyage into
"perilous seas, in faery lands forlorn" (70).

CHAPTER 7

Perilous Seas: The Odes of Spring

I "Ode to Psyche"

B Y May 1819 the futile attempt to escape into a supernal realm
with its subsequent disillusion has become the standard pattern
for Keats's poems. The "Ode to Psyche," however, exhibits a brilliant
flight into visionary experience followed by a barely perceptible
movement of return. Keats was acquainted with the myth, as told by
Apuleius in the second century, of Cupid's nightly visits to Psyche in
a miraculous palace, her disobedience of his command not to look at
him, her tribulations, and her ultimate reunion with Cupid. In the
ode (copied 30 April 1819) Keats narrates his vision of the goddess
Psyche in the arms of Cupid, goes on to deplore how she was deified
too late to become part of Greek religious ritual, and promises, now
that in any case all Greek deities have faded, to build a temple for her
"In some untrodden region of my mind" (51). The pattern of loss and
compensation is reminiscent of Wordsworth's "Immortality Ode," to
which Keats may have looked as a model for his great odes,[1] and like
Wordsworth's Ode (and like "Tintern Abbey," to which Keats repeatedly referred) "Psyche" contains an undercurrent of doubt as to
whether the compensation is adequate. The marriage of Cupid (Eros,
god of love) and Psyche (soul, mind), which traditionally represents
the openness of the soul to love and the union of feeling with mind, or
physical with spiritual love, would seem, in addition, to symbolize for
Keats the fusion of sensation and thought, the heart's schooling of the
intelligence in the vale of soul-making and, above all, the stimulation
of the imagination by the heart's affections (*Letters*, I, 184–85; II,
102). For the myth not only provides Keats with another opportunity
for celebrating "the warm Love" (67), but seems to raise hopes that
such love will become an inspiration to his poetry.

The vision of the opening stanza (1–23) comes as a sudden flash of
revelation to the poet, arrests the action (his wandering through the
forest), and transports him into the timeless world of gods. Although

119

the concentrated sensuousness, compounded by delicate synaesthesia, brings to life a natural landscape with "whisp'ring roof / Of leaves and trembled blossoms" and "hush'd, cool-rooted flowers, fragrant-eyed," and although Cupid and Psyche are represented in an earthly picture as "couched side by side / In deepest grass," these two "calm-breathing" figures inhabit the divine realm of an eternal present. Frozen in a tableau[2] of "soft-handed slumber" they convey none of the voluptuousness which flushed Porphyro "like a throbbing star" as he blended in "Solution sweet" with Madeline in "St. Agnes" (318–22), for Cupid and Psyche's love-making is in the past and the future rather than in the moment pictured here. The untouching lips heighten the feeling of the reader (or the observer of Keats's sculpture) in anticipation of "warm Love" and at the same time the suspension between the fulfillment of past kisses and the promise of more to "outnumber" them spells constancy. The potential future kisses are inexhaustible and forever new like those of the lover and the songs of the unwearied melodist in the "Grecian Urn."

The leaf-embowered, grass-embedded posture of Cupid and Psyche and the luxuriant language of this stanza bring to mind Keats's period of Flora and old Pan; and indeed some of the phrases have been repeatedly attacked as regression to Keats's early sentimentality. But in our discussion of Book Three of *Hyperion* in the last chapter we saw that Keats's reversion in his mature poetry to the style of 1816–17 is functional, a view which here gains support from the poet's claim in his journal-letter that "Ode to Psyche" is the only poem with which he has "taken even moderate pains" (II, 105). The oft-censured expression "happy, happy dove" (22), for example, like the "happy, happy boughs" and "happy, happy love" of the "Grecian Urn" (21, 25), is too emphatic (as are the "happy, happy tree" and "happy, happy brook" of "In drear nighted December" [2, 10]) to be a mere lapse in diction: it is intended to convey that naive faith in the perfect bliss of immortals which the self-conscious poet has lost. In the last stanza, depicting the interiorized landscape which is to replace the loss, simplicity is counterbalanced by convoluted expressions and descriptions suggesting strenuous effort, such as "those dark cluster'd trees" which "Fledge the wild-ridged mountains steep by steep." There the image of softness ("Fledge") is underpinned by the firmness of the jagged mountains, whereas in stanza one all is smooth, tender, and delicate. The soft expression "At tender eye-dawn of aurorean love" (20) has frequently been deprecated—a modern critic considers it one of the "Huntian excesses" though Hunt himself condemned the line.[3] The use of both "tender" dawn and Aurora may at first sound weak, precious, and awkwardly tautological, but upon closer examination proves to be an apt and compact double analogy comprising dawn, opening eyes, and reviving love.

The inaccessibility of this transcendental realm is the ultimate cause of Keats's sense of privation. Many readers have observed that the poet's lament over the neglect of Psyche and the loss of the simple faith of the Greeks hides a deeper concern. If the expressions "two fair creatures" lying "side by side" (9) remind us of the Adam and Eve of *Paradise Lost* (IV, 741, 790), we feel Keats bewailing the loss of Eden. But Milton's faith is no more valid for Keats than "all Olympus' faded hierarchy" (25), and the poem encompasses, in Homer Brown's words, "the mortality of all cultures." [4] Other recent interpretations, which, like Brown's, stress Keats's awareness of the burden of the poetic past, see him yearning for what Sperry calls "the state of poetic innocence, . . . the great myths of the past in the fullness of their simplicity," or, in Bloom's "revisionary" terminology, struggling as a belated poet with the shadows of his precursors, specifically Milton's and Wordsworth's, and "clearing an imaginative space for himself." [5] Keats probably models his yearning for the holy "haunted forest boughs" (38) of pagan mystery on the fourth book of *The Excursion*. As he promised Reynolds exactly a year ago, he is following Wordsworth into the "dark passages" leading out of the "Chamber of Maiden–Thought" (*Letters*, I, 281). Although this self-conscious modern stance comprises condescension toward "the fond believing lyre" (37) as well as envy, Keats now gives more explicit expression to his longing for what in the Ode to Maia he called "the simple worship of a day." Like Wordsworth Keats seems to regret the loss of an earlier stage within himself when his instinctive response to nature had not yet been undermined by speculations on mutability (we have heard the period of Flora and old Pan echoed in the *Endymion* vocabulary of the first stanza). But underlying the nostalgia for the naive "happy pieties" (41) of antiquity, for his own former life of pure sensation, and for the relatively unfettered sensibility of his poetic precursors, is Keats's desire to be wedded to immortality. Like the other odes "Psyche" attempts to cope with the inescapability of human ephemerality,[6] and, like most of Keats's works after *Endymion*, to reconcile the poet to a world in which love does not immortalize.

In his quest for permanence Keats turns to art. Although his poems, in particular "La Belle Dame," the "Ode to a Nightingale," and *Lamia*, show him growing increasingly skeptical of the powers of imagination, although he has laid aside for the moment the epic which should have depicted the ultimate triumph of the god of poetry over Hyperion, and although "St. Agnes" has hinted and the "Grecian Urn" illustrates more explicitly his awareness of art's limitations, Keats repeatedly tries to make art a surrogate for conventional religion. The internalization of Psyche worship, characteristic of the poet's modernity, indicates the supreme position he still allocates to the poetic imagination. According to Mario D'Avanzo, "Psyche, the winged soul of imagination, serves as the central symbol around which cluster thirteen distinct metaphors for poetry and the imaginative process. Love, dream, flight, the fountain stream, light, architecture, the bower, music, the labyrinth, wind, flowers, weaving, and pain form a network of linkages to describe that process and product of imagination." [7]

In his letter to Bailey of November 1817 Keats used the dream-come-true of Milton's Adam as analogue for the miraculous creativity of the imagination (I, 185), and the self-fulfilling dreams of Endymion and Madeline also illustrated the concept. In "Ode to Psyche" the miraculously realized dream is the poem's premise, expressed in the scene of the opening stanza by the palpable reality the poet bestows upon the two "fair creatures" of his vision, and, paradoxically, by the portrayal of a no longer human "winged Psyche" (6) who has already secured that immortal love of which ordinary mortals can only dream. But having realized his dream vision once, the poet intends to recreate it in his mind, so that the scene of the first stanza (a dream that has become reality) assumes the prophetic function of Endymion's dream of Cynthia: it is a goal to be pursued. When in the final stanza Keats promises to reenthrone Psyche, he not only purposes to retrieve from oblivion the Olympians' "latest born and loveliest vision far" (24), but also to revalidate and give permanent significance to his own visionary experience. Keats wants to demonstrate how his dream will come true once again, a more arduous task than the spontaneous rehearsal of the dream which created the two embracing immortals "on the bedded grass" (15). In stanza one he simply told his dream; now he intimates how a poet's dream becomes truth, that is, how his imagination works.

In the concluding stanza's internalization of the luxuriant natural bower of the opening vision we see the poet's fancy breaking ever new ground and "breeding" ever new flowers in an "untrodden region" of the mental landscape. The tranquil and sheltered "rosy sanctuary" will furnish the conditions for the reunion of Cupid and Psyche, feeling and mind, sensation and thought, heart and imagination. The "wide quietness" and open casement suggest the creative receptivity conducive to soul-making and the poetic process, in which the sensuous beauty of "zephyrs, streams," and "moss-lain Dryads" bring the imagination into play. Like all births the production of a work of art is a laborious process which involves joy and pain, a "pleasant pain," reflected in a mountain image that conjures up an exhausting climb and is echoed in the tortuous, difficult-to-articulate consonant clusters. (The joy and pain of composition are already conveyed by the "sweet enforcement" of the opening apostrophe.) Yet the thoughts making up a poem grow organically, like the branches of a tree—"as naturally as the Leaves to a tree" was the phrase Keats used in February 1818 (*Letters*, I, 238)—though ultimately they remain as vague and elusive as shadows. The thought of a "working brain" seems to encroach upon the pure sensation experienced during the poet's thoughtless wandering through the forest and his intuitive retelling of the experience in the first stanza. Although "the gardener Fancy" is not yet represented as the "deceiving elf" of the "Nightingale," we hear in the word "feign" (which once merely meant "fancy," "imagine," "devise") an undertone of duplicity suggesting what Perkins calls "The Uncertainties of Vision." [8] But consecutive reasoning is held at bay lest the poet should suddenly awake on the cold hillside of reality to find that Psyche has escaped his temple. The "Ode to Psyche" ends in renewed vision brightly affirming the poet's high expectations of the consummation of "warm Love."

II   *"Ode to a Nightingale"*

In the justly celebrated "Ode to a Nightingale" (May 1819) the poet epitomizes his unappeased craving for permanence, his failure to escape the mutable world and die into a higher life. Overpowered by the attractions of a nightingale's melody, Keats hopes to follow it into the forest, leave behind the spectacle of human death and suffering, and die so as to perpetuate the ecstatic moment. Since this movement into an eternal realm of song is one of the most magnificent in literature, the poet's return to actuality is all the more shattering. Realizing that his death would only separate him from the immortal nightingale, he awakes to full consciousness and questions the reality of the whole experience. As in "Ode to Psyche," the poet tries to attain an imaginary realm through the eternalization of an intense moment of vision induced by a trancelike state midway between sleep and waking. The speakers in both poems yearn for and half envy a joyfully instinctive, unreflecting, and unselfconscious mode of existence. The "Nightingale," however, stresses man's consciousness of his own mortality and sharpens the contrast between sensation and thought, which was only suggested in "Ode to Psyche," into an irreconcilable conflict between the raptures of birdsong and the consecutive reasoning of the perplexing and retarding "dull brain" (34). Both odes extol the autonomous power of the imagination to create beauty as a compensation for life's losses, but the nightingale's song demonstrates how beauty comprises the "ecstasy" (58) of fulfillment as well as the "plaintive" (75) note of disillusion. The undertone of misgiving about the visionary experience which we detected in "Psyche" now becomes open distrust as Keats fails to sustain this experience to the end of the poem and is drawn back to life from the realm of fancy. The question "Surely I dreamt to-day, or did I see / The winged Psyche with awaken'd eyes?" (5–6), coming near the beginning of "Psyche," does not affect our sense of the reality of the scene which Keats's imagination has seized as truth so much as the similar question "Do I wake or sleep?" in the "Nightingale," where it concludes the poem and thus reinforces the undermining of the poet's song-inspired visionary flight and casts doubt on the whole nightingale episode. It is ironic that a reader who may never question the existence of the embracing grass-bedded Cupid and Psyche, pure products of Keats's imagination, will end in some uncertainty about a nightingale which, according to Brown, the poet had actually heard from their Hampstead home (*Keats Circle*, II, 65).

The poem opens with the speaker benumbed, drained, as it were, of all sensation through listening to the nightingale's song, yet paradoxically he experiences pain and heartache. The paradox is compounded by the poet's claim to share in the bird's happiness. This joy-pain paradox (to be resolved in "Ode on Melancholy" as an essential characteristic of the human condition) here suggests that the poet's happiness in empathy with the bird reaches such an extreme as to verge upon pain, and this painful happiness increases in intensity until the body is exhausted and overcome by "drowsy numbness." Free of "envy" for the bird's "happy lot," the poet can imaginatively participate in it at the moment as he would pick about the gravel with a sparrow before his window (*Letters*, I, 186); yet,

knowing that his desire to join the nightingale will eventually be
thwarted, he cannot avoid envy as he yearns for the unattainable state
of unearthly felicity enjoyed by the "Dryad of the trees." The happiness is caused by the momentarily shared ecstasy, the pain by fore-
knowledge of ultimate frustration. Similarly consciousness cuts with
pain across the drugged numbness of the opening lines before it
temporarily recedes to make room for the empathic identification
with the bird's "full-throated ease." E. C. Pettet has shown how the
dull half-rhyming nasals of the opening quatrain, interrupted by the
assonance of the *a* in "aches" and "pains" and modulating into the
clean, ringing long *e* and *o* sounds of "trees," "melodious," "beechen
green," and "full-throated ease" at the end of the stanza, reflect the
speaker's pain and numbness in contrast with the bird's happiness.[9]
But the oxymoron of painful numbness and the implied paradox of
drugged happiness convey a peculiar state divorced from everyday
reality with the poet poised for visionary flight.

In the second stanza the impulse to journey into the higher realm
of the nightingale becomes explicit. Wine is to be the vehicle. Just as
a moment ago we experienced the "full-throated" song from inside
the bird, as it were, so now we are drawn into the poet as his throat
anticipates "a draught of vintage," which brings into play all the five
senses. First, the complex synaesthetic imagery which, among other
things, conjures up heated mirthful song and dance in the cool taste
and bubbling sound of wine and then the seductive, sensual blushing
of Hippocrene suggest that, as in *Endymion,* the journey into transcendence leads through the life of the senses. But "the true, the
blushful Hippocrene" is the fountain of the never-dying muses and
symbol of poetic inspiration hinting, like the blushing Cynthia of
Endymion's dream (I. 635), at the journey's destination in the realm
of immortals, the home of the nightingale.

Stanza three sets up the Ode's dialectic pattern by opposing to this
imagined ideal our temporal world of human wretchedness, where a
fatally ill youth like Tom Keats, "with an exquisite love of life," falls
into "a lingering state" (*Letters,* I, 293) and "grows pale, and spectre-
thin, and dies." Some critics have disparaged this stanza for bad
"rhetoric" or attributed "weakness" to Keats's recollection of his
brother's death.[10] But there is no weakness in depicting the weakness
of one of the sides in a symbolic conflict between the worlds of time
and timelessness, the specter-thin pallor of human ephemerality
which the poet will ultimately fail to escape. Not only diction, imagery, and symbolism, but also what F. R. Leavis aptly calls the

"prosaic matter-of-fact" tone in this "completely disintoxicated and disenchanted" stanza,[11] and even the rhythm do exactly what Keats sets out to do: to dramatize the contrast between the nightingale's unselfconscious harmony with its natural habitat ("among the leaves") and man's desperate awareness of change and disappointment and disease and death, which leads to his alienation from all that surrounds him. The fluent rhythm of "What thou among the leaves hast never known" slows down with the first enumeration of human ills, "The weariness, the fever, and the fret" (a line probably influenced by "the weary weight / Of all this unintelligible world" and "the fretful stir / Unprofitable, and the fever of the world" of "Tintern Abbey," lines 39–40, 52–53). Movement comes to an abrupt halt with the emphatic "Here," and then the verse inches along with additional catalogues stressing human transitoriness ("few, sad, last gray hairs," "pale, and spectre-thin, and dies"), its flow further checked by the repeated "Where." When we return from fancy to reality we tend to find with Endymion that "the stings / Of human neighbourhood envenom all" (I.621–22). The ode explains why fellowship in suffering exacerbates pain instead of providing comfort: the burden of consciousness is reinforced when agony is echoed in another's groan. By fading away into the nightingale's forest the poet would overcome his "leaden-eyed despairs" and see none reflected in the faces of his fellows. Unlike Byron, Keats does not wear his acute sense of transience as a badge of superiority over ordinary humanity, but his visionary flight from the community of suffering mankind toward a Dryad's "forest dim" (20), the magic realm of "Queen-Moon" and "starry Fays" (36–37), or "easeful Death" (52) is a no less paradoxical and no less futile quest for permanence and unconsciousness.

The equivocal death-wish of stanza six is prepared by the numbness, the hemlock, and Letheward movement of the opening stanza, the desire to "dissolve, and quite forget" (21), and the "embalmed darkness" (43) and leaf-buried "fast fading violets" (47) of a landscape felt rather than seen, a half-supernatural bower where keen sense perception penetrates to the essence of things giving an intimation of transcendence, as if the "happiness on Earth" experienced in the first stanza were here "repeated in a finer tone" (*Letters*, I, 185). The easeful, painless transition to a higher mode of existence now anticipated by the poet is very different from the death-menacing, palsy-ridden old age or the specter-thin consumptive patients summoned up in the third stanza. For the death that "would take into the air" the poet's "quiet breath" while the nightingale is "pouring forth [its] soul

abroad / In such an ecstasy" seems to be exceptionally "rich": in their
joint exhalation of breath, song, and soul the poet would die into the
eternal music of the nightingale.
But death only "seems" rich. Despite his earlier claim, "Already
with thee!" (35), the speaker has never really left earth, and if he has
been entrancedly gazing in the direction of melodious sound, his
dull, consecutively reasoning brain now dumps him to the ground
with a brutally truncating monosyllable by telling him that in death
he would simply "become a sod."
It is the recollection of this inescapable earthbound condition
ending in the silence of death that provokes the poet into describing
the sounds he hears—and thus the nightingale—as immortal. Since
Keats is primarily trying to convey his own longing for transcendence, a feeling inexpressible in the language of consecutive reasoning, it matters little in what sense he conceives of the nightingale's
immortality when he exclaims at the opening of stanza seven (in a
tone in which envy now clearly prevails over shared happiness):
"Thou wast not born for death, immortal Bird!" Critics, however,
have repeatedly debated whether the nightingale is immortal because of its imperishable song (Colvin), because it stands for its
species (Lowell), because it is a Dryad (Garrod), because it symbolizes poetry (Muir) or art (Hough), or because it "lacks man's self-
consciousness" and "is in harmony with its world" (Brooks and Warren), an idea recently developed by Andrew J. Kappel, who sees the
bird's immortality in its "native naturalness," its "obliviousness to
transcience" [sic], its "more satisfying experience of time." [12] Ruth's
homesickness (a trait not mentioned in the biblical story) has also
roused much discussion. While several commentators have accepted
Garrod's suggestion that the idea of the homesick gleaner came to
Keats via Wordsworth's "Solitary Reaper," Victor J. Lams, tracing
the influence of Milton's nightingales in the ode, finds that the
"alteration of Ruth's situation and emotion helps Keats to repudiate
dramatically Milton's Christian consolation." [13] But there is no need
to be surprised at Ruth's homesickness and alienation; indeed it
underlies a story whose whole point is the victory of a new faith and
loyalty over the natural feeling of estrangement everyone experiences in an "alien" land. Just as the nightingale's immortality fills the
void left by Keats's recognition of his own mortality, so Ruth "sick for
home" standing "in tears amid the alien corn" mirrors the poet's need
for perfect union with the ideal other, his yearning for the nightingale's harmony with its environment, and his estrangement from the

natural world in which the unconscious grain achieves fulfillment by being harvested.

The last stanza, by representing fancy as a cheat, prepares the poet for the acceptance of nature's cyclical process of death ("fading violets") and birth ("The coming musk-rose") depicted in stanza five. But this recognition of the inevitability of death does not obviate the poet's longing for immortality: he still hungers for a timeless realm while realizing that fancy, which seemed to have carried him there, is a "deceiving elf." The shock of recognition neither destroys him nor leads him to a serenely resigned contemplation of a world of time, process, and death. Only for a brief moment is the speaker "Forlorn." With his concluding questions he stands halfway between the "haggard" and "woe-begone" knight of "La Belle Dame," lost after missing the harvest during his journey through elfin-land, and the fulfilled Ruth figure who appears as the gleaner playing her part in the natural process in "To Autumn."

III   *"Ode on a Grecian Urn"*

A similar pattern of escape into another world and return to actuality recurs in the sublime "Ode on a Grecian Urn" (also probably written May 1819); but whereas in the "Nightingale" we sensed Keats's continued allegiance to a transcendence which had proved inaccessible, he now establishes a delicate balance between longing and acceptance. The poet creates a timeless realm by fusing into an imaginative whole various figures and scenes reminiscent of those he may have seen on different vases such as the Townley and Sosibios vases, in paintings by Claude Lorrain and Nicolas Poussin, and among the Elgin marbles.[14] We are, however, meant to imagine that Keats is describing an actual urn. On one side this urn depicts a "Fair youth" playing a song on a pipe while a "Bold lover" is pursuing a maiden (stanza two) and on the other a priest leading a heifer in a sacrificial procession (stanza four). Hypnotized by the enduring beauty of this immaculate work of art (a "still unravish'd bride") and transported by the "wild ecstasy" it conveys (stanza one), the poet attempts to enter into the immortal and uncloying state of the "happy boughs," the "happy melodist," and the "happy love" on its frieze (stanza three) until he remembers that the urn is no more than a "shape," an "attitude," or a "silent form," and that the figures carved on it are of marble and therefore cold and dead (stanza five). Keats's architectonic sense produces something of the circular perfection of

an urn, as it were, by letting the scenes pictured on it revolve before
our eyes (like the rotating "figures on a marble urn" twice "shifted
round" in the opening stanza of "Ode on Indolence"). (On the other
hand there is also an impression of inward movement toward the
figures followed by withdrawal.) The poet further enhances the urn's
completeness by balancing a scene of Dionysian ecstasy against one
of solemn order, a scene of love and renewal against one depicting
sacrifice and death. At the same time he pits the lasting realm of the
urn against our world of wasting generations. The symbolic debate
pervading the great odes finds its most paradoxical expression[15] in
the ultimately unbridgeable gulf between art and life as seen here:
Keats juxtaposes a lifeless immortality and mortal life, a love portrayed on an inanimate but perpetually beautiful artifact and the
"breathing human passion" (28) which, however brief, belongs to
men and women who are *alive.*

The latent paradox diffused through the first stanza with its un-
ravished bride-child, the marble storyteller conveying violent struggle amidst frozen silence, becomes the bold assertion, at the opening
of the second stanza, that "Heard melodies are sweet, but those
unheard / Are sweeter." Keats's preference of "the spirit" to "the
sensual ear" is not to be construed as rejection of the life of sensations, but rather shows imagination seizing beauty by playing upon
the auditory sense. As the first stanza has already made clear, the
wordless "flowery tale" expressed by the "Sylvan historian" in the
purely sensuous language of sculpture is superior to the poet's own
rhyme, which, however imaginative, consists of words, that is, abstract signs, and makes at least some abstract statements (like the one
just quoted which opens the second stanza or the aphorism in the
poem's last two lines); and the story told in the still remarkably
sensuous idiom of Keats's Ode is in turn more beautiful than would
be one narrated in the abstract speech of consecutive reasoning. As
the poet empathically moves toward the idealized melodist, he
leaves corporeality behind: transcendence triumphs over the mortal
world of "the sensual ear." On the other hand the next moment it
appears as if the poet laments the fate of this "Fair youth, beneath the
trees" who cannot leave his song and, more emphatically, the fate of
the lover: "never, never canst thou kiss / Though winning near the
goal." But the balance is immediately restored: "yet do not grieve; /
She cannot fade, though thou hast not thy bliss, / For ever wilt thou
love, and she be fair." This maiden pursued by the lover will not
wither into old age and death, and her eternal virginity is that of the

"still unravish'd" urn, which is not consumed but fostered by "slow time." Since, however, the poet's joy in the maiden's changeless beauty is qualified by his pity for her lover's frustration, we should at this stage have become aware of the ambivalence with which Keats treats the urn and the timeless realm the urn symbolizes.

In the third stanza the poet surrenders without reservation to his desire for transcendence. The ambivalent negatives of the second stanza now give way to enraptured incremental repetitions of "happy" and "for ever," which have sometimes been unjustly censured. But the strain felt in the repetition or cataloguing conveys a sense of human weakness which serves as foil to the immortal beauty captivating the poet. Keats leads up to a climactic opposition between the feverish and soon satiated passion of mortals and the urn's pictures of ideal love, briefly forgetting that the latter is uncloying because unconsummated. The urn, itself a product of Keats's imagination, has eternalized the features of the transient passion of mortals, and now Keats's imagination in turn animates the frozen eternity of the urn. Thus, for a moment, Keats combines life and eternity. His empathy (which does not preclude the undertone of envy we already observed in "Psyche" and "Nightingale") allows him to imagine the love of the cold marble figures as "For ever panting" and "For ever warm," because it is perpetually in that state of prefulfillment which in the human sphere would show the flush of anticipation. Whereas real "human passion" is followed by "A burning forehead, and a parched tongue" or subsides into painful satiety, the sculptured figures, frozen in the unconscious and unchanging happiness of an eternal present, know neither transience nor tedium: the leaves on the "happy boughs" never "bid the spring adieu" and love is "for ever young" and "still to be enjoy'd." In this sense the disembodied love represented in a work of art is "far above" the actuality of "breathing human passion." In the symbolic conflict between flesh and marble the latter is now ascendant.

But marble remains marble. In the last stanza the balance between the lifeless artifact and ephemeral humanity is restored as the poet (having stepped back to view the urn with greater detachment) recognizes that the seemingly warm rural idyll is really a "Cold Pastoral" consisting of dead, petrified figures. (Stone echoes through the repeated hard plosive of "Attic . . . attitude.") Already the fourth stanza stresses the limitations of the fixed figures, without the comfort stanza two offers the frozen lover whose beloved "cannot fade." Suffering, desolation, and death are now imported from everyday life into a transcendental realm, and questions about origin and destination suggest the before and after of temporality. The poet asks us to imagine a "little town" and a "green altar" which presumably are not on the urn he is describing (that is, creating imaginatively). He further lets us imagine a messenger who fails to "return" to this town because it does not exist and because he, too, if he were depicted on the urn, would be fixed to the marble like boughs and leaves, melodist and piper, lover and maiden, priest and heifer. The associative process of the imagination is mysterious: it casts logic overboard to "tease us out of thought / As doth eternity" (44–45). It is as if Keats were probing the limits of the mind by imaginatively seizing one beauty after another, which "must be truth—whether it existed before or not" (*Letters*, I, 184). Although the empty town did not exist before Keats imagined it, and he imagined it only after he had imagined the ritual procession which emptied it, the town is of the same order as the priest who is supposedly sculptured on the frieze: both are products of Keats's imagination. Messenger, town, priest, and urn itself did not exist before Keats created them, but being beautiful (beautiful pictures conveyed through melodious verse) they are true. Keats supplies no answers to the repeated questions in stanzas one and four or to objections raised by our consecutive reasoning and only suggests various possibilities. His "Sylvan historian" (3) does not write history, which (as we learn from Aristotle in the ninth chapter of the *Poetics*) relates particular events that have actually occurred; the urn narrates a "flowery tale" (4) (turning out to be a "Cold Pastoral" [45]) in the language of poetry (of art), which tells us "what may happen" (that is, anything seized by the imagination) and thus expresses the universal.

The truth-beauty equation in the concluding lines reminds us that like all works of art the urn conveys general validities or theoretical possibilities as distinct from historical particulars or actual facts. Whether or not Keats thinks of the words within quotation marks as an inscription on the urn, the latter addresses the reader in terms that have a bearing on its own nature: [16]

> "Beauty is truth, truth beauty,"—that is all
> Ye know on earth, and all ye need to know.

When in chapter 2 we discussed the letter to Bailey of 22 November 1817 in which Keats contended that "What the imagination seizes as Beauty must be truth" (I, 184), we identified truth with reality, with

actual phenomena. Through the urn Keats now asserts once more
that the imagination can create new realities: its beauty is truth. The
urn, however, also claims that truth is beauty. Truth must here stand
for more than everyday actuality, since not all actual phenomena are
beautiful. Garrod feels that his paraphrase of the urn's aphorism that
"there is nothing real but the beautiful, and nothing beautiful but the
real" has not resolved its difficulties. Garrod does not clarify what he
means by "real." Sir Maurice Bowra repeats Garrod's paraphrase
but, connecting the urn's dictum with various pronouncements in
Keats's letters, goes on to explain that "Truth is another name for
ultimate reality." [17] Keats is indeed developing his own earlier insights while integrating into his ode a Platonic commonplace as
adapted by various eighteenth-century thinkers, notably Anthony
Ashley Cooper, the third Earl of Shaftesbury, and perhaps, as Keith
Brown has recently suggested, Charles Batteux.[18] Many scholars
besides Bowra have linked the truth-beauty paradox with passages
from the letters such as those on "Things real—things semireal—and
no things" (I, 242–43), on "hovering . . . between an exquisite sense
of the luxurious and a love for Philosophy" (I, 271), on "axioms . . .
proved upon our pulses" (I, 279), on "the Chamber of Maiden-
Thought" (I, 281), or on "Soul-making" (II, 102);[19] and even more
often has the urn's aphorism been compared with the famous one on
the "truth of Imagination" (I, 184) and with other comments relating
truth to beauty (II, 19), or to the imagination (I, 218), or beauty and
truth to the intensity of art "making all disagreeables evaporate"
(I, 192). Thus Kenneth Muir writes: "Momentarily, and in response
to the beauty of the Urn, the poet can accept the proposition . . . that
beauty is an image of truth, and that therefore, if we see life steadily
and see it whole, the disagreeables will evaporate as they do in a great
work of art." [20] This is a carefully qualified formulation, and yet
perhaps it claims too much. "Beauty is an image of truth"—yes, but
beyond that it is doubtful whether a work of art can even momentarily
illuminate life "on earth" (though it may give us a glimpse of Heaven)
to the extent of making life's disagreeables evaporate. They but *seem*
to evaporate because we are so lost in the work of art that we do not
see them, whereas in the work of art itself the disagreeables have
indeed ceased to exist (or, more precisely, never existed). Truth is
beauty only in the world of the urn, where the pictured heifer led to
slaughter and the imagined desolate town are beautiful. The poet
may contemplate this beautiful world from the outside and even
imaginatively identify with its inhabitants, but it ultimately remains

closed to him. The speaker in the ode vainly tries to force his way into
the silence of the urn with his excited questions and, though perhaps
not "reaching after fact & reason," at least probes "doubts" and
"uncertainties" in an "irritable" and feverish attempt to ravish the
urn's "Penetralium of mystery" (*Letters*, I, 193–94). After repulsing
with marble indifference the insistent questions that threaten to
violate its secrecy, the urn consoles the questioner with a riddle
which is simply a pithy expression of its own nature: the urn's solace
lies not in what it says but what it represents. As lifeless perfection it
is a silent advocate of imperfect life. It illustrates that the highest
truths are paradoxical and not to be attained through persistent
questioning and the accumulation of hard facts, not through the
language of consecutive reasoning and science, but through feeling,
through instinct, through a sensuous perception that stimulates the
imagination, through (we may say) negative capability. Art allows us
to intuit the final mystery in which beauty and truth are one.

Whereas the consolation of the song of the nightingale passed as
soon as it faded, making the poet doubt whether he had heard it at all,
the ever-beautiful urn remains with him, "a friend to man," teaching
him in a marble-cold lesson to accept the weariness, the fever, and
the fret of transient and cloying but living human passion. Yet, as in
the "Nightingale," the speaker remains baffled by the burden of the
mystery and painfully aware of the gaping gulf between eternity and a
temporal realm in which old age wastes generations hungry for
permanence and perfection. The urn's advice that its riddle is "all ye
need to know" is little comfort to a poet who probably only two
months earlier wrote to his brother that "poetry . . . is not so fine a
thing as philosophy"(II, 81) and for a Romantic aspirer who strives for
ultimate enlightenment in an immortal world peopled with unfading
maidens and unwearied melodists and lovers.

An aphorism which reflects its paradoxical nature, a half-soothing,
half-ironic exhortation, the urn's speech is not, as has sometimes
been claimed, a didactic appendage "gummed hopefully on to an
alien substance." [21] Although abstract, the urn's statement is not
made in the language of consecutive reasoning, for the urn can only
speak the language of art, and its words relate art to life by recapit-
ulating its own poetic expression of how poetry in general (and this
ode in particular) functions. But, ironically, the poetic lesson for life
is embodied in a doubly lifeless object. While all works of art exist
outside the natural process of ripening and harvest, birth and death,
Keats's imaginary artifact, an ideal urn depicting ideal figures, does

so in a special sense: like all vases in poems it remains confined to the poet's and his readers' minds. Were it to die into the life of the temporal world, its purely sensuous sculptural language would not compensate for a loss of perfection which is based on unfulfillment. Although the ultimate mystery conveyed by its immortal beauty is inviolable, a real vase is "unravish'd" only so long as it remains intact. The "Cold Pastoral" in Keats's poem, on the other hand, will never be ravaged by time. But neither will its potential ever be consummated in the actuality of a real urn: its perfect design can never be executed by a sculptor. In this sense Keats's immortal urn will never "live"—it is like an "unravish'd bride" who, in every sense, will never "die."

IV   "Ode on Melancholy"

The theme of transience of beauty, expressed in the "Nightingale" and the "Grecian Urn" by the contrast between a mutable and immutable world, becomes explicit statement in "Ode on Melancholy" (written 1819 and also usually assigned to May). Keats had probably read quickly through Burton's *Anatomy of Melancholy* in April, and his intensive study and annotation of this work came later.[22] In the ode Keats tells the devotee of Melancholy not to seek Lethe, "the downy owl," and other paraphernalia of the Graveyard School (Keats wisely suppressed a first stanza with more horrible elements) lest his feeling should be submerged in the general gloom for lack of contrast (stanza one). He advises the victim of "the melancholy fit" to intensify his mood by gazing upon what is most beautiful and transitory, implying that his awareness of its ephemerality makes it all the more desirable (stanza two). The goddess Melancholy must be worshiped "in the very temple of Delight," where she dwells with transient Beauty and Joy (stanza three).

In this poem there is no bower of permanence luring the poet into a futile attempt to escape his ephemeral humanity, no eternal present of pure unconscious being to set off the fever and fret of hungry generations. But while the ode explicitly exhorts us to a fervent acceptance of earthy reality, the overprotest of the emphatically iterated negatives in the opening stanza gives evidence of the residual strength of a contrary drive: flight into despair, oblivion, or the numbing indifference resulting from satiated desire and repeated disillusion. The impetus is rejected. The only means of feeling that one is alive is to stir "the wakeful anguish of the soul."

The second stanza arouses us from the charm of melodious but deadening assonance with which Keats has just described the conventional melancholy addict's lapse into insentience. Revival occurs, paradoxically, with the fall of the "melancholy fit" and is as "Sudden" as this trochaic word at the beginning of the line has power to make it. The stanza's wealth of synaesthesia (visual impressions blend with sound, smell, taste, touch, motion, and even hunger) is in the service of mutability. For instance, the shroud image in the simile of the "weeping" but restorative and fostering cloud intimates that growth is toward death and depends on death. The ephemerality of the rose is enhanced by the epithet "morning" (with its pun on "mourning"). The wave, another common symbol of transience, is connected with the sand, which, though more solid than water, is not to be built on and therefore heightens our sense of impermanence; and the rainbow casts its glorious evanescence upon the evanescent sand-wave. The "globed peonies" are more tangible: we are impelled to cup our hands around them (as if we were imprisoning the live "soft hand" of the beloved), which, however, makes them no less ephemeral. But Keats is not only indulging our senses in luxuriant pleasantness, for he also evokes the pungent smell of the sea inviting us to taste its salt. In order to "glut" our feelings we cannot merely gaze upon the beautiful landscape but must, as it were, inhale, imbibe, or ingest it. The picture of the raving mistress is not "a lapse that recalls the very youthful Keats," and although it may be regarded as an example of "a masochistic sort of love-making" or of implied self-criticism of the frustrated "outpouring of a distracted spirit," it is to be seen primarily as one element in a series of beautiful transient objects (or, as Horace Posey suggests, "perceptions of the moment which must die" rather than "the *things* of beauty which perish").[23] As Keats wrote to his brother on March 19, even while hating a quarrel one cannot help admiring "the energies displayed in it" (II, 80). But let the reader judge for himself:

> Or if thy mistress some rich anger shows,
>   Emprison her soft hand, and let her rave,
>   And feed deep, deep upon her peerless eyes.

Has intensity not made "all disagreeables evaporate" (I, 192)? Seizing the beloved's hand the poet enjoys her "peerless eyes" a moment longer (the repeated long *e* forces us to linger) in a desperate attempt to arrest time. Here too he is not content merely to gaze: only by absorbing, by consuming the beautiful object will he appease the hunger of true melancholy while there is as yet no sign of satiety. And as his gaze consumes his "mistress," so is he consumed by her.

For, placed at the beginning of the final stanza to follow immediately upon this picture, the word "She" suggests that, like the goddess Melancholy, the raging woman "dwells with Beauty—Beauty that must die." The pronoun thus provides a subtle link between "mistress" and "Veil'd Melancholy," so that the "mistress" becomes at the same time the subject of the poem and one of several figures in it (very much like the "unravish'd bride" in the "Grecian Urn"). This superb stanza makes clear how futile it is to try to arrest time. Adamantly, in figure after figure, the poet reinforces the idea that there is no permanence on earth, no lasting beauty, joy, and pleasure. So in the line "She dwells with Beauty—Beauty that must die" he grants the existence of beauty in the first hemistich only to emphasize its transience in the second. At the end of the following line, for a split second we are deluded by the word "ever" that there may be something permanent about "Joy": perhaps the hand at the lips is a gesture of fulfillment? But no, the verse runs on, inexorably telling us that the "ever" sounds an eternal farewell. From the next personification we see that there is no one moment of pleasure we can isolate, only continuous movement. But pleasure is not only transitory: it turns to poison. The anticipation of pain which inevitably follows pleasure is here carried to its logical conclusion: the process which poisons pleasure begins with the onset of pleasure itself "while the bee-mouth sips." Hence pleasure is always, and by definition, "aching Pleasure." Honey is not even mentioned but only its expectation (in the sipping) and the result (the poison). The following figure formulates (still in striking personifications and not in the language of consecutive reasoning) the relation between melancholy and pleasure by defining melancholy's place as *inside* the "temple of Delight." Melancholy is an inextricable part of pleasure, it is at the heart of pleasure. Without glutting ourselves on what is most beautiful and pleasurable we cannot fully appreciate what melancholy is. The goddess Melancholy is seen only by someone who boldly breaks into the "temple of Delight," someone whose "strenuous tongue / Can burst Joy's grape against his palate fine." (We hear the bursting of eleven plosives in these ten words.) Among other things the image has been said to convey an "orgasmic climax" or "the act of deflowering" [24] (with inevitable satiety following upon fulfillment), but that is not its main impact: there is more of a movement toward sexual penetration in the speaker's relation with the "unravish'd bride," the womblike urn. Stephen Reid claims that "Ingestion is Keats's primary mode of experience," [25] and this is certainly true of the "Ode on Melancholy." It is after all the tongue that tastes, bursts, and prepares to consume the grape just as it would taste and dissolve the salt of the sand-wave. The burst grape repeats the paradox conveyed in the "Grecian Urn": the consummation of life demands a readiness to sacrifice life.

For the ode's triumphant tone of acceptance (which should long ago have dismissed the charge of decadence still occasionally leveled at it) tells us that life is worth its deaths. Death, "life's high meed" ("Why did I laugh tonight?"), is the necessary fulfillment of existence. The opening stanza warned against a self-pitying, easy glide into oblivion, but not against the rich death that affirms life. John Jones aptly writes that "transience has been articulated through taste," [26] but so has the fulfillment that can only be attained through total involvement in process and finally through death. Thus although a person who bursts Joy's grape will taste Melancholy's might and become her victim, he has also won a victory—he has lived life to the full. "Ode on Melancholy" cautions against retreat into insentience, against the temptation to despair of a life in which all joy is frustrated by the pain at its core, by the ephemerality of beauty, and by the awareness of death. Only the imagination can overcome the limitations of natural process. For as the poet imprisons the soft hand of his mistress he captures the fleeting moment of her "rich anger." Whereas in the third stanza of the "Grecian Urn" the lingering implied by the repeated "happy, happy" helped to animate frozen figures, here the delaying repetition and assonant long vowels reinforce the attempt to freeze a living woman into timelessness. By suspending time and transforming anger into poetry Keats illustrates how fancy creates enduring art from ephemeral experience. The realm of timelessness thus hovers after all in the poem's background, but it no longer provides a serious challenge to the world of mutability. Time is held off only for a brief moment as Keats seizes his lady's hand and fixes his gaze upon her "peerless eyes."

The central conflict in "Melancholy" is not the one between the realms of nature and vision which underlies the other odes of spring, "La Belle Dame," and *Lamia.* As in "To Autumn," the focus is now on the world of natural process. Keats's votary of Melancholy conquers the despair of wasting generations and the numbing indifference threatened by cloying pleasure: he achieves a tragic triumph by firmly accepting the mutability and aching joys of earthly life.

V   *"Ode on Indolence"*

Although a letter to Teignmouth of 9 June 1819 tells us that what Keats has "most enjoyed this year has been writing an ode to Indolence" (II, 116), he apparently did not think highly enough of the poem to publish it. The "Ode on Indolence" (spring 1819) indeed falls below the five great odes of 1819, but not so far as to warrant the neglect or disparagement it has suffered at the hands of most critics. In this poem Keats narrates how, lying in a drowsy trance, he was interrupted by the appearance of three shadowy figures who twice swept past him unrecognized, revealed themselves on their third entrance as Love, Ambition, and Poesy, and then vanished. Ostensibly about ordinary idleness, the ode celebrates that fertile receptivity which enables the poet to behold a vision of Cupid and Psyche, to respond to the nightingale's song, or to recreate a work of art like the Grecian urn. The wise passiveness depicted in the poem represents for Keats (as for Wordsworth) the more meaningful existence he has already praised as "delicious diligent Indolence" in the letter to Reynolds of 19 February 1818, in which he advocates the receptivity of a flower over the impatient buzzing of the bee (I, 231–32); and he refers to this mood again on 19 March 1819 in a passage describing the experience in which the ode must have originated (II, 78–79).

The three ghostly figures which threaten to arouse the poet from his drowsy numbness are eventually repulsed. Before their third appearance, however, the speaker seems to regret that they have not divulged their identity, leaving him in his indolent mood "without a task"(14).[27] Only in retrospect he deplores that the three apparitions "did . . . not melt" (19) right then and instead passed by a third time turning their faces toward him to be recognized. When the figures fade again and appear to become an unattainable goal, the poet is momentarily overcome by a desire to pursue them and, like Icarus and Endymion, "ached for wings" (24)—one of several images and expressions echoing the other odes.[28] In the fourth stanza[29] Keats discards this aspiration as folly. His rejection of the "fever-fit" of "poor Ambition" (33–34) and celebrity (possibly to be attained through mediocre poetry) as the public's "pet-lamb" (54) is not surprising after the two recent sonnets "On Fame," but his renunciation of love and poetry in general can only be explained as resulting from a conflict in which a superior good conquers: the "honied indolence" foreshadowing "an age so shelter'd from annoy" (37–38) that the poet would barely be conscious of the passage of time. When, in the beautiful fifth stanza, Keats repeats his lament that the figures came by for the third time, he explains why he regrets the discovery of their identity:

> My sleep had been embroider'd with dim dreams;
> My soul had been a lawn besprinkled o'er
> With flowers. . . . (42–44)

The use of the pluperfect tense takes us back to the ripeness of the "drowsy hour" and the relaxed state of "summer-indolence" (15–16) prior to the third encounter and emphasizes the sharp break in mood caused by the recognition. Ironically Keats longs for the "dim dreams" which the third intrusion interrupted, the shadowy figures being of course dream visions themselves. But apparently the three figures have been part of the "dim dreams" only so long as they remained unrecognized. When they appeared "side-faced" (2) like "figures on a marble urn" (5), they were characteristic of the indeterminacy and lifeless eternity of beings outside our world of process. Upon turning their faces toward the speaker and becoming, as it were, three-dimensional they lose the other-worldly aura pervading the silent shapes carved on the Grecian urn and enter the poet's earthly realm, in which he recognizes them as his preoccupations. He does not permit his reverie to be disturbed by the irritable reaching of earthly ambition but, paradoxically, delicious indolence is conducive to overreaching aspirations for visions of a transcendental realm. This realm, however, is not represented (as it is in the "Nightingale" and the "Grecian Urn") as being in irreconcilable conflict with earthly actuality: in "Indolence" earth-rooted ripening leads to vision. Unlike the speakers in the "Nightingale" and the "Grecian Urn" who are drawn into the beyond and forced back to earth, in "Indolence" the poet expresses a momentary desire to leave his pure flowerlike state for the bee-buzzing voices of "busy commonsense" (40), but by an act of choice remains in vision's antechamber. The poem ends before the speaker has embarked upon a voyage beyond his "dim dreams" into more perilous seas of imagination, so that he need not yet entertain the sobering thought of eventually being cast back upon the shores of reality.

CHAPTER 8

Mellow Fruitfulness:
Summer and Autumn 1819

I   Lamia

THE symbolic conflicts of the odes of 1819, which bring out the inextricability of pain and pleasure, the sorrow caused by perplexing thought, and the futility of the attempt to escape natural process, are given more openly dramatic expression in *Lamia*, Keats's superb narrative in pentameter couplets. The chief source of the main plot is a passage from Burton's *Anatomy of Melancholy*, which Keats appended to the poem.[1] The Corinthian Lycius, living in undisturbed happiness with the serpent-woman Lamia in an illusory world of her own creation, displays his beautiful bride at a banquet, where her magic is penetrated by the philosopher Apollonius, Lycius's former tutor. As in Burton Lamia vanishes when found out by Apollonius, but in Keats's version Lycius dies. The addition of an opening episode (probably influenced by Ovid's *Metamorphoses*), in which Hermes transforms Lamia from serpent into woman, greatly enhances the story's potential for dramatic contrast without diminishing its ambiguity.

Keats exploits this contrast and ambiguity in full. Lycius and Apollonius see Lamia from two opposing points of view: for Lycius she is the woman, for Apollonius the serpent; Lycius is captivated by her, Apollonius sees through her. Evidently all three characters are flawed: Apollonius is cold, Lycius is blind, and Lamia is deceptive. Point of view and sympathy shift within Keats's narrative, leaving open the question of how to take each of the three. Least can we pin down Lamia, who is a bundle of contrarieties: human being and snake, beautiful and destructive, a "goddess" (I.336) and "the demon's self" (I.56), a mistress whose love enchants and eventually kills. Lycius is both a victim of magic and a blinded, self-destructive

fool. Apollonius is a trusted philosopher-guide and a cynical mur-
derer. But although there are different (and even contrary) interpretations for all three characters, depending on which of their
features are emphasized, in each case two of the figures are opposed
in relation to the third. With Lamia at the apex of the triangle
Lamia-Lycius-Apollonius the contest is between the young dreamer
and the old realist; with Lycius at the apex of the triangle Lamia and
Apollonius fight for his allegiance; and until the story's climax Apollonius is trusted by Lycius and instinctively feared by Lamia. Lamia is
the rainbow which Lycius admires and Apollonius unweaves and lists
"In the dull catalogue of common things" (II.233). Lamia is the
palpitating life which Lycius drinks up and Apollonius murders to
dissect. Lamia is the dream dreamt by Lycius from which he is
awakened by Apollonius. If Lamia is Fanny Brawne, then Apollonius
may stand for Charles Brown admonishing Lycius-Keats to free
himself of love's fetters and enchantment and concentrate on his
poetry or get down to the mundane tasks of everyday existence. If, on
the other hand, Lamia's magic which produces palaces and banquets
symbolizes the powers of imagination or the poetic process, then for
Lycius her beauty is truth and her lovely creations are real whereas
for Apollonius both are illusions, "a mere Jack a lanthern to amuse
whoever may chance to be struck with its brilliance" (*Letters*, I, 242).
Lamia's initial success in drawing Lycius into her dream world makes
Apollonius seem "The ghost of folly" (I.377), but of course the philosopher's realism finally triumphs over illusion. The poem's conflicts
dramatize Keats's inner tensions between sensation and thought,
unreflecting love and responsibility, poetry and philosophy, the
attractions of fancy's fairy lands and the compulsions of cold actuality.
These conflicts remain unresolved. For the victory of truth over
illusion, Apollonius's liberation of his protégé Lycius from enthrall-
ment to Lamia, becomes a pyrrhic victory with the death of Lycius.
When Apollonius solves the "knotty problem" of the sudden appearance of Lamia's palace by thawing or melting its "tender-person'd"
builder into a shade (II.160–62, 238), the poet may indeed be presenting, as Garrett Stewart suggests, "the antiscientific case restated
by verbal ambiguity: to solve the mystery is to dissolve the beauty." [2]
Or, on the contrary, Keats may be pleading the case for philosophy
against his "exquisite sense of the luxurious" (*Letters*, I, 271) and for a
resigned acceptance of the hard facts of earthly reality against futile
attempts to escape into the beauteous realms created by the visionary

imagination. These conflicting attitudes and the ambivalence with which Keats treats his characters exhibit an unusual degree of negative capability.

Nevertheless this poem once more demonstrates a mortal's inability to sustain visionary experience. But now Keats suggests that it is not only the gravitational pull of everyday existence but, in addition, man's Faustian restlessness that cuts short all happiness, even unearthly happiness. Whereas in "La Belle Dame," the "Nightingale," and the "Grecian Urn" the protagonist or speaker is driven back from a transcendental world to drear actuality, in *Lamia* the return is the hero's choice: indeed he enforces his will against the warning of his paramour. Keats implies that a mortal will eventually grow weary even of a goddess. After winning a supernatural love Lycius still suffers from "a want / Of something more" (II.35–36): he continues to fret feverishly after further goals even in his ideal world of wish-fulfillment.

And so old loyalties and "the noisy world almost forsworn" (II.33) reassert themselves. "Almost forsworn," but not quite. A "thrill / Of trumpets" startles Lycius and leaves "a thought, a buzzing in his head" (II.27–29), the disastrous plan for a public ceremony. By setting the process of disenchantment in motion Lycius becomes the unwitting ally of Apollonius. He again unknowingly takes the initiative in Lamia's destruction by beseeching a glance from Apollonius at the banquet, and finally he causes her to vanish by echoing the words "A Serpent!" (II.305). This expression and his curse of the philosopher with the words "Begone, foul dream!" (II.271) may (as Gene Bernstein has recently argued)[3] suggest a similarity between Lamia and Apollonius in their serpentine and demonic characteristics, but these two exclamations certainly highlight the irony of Lycius's involuntary cooperation with his former tutor in the exorcism of the dream that is Lamia. Lamia can never be more than a dream to Lycius because she is a supernatural creature who has the knowledge to "unperplex bliss from its neighbour pain" (I.192), that is, she is beyond the pale of humanity for whom every joy is an aching pleasure.

For unmixed joy is the prerogative of a self-satisfied deity like Hermes. "Real are the dreams of Gods" (I.127), not those of mortals. The chief function of the opening episode of Hermes, nymph, and Lamia is to serve as foil to the mortal world in which lovers grow pale (I.145). As Bernice Slote points out, "in the first encounter of the story, Lamia, Hermes, and the nymph all win. In the last encounter (Lamia, Lycius, and Apollonius), all lose."[4] Unlike the nymph,

Lamia as a human lover *does* grow pale, "a deadly white" (II.276), and although she is transformed into a "a lady bright, / A full-born beauty" (I.171–72), in comparison with her transcendent nature her temporary humanization leaves "Nothing but pain and ugliness" (I.164). Whereas Hermes and the nymph find self-sufficient contentment in the natural bowers of "green-recessed woods" (I.144), Lamia's supernatural home leaves her human guest dissatisfied, and her illusory palace with its "secret bowers," in which art mimics nature (II.125, 149), provides no asylum for the lovers. The cynical opening of part two, which is sometimes criticized as an unsuccessful attempt to imitate Byron (the first two cantos of *Don Juan* were published on July 15), surely provides a masterful introduction to earthly disillusionment. The slightly flippant tone covers up a tragic recognition of the double curse (and ambiguous boon) of transience and tedium: brevity alone prevents an idyll from degenerating into a cloying love affair and finally into "distrust and hate" (II.10). Only in Keats's *Endymion* phase might Lamia have concluded happily at the end of part one with the retreat of Lycius and his unearthly mistress into an enchanted domicile. *Lamia*, too, might then have expressed the fulfillment of man's quest for permanence and the immortalizing power of love.

II   The Fall of Hyperion: A Dream

The Fall of Hyperion (hereafter *The Fall*) resumes the earlier *Hyperion*'s theme of the conquest of time by poetry and, like "Ode to Psyche," takes a closer look at the poet's mind and at the nature of the poetic process. By differentiating between mere dreamer and poet Keats now clarifies his ambiguous attitude toward vision. Approximately the last third of *The Fall* repeats the account of the fallen Titans of *Hyperion: A Fragment;* the remainder concerns the poet: the initiation into his art, his distinction from the mere dreamer, and his relation to his muse. Like the earlier version *The Fall* is a poetic fragment but a thematic whole. Those parts of the first version which were incorporated into the second are not the signs of Keats's flagging powers they were long considered to be, but, on the contrary, a skillful and disciplined reworking of his earlier imaginative fruits into his developing theme. While Keats's abandonment of *The Fall* has repeatedly been explained as a failure to reconcile the objective epic mode with the subjective dream vision, in particular the poet-figure of Apollo with the dreamer-narrator's part, it is probably (as we have already observed) because of its theme that he gave up the whole *Hyperion* project. Keats must have recognized that the poem was a thought-out attempt to reinterpret and transform Miltonic concepts rather than an experience felt on his pulses.

At the beginning of his dream-vision the narrator finds himself in a luxuriant garden reminiscent of the Eden of "our mother Eve" (i.31), probably symbolizing the first stage in the dreamer's development toward full poetic consciousness. If the "refuse of a meal" (the trace of disgust in this daring image makes the appetizing banquet all the more palpable) stands for the poetry Keats's precursors have not exhausted and left him to write, then he need not feel overburdened by their heritage, for "Still was more plenty than the fabled horn / Thrice emptied could pour forth" (i.30, 35–36). The intoxicating potion which quenches the poet-pilgrim's thirst becomes the "parent of [his] theme" (i.46) by transporting him from one imaginary realm into another, in which the action will take place: "an old sanctuary with roof august" symbolic of eternity and incorruptibility (i.62, 71, 75). The priestess ministering at an altar at the feet of a gigantic statue (which will turn out to be Saturn) is Mnemosyne (Memory)—in *The Fall* usually called Moneta (Admonisher)—who describes the dreamer's tormented struggle across the pavement and his ascension of the altar steps of her temple as a death and rebirth (the poet's shriek reminds us of Apollo's dying into life) and a test of his humanity (i.126, 141–53). The experience in the arbor and the temple may perhaps hint at the preparation of the poet first for the realm of Flora and old Pan and then for the strife of human hearts, but the successful passing of the second stage is an explicit condition of the poet's survival. The narrator is put to a further test when he must bear the motionless suffering of the statuesque Titans (i.382–99).

By means of these trials the mere dreamer becomes a poet. Dreamers gain admittance to Moneta's temple to compensate them for their tragic anticipation of disillusionment, which turns pleasure "to poison while the bee-mouth sips," as Keats said in "Ode on Melancholy" (24), for ordinary men and women, free of the dreamer's excessive burden of consciousness, experience "the pain alone; the joy alone; distinct" and "Only the dreamer venoms all his days" (i.174–75). In lines which Keats apparently intended to erase or revise (i.187–210) Moneta distinguishes between a dreamer like the narrator, an escapist who merely vexes mankind, and his "sheer opposite," the poet, who "pours out a balm upon the world" (i.198–202). The pilgrim now telling his dream-vision indeed belongs to the "dreamer tribe"—only we, his listeners, already know at this point that he must eventually also have become the poet whose poem we are reading. Unless Moneta's taunt is but another test (and perhaps even then), the disputed lines, whether intended to stand or not, seem to betray a final crisis of self-confidence—however shortlived—as severe at the end of Keats's poetic career as in parts of the "Sleep and Poetry" of 1816.

After subjecting the dreamer-poet to trial and humiliation, the priestess Moneta reveals herself as his muse. As "Shade of Memory" (i.282) who lives simultaneously in the past and the present, she preserves "scenes / Still swooning vivid through [her] globed brain" (i.244–45), and provides the raw materials upon which the poet works with his imagination. Change and permanence, mortality and immortality are reconciled in her:

> Then saw I a wan face,
> Not pin'd by human sorrows, but bright-blanch'd
> By an immortal sickness which kills not;
> It works a constant change, which happy death
> Can put no end to; deathwards progressing
> To no death was that visage. . . . (i.256–61)

Whether inspired by the unveiling of Beatrice at the end of the thirty-second canto of Dante's *Purgatory* (in this dream vision Moneta combines the functions of Dante's Virgil and Beatrice), by "the face of the agonized Christ," by St. John's "initial vision of the risen Christ," or by Keats's "dead mother, shrouded for her coffin," [5] these justly celebrated lines combine the deathward movement of all things in the world of time and process with the immortality of gods in the realm of timelessness. Immune from death herself, Moneta seems to share the human consciousness of earthly transience. The whiteness of her face mirrors both the pallor of mortality and the gleam of eternity. Although her "sorrows" and "immortal sickness" are unknown to humanity, they are expressed in piercingly human terms: "happy death" would be a release. The concentrated paradoxes reflect the whole mystery of suffering which the mortal poet cannot hope to resolve. Apollo, the poet's divine counterpart in *Hyperion*, presumably did achieve this feat, and his newly gained insight was immediately submitted to human pain experienced on his pulses. The portrait of Moneta exemplifies the "wondrous lesson" and "knowledge enormous" Apollo drew from Mnemosyne's face in

Hyperion by subsuming Thea's sublime "Sorrow more beautiful than Beauty's self" and Apollo's Christ-like agony as he dies into life (III.112–13; I.36; III.130).

As the poet's muse Moneta enables him to bear the burden of the mystery by helping him to translate it into art. Apollo's "knowledge enormous" is now discovered to be the power to visualize scenes conjured up by the memory-goddess and to transform them imaginatively:

> . . . there grew
> A power within me of enormous ken,
> To see as a God sees, and take the depth
> Of things as nimbly as the outward eye
> Can size and shape pervade. (i.302–306)

The first few words in Moneta's commentary giving the picture of Saturn's overthrow are enough to inspire the poet's "lofty theme," which, like the "vast idea" in "Sleep and Poetry" (291), is as yet a "half-unravel'd web" (i.301–302, 306–308). His imagination first seizes Moneta's unfolding vision as if it were a scene observed from nature and then explores and interprets the "huge cloudy symbols" ("When I have fears") which this vision supplies. In *The Fall* Keats exploits his own *Hyperion* to illustrate the workings of the poet's mind and sacrifices the potential for dramatic conflict to a more incisive probe into the timelessness of art and its relation to the world of mutability. The second fragment breaks off before Oceanus' allusion to his surrender to Neptune and Enceladus' incitement to rebellion, and the dreamer-narrator who replaces Apollo does not stand for one side of two warring factions. Whereas in *Hyperion* the Titans' enslavement and Apollo's victory over time furnished a clear-cut contrast between the representatives of time and timelessness, in the dream-vision the relationship between change and permanence becomes more complex. These contraries, poetically reconciled in the sublime countenance of a goddess, reappear in a mortal's imaginative endeavor to eternalize the transient moment.

In *Hyperion: A Fragment* the Titans fell and became conscious of time. In *The Fall* Keats has toned down the Titans' growing awareness of temporality and Saturn's loss of identity as god of time by transferring the burden of time-consciousness to the priestess-muse who recalls and the dreamer-poet who recreates and relives the Titans' fate. Thus Thea's references to "aching time" and the passing of "moments big as years" (I.65–65) are omitted, and the word "con-

scious" in "conscious of the new command" (I.60) is changed to
"captious" (i.362). In Saturn's fundamentally rewritten speech there
is no mention of being "nurtur'd" and of "ripe progress" (I.104, 125),
no heightened consciousness implied by the "doom" to be read in
Thea's face and by the recognition of a former illusion of power over
fate (I.97, 105), and no loss of "strong identity," of a "real self" (I.114).
It is no longer Saturn who appears to feel time in motion in his own
"wrinkling brow" (I.100) but Moneta, who, as it were, saw a fall from
eternity into time when Saturn's "carved features wrinkled as he fell"
(i.225). And it is now the narrator describing Saturn's speech who
betrays his awareness of transience when he calls trees "time-eaten,"
an abstraction wedged between typical Keatsian expressions of tangible in-feeling: "Even to the hollows of time-eaten oaks, / And to the
windings in the foxes' hole" (i.408–409).

It has often been noted that Saturn seems more impotent and
enfeebled in the revised version, but this observation requires qualification. Granted, the attempt at repossession (I.123), the assumption of command accompanied by a pantomimic "struggle in the air"
(I.133–36), and the desire, frightening to the three rebel Olympians
Jupiter, Neptune, and Pluto, to create "another universe" from chaos
(I.141–47) give way in *The Fall* to Saturn's lament over a cosmos
unchanged after his fall (the words "moan" and "still" recur several
times) and to a prophecy of death (i.412, 417–30); and whereas in
Hyperion Saturn's speech inspired "a sort of hope" (I.148), now
Moneta emphasizes that the Titan families "waste in pain / And
darkness for no hope" (i.462–63). Saturn's external appearance,
however, is as sublime as in the first *Hyperion*, where his reference
to himself as "this feeble shape" (I.98) is a little incongruous. In *The
Fall* Keats sharply distinguishes between sight and sound, between
the majesty of "large-limb'd visions" and the frail voice of "some old
man of the earth / Bewailing earthly loss" (i.440–45). Saturn's imposing size reminds us that he is still a god, whereas the lament is that of
the old Lear who has lost his kingdom and discovered his vulnerable
humanity. Both versions represent Saturn's fall as a forced withdrawal from active intervention in the affairs of planets and men, bringing
to an end the period of Saturn's sovereignty, his supreme divine
prerogative of expressing love through "influence benign" and
"peaceful sway" (*Hyperion*, I.107–12; *The Fall*, i.413–17). Saturn
overthrown remains immortal, but his influence upon events is as
dead as that of figures on a Grecian urn or the huge statue of him in
Moneta's temple. *The Fall* clarifies this distinction and represents

timeless Saturn's subjection to time by symbolizing his immortality
in the "large-limb'd visions" and his loss of power in an old man's
feeble voice.

Ironically, it is the time-bound and time-conscious poet who res-
cues timeless gods from oblivion. Having been, as it were, "swal-
low'd up / And buried" (i.412–13) and transformed into stone images,
the Titans are restored by the poet to their former life and activity.
Whereas the victory of the Olympians over the Titans is a temporal
event, the concepts which such victory might symbolize—the dis-
placement of the old by the young, of the powerful by the more
powerful, and of the beautiful by the more beautiful—are eternally
valid. By retelling the story of the Titans the poet perpetuates
transient incidents from the distant past and revives the dead abstractions which once lived in them.[6]

So long as the poet is aided by Moneta's visions and commentary,
his task is to record and imaginatively reinterpret them. Moneta,
however, is not only the stewardess of the past and the narrator's
source of inspiration, but as the last of the Titans, "the pale omega of a
wither'd race" (i.288), she herself becomes a participant in their
story. Her dual role is reflected in the inconsistent description of her
size: as priestess dwarfed by the colossal statue of Saturn her dimen-
sions seem to be those of an ordinary woman, but upon entering the
stage from the sidelines she assumes Titanic proportions and is only a
head shorter than Thea (i.337). When Moneta falls silent and becomes part of the spectacle before the narrator, the action is suspended and must be renewed by his independent effort. In this
severest of trials the burden placed on the poet-dreamer threatens to
crush him:

> Without stay or prop
> But my own weak mortality, I bore
> The load of this eternal quietude,
> The unchanging gloom, and the three fixed shapes
> Ponderous upon my senses a whole moon. (i.388–92)

He must sustain, as it were, the gigantic inert bodies of Saturn and
Thea; and instead of helping him carry the load as hitherto, immortal
Moneta adds her own weight to be borne by the poet's "weak
mortality" alone. The Titaness Moneta, for whom the power to
conjure up the humiliation of the Titans is "still a curse" (i.243),
promised the uninvolved dreamer that he should behold the spectacle "Free from all pain" (i.248). But now the poet has attained a

negative capability letting him completely identify with the characters, so that he takes the Titans' agony upon himself. Moneta is linked to the Titans by blood, the poet only by his sympathetic imagination which permits him to assume Moneta's and Apollo's former Christlike role. His vicarious suffering is intensified by the three immortals' "eternal quietude," which a time-bound mortal cannot endure indefinitely. While the "three fixed shapes" remain unchanged, the poet tells how "day by day" he grows "More gaunt and ghostly" (i.395–96); and if his "despair / Of change" (i.398–99) were justified, he would eventually succumb in the continued endurance test imposed by the frozen changelessness of the Titans. To regain control over the immortal figures he must bring them back into his own realm of time. If he really wants to "take the depth" of sculptured figures whose "size and shape" his "outward eye / Can . . . pervade" (i.304–306), he must not only bear their agony but also recreate the life concealed in the stone, a feat accomplished when "old Saturn rais'd his faded eyes" (i.400) and the story moves on.

This poignantly suggestive episode may represent a temporary lapse of inspiration (Moneta, the Muse is silent), and yet expresses what has been called a "consummation of the poet's will to poetry," and whereas Murry finds in it Keats's own torment and Sperry a despair paralleled only in Keats's last letters, others see it as conveying acceptance of "naked truths, / And . . . circumstance" (*Hyperion*, II, 203–204), of "eternal quietude," or simply of "sorrow and death." [7] No doubt the scene reflects the agony and self-sacrifice involved in the creative process. Following the general revisionist readings of Bloom and Sherwin, which see Moneta as the presider over the canon of poetry and her sanctuary as the monument of literary tradition, [8] we might interpret Saturn's reanimation in this specific passage as symbolizing the successful revival and transformation of Miltonic verse: by creatively "misreading" him, Keats feels himself outgrowing the deadening aspect of Milton's influence. (But in order to free himself entirely of Milton, and not only of "Miltonic inversions," he will have to abandon the poem.) Geoffrey Hartman suggests that the poet has to overcome an "ingrained sense of trespass or intrusion," and his lonely ordeal certainly seems to indicate that "he must take responsibility" for his creation. [9] Above all the poet's accomplishment without the aid of Moneta-Memory illustrates the independence and infinite might of the imagination. Keats has again teased us out of thought into a series of imaginary realms. His fancy projects the hidden life of a sculpture which has been conjured up in the mind of a priestess whom he has met in a vision induced by a drink imbibed in a dream which itself is the invention of the poet's fancy.

At the same time this passage highlights and boldly reformulates the traditional Keatsian contrast between a poet's "weak mortality" and the eternity of gods. The irony of granting the mortal poet the gift of reviving immortals is compounded by letting Saturn, who himself has fallen prey to time and change, appear in the guise of an eternal and changeless monument. Saturn's stillness, however, like the frozen silence of the figures on the Grecian urn, is a sign of lifelessness. The Titans' motionless posture, expressed in *Hyperion* in the beautiful picture of "natural sculpture in cathedral cavern" (I.86), becomes in *The Fall* a more functional "sculpture builded up upon the grave / Of their own power" (i.383–84), which provides a gloss on Saturn's own description of himself as "buried from all godlike exercise / Of influence benign" (*Hyperion*, I.107–108; *The Fall*, i.413–14). In our discussion of *Hyperion* we saw a possible analogy between the eating of forbidden fruit in Eden with its concomitant awareness of death, and the defeat of the Titans. In *The Fall* the burden of awareness is the poet's; but on the other hand the more explicit imagery of grave and monument to the dead suggests that Saturn's subjection to time and the loss of his dominion and his vitality symbolize human ephemerality. The poet's thawing of the frozen immortals to let them relive their former ascendancy and overthrow then represents his victory over mortality. As in *Endymion*, the imagination makes a man "see as a God sees"; as in "Isabella" and "The Eve of St. Agnes," the poet's fancy creates an eternal work of art by reviving ephemeral scenes from the past; like Apollo's dying into life, the narrator's agony prepares for the conquest of time by poetry; as in the worship of Psyche, the life of immortals depends on the persistent and painful imaginative effort of the mortal poet; as in the "Nightingale," the poet's weak mortality temporarily sustains an immortal burden in a symbolic battle against the world of timelessness; and as in the "Grecian Urn," the artist eternalizes the transient and animates the lifeless. The *Fall of Hyperion* is Keats's culminating attempt to establish the immortalizing power of the artist.

III   "To Autumn"

In a recent article Annabel Patterson aptly says of "To Autumn" (19 September 1819) that "Its place in Keats's mythic career has given it status as a finale."[10] Although many readers have voiced preferences for the "Nightingale" or the "Grecian Urn," we might well now accept the judgment of those critics, among them Arnold Davenport, William Walsh, Robin Mayhead, John Jones, and Christopher Ricks, who regard "To Autumn" as the greatest of Keats's odes.[11] The technical perfection is beyond dispute, conveying the ode's movement toward evening, toward winter, and toward the completed harvest,[12] with the first of the three stanzas portraying opulent fruition, the second personifying autumn in four harvesting pictures, and the third depicting "stubble-plains" at sunset and alluding to the winter migration of swallows.

In the opening stanza autumn, apostrophized as "Season of mists and mellow fruitfulness," supervises the ripening process in partnership with a sun which is ambiguously described as if it, too, were "maturing" toward noon or late summer. The convoluted phrase "bless / With fruit and vines that round the thatch-eves run" with its inversion and difficulty in articulation makes the tongue imitate the entwining creepers as they hug wall and roof. Christopher Ricks draws attention to the feeling of downward pressure of vines and apples, pressure inward to "fill all fruit with ripeness to the core," and pressure outward in the swelling and plumping, and shrewdly points out how our delight in the bee hive is strengthened by the distasteful possibilities inherent in the word "clammy."[13] The process of ripening is portrayed insistently as if everything in nature might ripen to surfeit, be rounded out to bursting, filled to overbrimming, and sweetened to cloying, which makes us wonder whether the load of fruit is all blessing. The mistake of the bees, who "think warm days will never cease," reminds us that we know better.

What the "conspiracy" of autumn and sun is becomes clear in the second stanza where we see that the process described is one from which the hook temporarily "spares" grain and flowers: the bosom-friends autumn and sun (or the harvest goddess Ceres and the sun-god Apollo) conspire to murder. In this stanza the ripening process is complete. Part of the balanced effect of the poem is that the first stanza, in which the fruit passively awaits time's harvesting hand, depicts an activity of loading, bending, filling, swelling, plumping, and budding, whereas the harvesting process itself is represented in the second stanza in the form of four tableaux, each with a passive autumn figure. Autumn is first seen "sitting careless on a granary floor" with "hair soft-lifted by the winnowing wind" (the onomatopoeia introduces a striking sound into the predominantly

visual imagery of the stanza and anticipates the music of stanza
three), then lying asleep, then crossing a brook, and finally patiently
watching a cider-press. Each of these four pictures arrests time: the
most poignant is the stay of execution granted by the sickle suspended in mid-air (rather than lying beside the sleeper) as it "Spares
the next swath and all its twined flowers" which have readied themselves for the sacrifice. The "steady" head of the "gleaner" (one of
several expressions conjuring up the biblical Ruth) seems to fix her in
the middle of the act of crossing a bridge or recovering her poise as
she steps over the stones of a brook, a boundary symbol for the
separation of the past from the future.[14] Keats is freezing the harvest
landscape, as if filmically, into a still picture. Thus also the two scenes
of the autumn figure on the granary floor and beside the cider-press.
The "last oozings" of the press are reminiscent of the "clammy cells"
of stanza one with their imperceptible movement and the repug-
nance they might possibly induce. Slowly but inexorably the film is
set in motion again, as if with time lifeblood were trickling out.

The last stanza shows that the merciful gesture of the sickle sparing
the flowers was futile. The picture of the grain-field with "all its
twined flowers" has been replaced by that of the harvested stubble-
plain which Keats admired in his Sunday walk around Winchester.[15]
But the death symbolized by stubble, sunset, mourning gnats,
changing wind, and winter announced by gathering swallows is part
of a process that portends new life. The "soft-dying day" accompanied by autumnal music is reborn in the "barred clouds" that open up
like blooming flowers. We now remember the "sweet kernel" of
hazels, the "ripeness to the core" of the first stanza, and realize that
the conspirators autumn and sun have not neglected to provide the
seed for future life (and their victims of the coming years) in an
eternal cycle of death and rebirth.

It is generally recognized that "To Autumn" conveys its theme
more implicitly than Keats's other odes. Here the poet adds no
explanation or definitions. Nor does he exhort against escape into
numbing indifference or despair, as he does in "Ode on Melancholy,"
in order to render his unqualified acceptance of mutability. And yet,
contrary to general critical opinion, "To Autumn" returns to the
symbolic conflicts that pervade the odes of spring. When the film
about harvesting is stopped to project a still picture of the spared
"swath and all its twined flowers" (18), death is held off for a brief
moment. This still on the screen, a single frame which can be cut out
of the film, represents a timeless realm in which apples never rot,

flowers never fade, and love is for ever young. Like Keats's imagined urn, the four tableaux in "To Autumn" are works of art created by the poet to vie with nature within the larger work of art that constitutes the whole poem. In the "Grecian Urn" Keats established a delicate balance between time and eternity; here time conquers. (Although the art of Keats's poetry will never bow to time, within a given poem nature may be represented as triumphing over art.) Like the transfigured anger of the raving mistress in "Ode on Melancholy," the timeless element introduced by the four still pictures does not distract us from the poem's focus on mutability. Just when Keats is abandoning his final attempt, in the second *Hyperion*, to dramatize the victory of poetry over mortality, he composes the ode "To Autumn," a consummate expression of the triumph of nature's process over the artist's endeavor to eternalize the fleeting moment.

This triumph, however, is won at a tremendous cost. The "Grecian Urn" showed why life must be paid for by death; now Keats illustrates further how life is cut off at its most beautiful moment. But this price is worth paying. The apple, at its ripest, is saved from decay; the flower cut when it is loveliest is about to fade in any case. To fulfill its destiny a rose must be plucked when it is completely opened up, for the seasonal progression does not permit it to "shut, and be a bud again" ("The Eve of St. Agnes," 243). While Keats cannot resist the temptation of prolonging the moment of fulfillment (a tendency which Bate has shown to be reinforced by the structure of the eleven-line stanza),[16] he nevertheless firmly accepts the inevitability of the natural process.

Having tried four times to arrest the progression of autumn he attempts briefly to escape the present by turning back the march of time: "Where are the songs of Spring? Aye, where are they?" (23) This residual escape pattern of the earlier odes is immediately rejected: "Think not of them." Thought threatens to destroy the natural beauty of autumn's subdued music, as it put an end to the illusory paradise of Lycius in *Lamia*. When the bees are said to "think" they are deluded: knowing nothing of winter they live as if "warm days will never cease" (10); that is to say they do not "think" at all but live purely in the present warmth. In their lack of consciousness the bees are like the flowers. (Until the following line the "they" of line 10 might refer equally to flowers and bees.) In "To Autumn" the bees are not "buzzing here and there impatiently from a knowledge of what is to be arrived at" (*Letters*, I, 232): they have learned their lesson from the flowers. And so has the poet. Unable to escape the human consciousness of past and future, Keats here does his best to prevent this consciousness from undermining the pure enjoyment of the present moment. At least he overcomes the paralysis of nostalgia and seeks the compensations inherent in the seasonal progression. For with the harvest stored in the granary everything is attained. "To Autumn" satisfies the speaker's hunger, left unappeased in the "Nightingale" and the "Grecian Urn." Here we are finally enticed to relinquish our Faustian aspirations in favor of dying beauty, to affirm, almost to extol the natural process of mutability. Nothing in nature is excluded from this all-embracing acceptance. Looking at life objectively from the outside and recognizing progress toward death and rebirth as one movement, Keats's imaginative sympathy encompasses the exquisitely visualized "twined flowers" and the equally palpable "hook" (17–18), the victim as well as the executioner. In "To Autumn" Keats wonderfully conforms to his idea of "the poetical Character" which "enjoys light and shade" and "has as much delight in conceiving an Iago as an Imogen" (*Letters*, I, 386–87); and here he produces the most glorious illustration in literature of Edgar's words to Gloucester in act 5, scene 2 of *King Lear*:

> Men must endure
> Their going hence, even as their coming hither:
> Ripeness is all.

IV *Epilogue*

"Ripeness is all"—Keats was proving it on his pulses. There remained only a few months of health and less than a year and a half of life when Keats composed "To Autumn," and little of that poem's serenity and acceptance emerges in the scattered lyrics apparently written afterwards (such as "I cry your mercy" and "What can I do to drive away"). Middleton Murry says of "To Autumn": "how deeply Shakespearean that perfect poem is—Shakespearean in its rich and opulent serenity of mood, Shakespearean in its lovely and large periodic movement, like the drawing of a deep, full breath." [17] It is fitting that Keats's poetic career should virtually have ended with the poem most frequently mentioned when his Shakespearean strain is discussed, for the Shakespearean magic is what seems to impress discerning critics more than anything else about Keats. Aileen Ward ended her 1963 biography of Keats with Arnold's often-quoted eulogy: "he is with Shakespeare"; and in the same year Bate concluded his magisterial study with the quotation from Keats's letter to Haydon of 10 March 1817, which Murry had already cited in 1925 at the end of his *Keats and Shakespeare*:[18]

> I remember your saying that you had notions of a
> good Genius presiding over you—I have of late had the
> same thought. . . . Is it too daring to Fancy Shakspeare
> this Presider? (I, 141–42)

Keats openly recognizes Shakespeare as master of the negative capability that he seeks to emulate (I, 193) and implicitly acknowledges him as his model for his all-pervasive harvest image when he quotes the second quatrain of Sonnet 12 with the comment: "Is this to be borne?" (I, 188–89). Judging from the passages underlined in his Shakespeare, Keats was sufficiently impressed by the thrifty use of words and concentration of meaning to encourage him (and advise Shelley) to " 'load every rift' of your subject with ore" (II, 323), and by those Shakespearean images which convey motion arrested (as much as by Miltonic stationing) to induce him to capture a scene in suspended movement, a dynamic poise, or energy in repose, as we have seen him do repeatedly with superb effect.

It is tantalizing to speculate whether Keats, had he lived, would have fulfilled his ambition of making "as great a revolution in modern dramatic writing as Kean has done in acting" (II, 139), and whether Shakespeare's influence would have aided or hindered this endeavor. Some sketches of individuals in his letters, especially in those of the Northern Tour, show Keats to be a master in characterization, and "The Eve of St. Agnes," the great odes, and *Lamia* exhibit his gift for dramatic balance and contrast. The little he did accomplish in drama proper, however, is not decisive. During July and August 1819 Keats wrote *Otho the Great*,[19] a historical tragedy for which he "only acted as Midwife" to a plot suggested by Brown (*Letters*, II, 157). He composed the first four of the five acts "scene after scene, never knowing nor inquiring into the scene which was to follow" (*Keats Circle*, II, 66) in the hope of having Kean act in it and making money, a hope which was disappointed. The play is more successful in its presentation of a cluster of harvest imagery than in its more obvious Shakespearean echoes, its dramatic structure, or its exploitation of the tragic themes of parental mistrust and love betrayed. The four scenes of the fragment *King Stephen* [20] (late August–November 1819) with their prompt exposition and their potential inner conflicts in the title hero and in Gloucester show more promise than the opening scenes of *Otho*. Toward the end of 1819 Keats also wrote an unfinished satire in Spenserian stanzas entitled *The Jealousies* or *The Cap and Bells*,[21] in which he may have been ridiculing George IV and seems to be mocking Byron, whom he quotes in stanza sixty-eight (as Byron quoted other poets). Most probably Keats is also parodying himself. The hero is an immortal with mortal aspirations: Elfinan, emperor of a fairy city, chooses as object of his affection the mortal Bertha, because "He lov'd girls smooth as shades, but hated a mere shade" (9) despite his parliament's remonstrance "that shade with shade should meet" (23). ("For shade to shade will come too drowsily," Keats had written in the first stanza of "Ode on Melancholy.")

These three works were not printed in Keats's lifetime. There was no new edition of his poems in England until 1840, but one appeared in Italy in 1829 in a volume containing also the works of Coleridge and Shelley. In 1848 Richard Monckton Milnes (later Lord Houghton) published the first biography in his *Life, Letters, and Literary Remains, of John Keats*, which did much to raise the poet's reputation, and it has been rising ever since. Keats soon became the poet's poet. What Spenser had been to him and to previous generations, Keats became for poets of the nineteenth and twentieth centuries from Tennyson through the Pre-Raphaelites to Wallace Stevens. More than any of his great contemporaries Keats escaped the general onslaught on the Romantics by some of the New Critics.[22]

Keats nevertheless is very much a son of the Romantic age. It is not just that he is on "the Liberal side" (*Letters*, II, 180), that he attacks Augustan verse ("Sleep and Poetry," 181–206), absorbs the Wordsworthian interchange of man and nature, withdraws into isolation, makes the poet the protagonist of his poetry, extols "the truth of Imagination" over what he calls "consequitive reasoning" (*Letters*, I, 184–85), luxuriates in aching pleasure, and shows an interest in medievalism and the Gothic strain ("The Eve of St. Agnes") and the ballad genre ("La Belle Dame sans Merci"). Keats also participates with his contemporaries in a quest for permanence in an age that no longer finds comfort in conventional religion and shares the Romantic tension between the desire for reality and the yearning for infinitude. He too is overwhelmed by self-consciousness and longs for a life of sensations rather than of thought. Even more than other Romantics he is aware of the burden of the poetic past resting on the shoulders of a modern poet because of the need for constantly clearing new space and breaking new ground on the "grand march of intellect" (*Letters*, I, 282). Among the English Romantics he is perhaps the most acutely sensitive to the gap which particularly German thinkers, critics, and poets (Hegel, the Schlegel brothers, and, above all, the "Classical" Schiller of *On Naive and Sentimental Poetry*) saw between earlier, more primitive, happy, and unselfconscious ages and their own cursed self-consciousness. The escape Byron tries to find in oblivion, and other Romantics, especially Wordsworth, in nature, Keats seeks in the realms of imagination and art.

But ultimately Keats retains a firm grip on reality. Unlike Shelley, for example, even when his gaze flies skyward, Keats ultimately remains "on the shore / Of the wide world" ("When I have fears"), on "earth's human shores" ("Bright star"). Keats's steadfast star has not the power to make the poet forsake his native earth in the "Bright star" sonnet (long thought to be Keats's last poem because he wrote it down again on his journey to Italy, but most probably composed well before the end of 1819, possibly as early as 1818). On the other hand the star imagined by Shelley ("The soul of Adonais" at the end of Shelley's elegy on the death of Keats) lures the poet into the sky as it "Beacons from the abode where the Eternal are"; and the West Wind, "The breath whose might" Shelley has "invoked in song," drives his "spirit's bark . . . / Far from the shore" (*Adonais*, last stanza). "Bright star" repeats the flight-and-return pattern of the great odes in miniature with the return movement beginning in the second line. Once more Keats would eat his cake and have it, too: the star's permanence without its cold solitude and breathing human passion without its ephemerality, or the immortality of the lovers on the Grecian urn without their lifelessness. He longs to draw out the earthly "ripening" process to eternity; but since he knows that all ripening is deathward, he also welcomes death, the culmination of the "soft swell and fall," the "sweet unrest" that is human love and every living experience. In the course of the long struggle through which he assimilates this awareness the balance between his craving for transcendence and his acceptance of natural process gradually shifts toward the latter.

Keats's gradual assumption of a more ambivalent attitude toward the realm of vision also applies to his own art. Except in his earliest works such as "Calidore" he tends to give us more truth than is required of a work of fiction, does not rest content with what Coleridge calls "willing suspension of disbelief," and encourages us to examine the artistic process. We have seen him invoking "Truth" in

Endymion in order to justify his delay in enskying the hero (IV.770–73) and temporarily hold off the legitimate fiction of the mythological ending. In the last stanza of "The Eve of St. Agnes" he reminds us that he has written a story of wish-fulfillment and has been manipulating us in romance fashion, and in "La Belle Dame" he draws our attention to the mystery of the ballad genre. In *Lamia* Keats's truth no longer permits him to ensky an earthling or embower him in some magic palace for all eternity:

> And but the flitter-winged verse must tell,
> For truth's sake, what woe afterwards befel,
> 'Twould humour many a heart to leave them thus,
> Shut from the busy world of more incredulous. (I.394–97)

The love stories of "Isabella," "St. Agnes," "La Belle Dame," and *Lamia*, which make it clear that retreat "from the busy world" is temporary, increasingly insist that the poet's "verse must tell, / For truth's sake" of the "woe" which inevitably succeeds love's consummation but which romance seeks to conceal. Keats refuses to leave us with the belief that there was nothing to follow the illusory happy ending of part one of *Lamia*. The introduction of the concept of incredulity momentarily threatens to undermine our willing suspension of disbelief and thus announces the victory of reality over illusion in part two. This device, moreover, seems to support the case for Apollonius against Lamia, Lycius, and the rainbow. *Lamia* leaves the case undecided, but the increasing subtlety of such artistic distancing effects from his fictions may be symptomatic of the evolution of Keats's poetry as a whole toward a philosophical resignation to the inevitable triumph of mutability over love, beauty, and happiness, and of actuality over a poet's visions.

What allows Keats to confront mutability with equanimity and continue to tell us his poetic dreams is a "knowledge of contrast, feeling for light and shade" (*Letters*, II, 360), his negative capability, his avoidance of "any irritable reaching after fact & reason" (I, 193), which probably more than anything distinguishes him from his great contemporaries. The doubts and mysteries conveyed by the poetry transcend the poet's own conflicting impulses and seem to resolve the paradoxes of life. Granted, to speak of the capability "of being in uncertainties" and "remaining content with half knowledge" (I, 193–94) does not do full justice to Keats's growing affirmation of process, for what is the ode "To Autumn" if not an assertion, however implicitly rendered, that all living things should gladly surrender to the sickle when the time is ripe? But the mystery (which will become an unbearable burden on his deathbed) is always there. By giving us a sense of the weary weight of the unintelligible world Keats's poetry also lightens it, most in the moments of serenity when he probes least. "To Autumn" is a poem about death and mutability in which Keats neither longs for death nor laments mutability (just as in this ode of departure there is no bidding "adieu," a word that appears in all the odes of spring). In a less serene mood, in "Ode to a Nightingale," for example, Keats feels it would be "rich to die" at midnight (55–56) and yet bemoans a world "Where youth grows pale, and spectre-thin, and dies" (26). The two sentiments are mutually exclusive despite their different circumstances, for death makes a sod of the speaker no less than of his palsied and specter-thin fellow-men: yet both are, must be, there. Keats here expresses a paradox exhibited more openly in the works of other Romantics (in Goethe's *Faust* or Byron's *Cain*, for instance) of a death-wish concurrent with a lament over the brevity of life. The Romantic quest for immortality is not only rebellion against human transience but also represents the thirst for absolutes: it is an attempt to overcome the limitations that cause the agony of ignorance. The futility of this quest spells despair: a life that ends in death is not worth living.

But whereas for most European Romantics—Byron, Goethe, and Hugo are representative of this trend—it is the sense of futility and despair that induces world-weariness, in Keats it is more often the cloying excess of the absolute, expressed as pleasure, then excessive pleasure, that leads to tedium. We have seen the mellow fruitfulness of "To Autumn" with its oversweetness that just stops short of cloying and its muted description of the imperceptible but inexorable passage of time providing Keats with an antidote to the double bane of tedium and transience: prepare to die before decay sets in.

In February 1819 Keats wrote to his brother and sister-in-law in America:

A Man's life of any worth is a continual allegory—and very few eyes can see the Mystery of his life— . . . —Shakspeare led a life of Allegory; his works are the comments on it—(II, 67)

Every reader must be struck by the appropriateness of these words to Keats himself. The man wasted away with tuberculosis, embittered that death should cut him off before he had consummated the joys of life and gained renown; but his poetry incarnates the fulfillment of "a Life of Sensations," which to him was " 'a Vision in the form of Youth' " (I, 185). Part of the allegory that is John Keats is the flower imagined as readying itself for the sickle at the moment of its most intense beauty.

Notes and References

Chapter One

1. Robert Gittings, *John Keats* (London, 1968), p. 27; Charles Cowden Clarke, "Biographical Notes on Keats, 16 March 1846" in *The Keats Circle*, ed. Hyder Edward Rollins, 2nd ed. (Cambridge, Massachusetts, 1965), II, 147, hereafter cited as *Keats Circle*.
2. Aileen Ward, *John Keats: The Making of a Poet* (1963; rpt. New York, 1967), p. 13. James W. Hamilton, "Object Loss, Dreaming, and Creativity: The Poetry of John Keats," *The Psychoanalytic Study of the Child* 24 (1969): 529, invokes Freud to support his claim that "Keats resorted to poetry in an attempt to . . . make restitution for the lost object, most importantly his mother . . ."; and Stephen A. Reid, "Keats's Depressive Poetry," *Psychoanalytic Review* 58 (1971): 398–99, traces Keats's poetry to what Melanie Klein calls the "depressive position": the infant's conflicting attitudes towards his mother's breasts.
3. *The Letters of John Keats, 1814–1821*, ed. Hyder Edward Rollins (Cambridge, Massachusetts, 1958), I, 293; I, 279; II, 312. All references to Keats's letters are to this two-volume edition and are cited, where necessary, as *Letters*. Gittings, *John Keats*, pp. 209–10, comments on I, 279 and I, 293. There is only one other allusion, probably insignificant, to either of Keats's parents in his letters—in connection with their initials on his seal (II, 133).
4. See the article on Keats in *Encyclopedia Britannica*, 8th ed. (1857), partly reprinted in *Keats: The Critical Heritage*, ed. G. M. Matthews (London, 1971), p. 365.
5. For two conflicting accounts of the role of Isabella Jones in Keats's life compare Robert Gittings, " 'Bright Star' and the Beautiful Mrs. Jones" and " 'Hush, Hush' and Isabella Jones" in *John Keats: The Living Year, 21 September 1818 to 21 September 1819* (1954; rpt. London, 1968), with John Middleton Murry's reply "Keats and Isabella Jones" in *Keats* (1955; rpt. [London,] 1968).
6. "Psyche," "Nightingale," and "Indolence" were written in spring, but of the "Grecian Urn" and "Melancholy," which, following tradition, we also place with the odes of spring, we know for certain only that they were written

in 1819 (see Jack Stillinger, ed., *The Poems of John Keats* [Cambridge, Massachusetts, 1978], pp. 647, 651–55).

7. Cf. Walter H. Evert, *Aesthetic and Myth in the Poetry of Keats* (Princeton, 1965), p. 31, part of a full treatment of the Apollo figure (pp. 23–87).

8. H. W. Garrod, *Keats*, 2nd ed. (1939; rpt. Oxford, 1957), pp. 80–87.

9. The relative stylistic looseness of Keats's early work is discussed in detail by Walter Jackson Bate, *The Stylistic Development of Keats* (1945; rpt. New York, 1962), pp. 8–28, 194–201: Keats uses more hiatus, feminine rhymes, pyrrhics, and trisyllabic feet than in his later work.

10. Christopher Ricks, *Keats and Embarrassment* (Oxford, 1974), p. 108.

11. For Titian's *Bacchus and Ariadne* see Ian Jack, *Keats and the Mirror of Art* (Oxford, 1967), pp. 130–31 and plate XIII. For the gleaner in "To Autumn" Jack suggests a painting by Poussin, *Autumn, or The Grapes of the Promised Land* (p. 237 and plate XXXIX).

12. Ricks, p. 209.

13. Bate, *Stylistic Development*, pp. 50–65, and *John Keats* (1963; rpt. New York, 1966), pp. 413–17. Cf. also E. C. Pettet, *On the Poetry of Keats* (1957; rpt. Cambridge, 1970), especially pp. 92–93. On Keats's imitation of Chatterton's vowel play see Nai-Tung Ting, "Chatterton and Keats: A Reexamination," *Keats-Shelley Journal* 30 (1981): 101–105.

Chapter Two

1. See Gittings, *John Keats*, p. 451.

2. T. S. Eliot, *The Use of Poetry and the Use of Criticism* (1933; rpt. London: Faber, 1975), p. 100.

3. Ricks, p. 219.

4. For detailed analyses of this letter see Newell F. Ford, *The Prefigurative Imagination of John Keats: A Study of the Beauty-Truth Identification and Its Implications* (Stanford: Stanford University Press, 1951), pp. 20–38, and Jack Stillinger, *The Hoodwinking of Madeline and Other Essays on Keats's Poems* (Urbana, 1971), pp. 151–57. See also chapter 4, sections III and IV, chapter 6, section I, and chapter 6, note 13 below.

5. Robert M. Ryan, *Keats: The Religious Sense* (Princeton, 1976), pp. 129–37.

6. James Ralston Caldwell, *John Keats's Fancy: The Effect on Keats of the Psychology of His Day* (1945; rpt. New York, 1965), pp. 155–56. See also R. T. Davies, "Some Ideas and Usages," in Kenneth Muir, ed., *John Keats: A Reassessment*, 2nd ed. (Liverpool, 1969), p. 135, and for a detailed discussion, Stuart M. Sperry, *Keats the Poet* (Princeton, 1973), pp. 3–29.

7. Most critics widen the concept of negative capability well beyond the letter in which the word occurs, although a few attempts have been made to narrow down the use of the term. Thus Leon M. Guilhamet ("Keats's 'Negative Capability' and 'Disinterestedness': A Confusion of Ideals," *University of Toronto Quarterly* 40 [1970–71]: 2–14) distinguishes the term from disinterestedness and Arthur Clayborough (" 'Negative Capability' and 'The

Camelion Poet' in Keats's Letters: The Case for Differentiation," *English Studies* 54 [1973]: 569–75) from the poet's lack of identity, but both scholars admit that the concepts overlap. The term "negative capability" occurs only once in Keats (*Letters*, I, 193).

8. S. R. Swaminathan, "Keats and Benjamin West's *King Lear*," *Keats-Shelley Journal* 18 (1969): 15–16, shows that Keats is probably referring to West's painting and not, as has been generally held, to Shakespeare's play.

9. Bate, *John Keats*, pp. 239–45, 255–60. See also Muir, "Keats and Hazlitt," in *Reassessment*, p. 142; M[eyer] H. Abrams, *The Mirror and the Lamp: Romantic Theory and the Critical Tradition* (1953; rpt. New York: Norton, 1958), pp. 134–36; John Jones, *John Keats's Dream of Truth* (London, 1969), p. 189. Caldwell, p. 175, and Herschel M. Sikes, "The Poetic Theory and Practice of Keats: The Record of a Debt to Hazlitt," *Philological Quarterly* 38 (1959): 407, equate the two terms outright. Robert Ready has shown in "Hazlitt: In and Out of 'Gusto,'" *Studies in English Literature 1500–1900* 14 (1974): 537–46, that Hazlitt's "gusto," referring chiefly to painting and pictorial effect in literature, is subservient to "interest" and "does not belong in the higher provinces of literary art" (p. 540). Keats's more comprehensive "intensity," however, is simply "the excellence of every Art," and Keats's letter as a whole stresses art's disinterestedness. Unlike "gusto," "intensity" excites "momentous depth of speculation" and leads to an imaginative apprehension of the beauty perceived as a truth. Whereas Keats draws attention to Shakespeare's "intensity of working out conceits" (*Letters*, I, 188), Hazlitt, in his brief discussion of literature at the end of his essay "On Gusto" (Geoffrey Keynes, ed., *Selected Essays of William Hazlitt* [1930; rpt. London: Nonesuch Press, 1948], p. 613), contrasts Shakespeare's gusto with his lack of intensity. Abrams rightly groups both Hazlitt's "gusto" and Keats's "intensity" with expressive theories of aesthetics under the title "Varieties of Romantic Theory" (p. 125) which break away from the mimetic and pragmatic theories of neo-classicism. On the other hand, as R. T. Davies, "Keats and Hazlitt," *Keats-Shelley Memorial Bulletin* 8 (1957): 4, has demonstrated, what Keats associates with intensity Hazlitt attributes to imitation. The shift toward a modern theory of the communication of experience is therefore more evident in Keats than in Hazlitt.

10. Sperry, pp. 44–46, quotes scientific dictionaries and treatises to show that Keats is borrowing terms from chemistry.

11. Most books on Keats refer to Wordsworth's influence. There are extended discussions in Clarence DeWitt Thorpe, *The Mind of John Keats* (1926; rpt. New York, 1964); Claude Lee Finney, *The Evolution of Keats's Poetry* (1936; rpt. New York, 1963); Murry's *Keats*; Thora Balslev, *Keats and Wordsworth: A Comparative Study* (Copenhagen: Munksgaard, 1962); and Miriam Allott, "Keats and Wordsworth," *Keats-Shelley Memorial Bulletin* 22 (1971): 28–43.

12. These words read like a gloss on Immanuel Kant's description of art as "purposiveness without a purpose" in his *Critique of Judgment* (1790), which Keats could hardly have read.

13. For Keats's idea that poetry, like "every mental pursuit takes its reality and worth from the ardour of the pursuer" (I, 242) see Bate, *John Keats*, pp. 241–42, 550; Helen Haworth, "Keats and the Metaphor of Vision," *Journal of English and Germanic Philology* 67 (1968): 376; George Borstein, "Keats's Concept of the Ethereal," *Keats-Shelley Journal* 18 (1969): 100–101; John Jones, pp. 75–76, 117, 122, 169; Bhabatosh Chatterjee, *John Keats: His Mind and Work* (New Delhi, 1971), pp. 283–84; Sperry, pp. 68–70; James Land Jones, *Adam's Dream: Mythic Consciousness in Keats and Yeats* (Athens, Georgia, 1975), pp. 36–38; Stuart A. Ende, *Keats and the Sublime* (New Haven, 1976), pp. 59–60; Ryan, p. 155; and Ronald A. Sharp, *Keats, Skepticism, and the Religion of Beauty* (Athens, Georgia, 1979), pp. 33, 48–50, 94, 100, 130. The poet's skepticism is discussed at length by Ryan and Sharp, the latter finding Keats more radically and consistently skeptical, seeing, for example, even in Keats's reference to the "here after" (I, 185) an "ironic perspective on immortality" (p. 19). Similarly Sharp (p. 172) disagrees with Ryan's view of the passage on "Soul-making" (II, 101–104) as showing that "Keats seems fairly confident about immortality at this time" (p. 209). Both scholars adduce cogent arguments, and although at least in the earlier of these two passages Keats does seem to be leaning toward belief in some form of afterlife, we cannot be sure whether his words indicate more faith than doubt; we receive only a half-knowledge of what the poet remains content to express as a mere "favorite Speculation" (I, 185) or to convey by means of taking immortality "for granted for the purpose of showing a thought which has struck" him (II, 102). Sharp repeatedly (and rightly) emphasizes Keats's "deep and abiding skepticism about the possibility of knowing with certainty any kind of transcendent or higher reality" (p. 5), but when he writes of "a conception of spirituality that does not depend on—that in fact *denies*—transcendent reality" (p. 4, italics mine), he imputes an un-Keatsian lack of negative capability to the poet.

14. E.g. by Douglas Bush, *John Keats: His Life and Writings* (London, 1966), p. 126, and Guilhamet, p. 9.

15. David Luke, "Keats's Letters: Fragments of an Aesthetic of Fragments," *Genre* 11 (1978): 222.

Chapter Three

1. John Middleton Murry, *Keats and Shakespeare: A Study of Keats' Poetic Life from 1816 to 1820* (1925; rpt. London, 1964), p. 14; Bush, p. 29.

2. Garrod, p. 150; Murry, *Keats and Shakespeare*, p. 15; Graham Hough, *The Romantic Poets*, 2nd ed. (London: Hutchinson University Library, 1957), p. 160.

3. The sonnet contains 16 visual and 19 nonvisual images: 8 organic, 6 auditory, 3 thermal, 1 tactile, 1 motor.

4. The poem was written in a friendly on-the-spot competition with Hunt. See Bate, *John Keats*, pp. 120–21.

5. Cf. "Ode to a Nightingale," 1. 74; "Ode on Indolence," 1. 30; "Ode on a Grecian Urn," 1. 45.

6. Marjorie Norris, "Phenomenology and Process: Perception in Keats's 'I Stood Tiptoe,' " *Keats-Shelley Journal* 25 (1976): 46.

7. Cf. M[eyer] H. Abrams, "The Correspondent Breeze: A Romantic Metaphor" in his edition of *English Romantic Poets: Modern Essays in Criticism*, 2nd ed. (London, 1975), pp. 37–54.

8. Michael G. Cooke, *The Romantic Will* (New Haven, 1976), p. 155.

9. See Matthews, ed., p. 62.

10. Stillinger (page 8, note 8) lists seven examples.

11. Murry, *Keats and Shakespeare*, p. 23.

12. See Jack, pp. 136–39.

13. J. Burke Severs, "Keats's 'Mansion of Many Apartments,' *Sleep and Poetry*, and *Tintern Abbey*," *Modern Language Quarterly* 20 (1959): 128–32.

14. Morris Dickstein, *Keats and His Poetry: A Study in Development* (Chicago, 1971), p. 35.

15. "I stood tip-toe," ll. 157–62, and *Endymion*, I.242–43; *Endymion*, II.936–1009; "Ode on a Grecian Urn," l.18.

Chapter Four

1. Benjamin W. Griffith, "Keats' 'On Seeing the Elgin Marbles,' " *Explicator* 31 (1973): item 76.

2. The discussion of this sonnet is indebted to E. B. Murray, "Ambivalent Mortality in the Elgin Marbles Sonnet," *Keats-Shelley Journal* 20 (1971): 22–36.

3. Ricks, pp. 104–105.

4. Murry, *Keats*, p. 175; John Jones, p. 182; G. Wilson Knight, *The Starlit Dome: Studies in the Poetry of Vision* (1941; rpt. London, 1964), p. 262.

5. Pettet, pp. 193–97.

6. On the "transfer of power from Apollo to Cynthia" see Evert, pp. 104–106.

7. E.g. by Bruce E. Miller, "On the Meaning of Keats's *Endymion*," *Keats-Shelley Journal* 14 (1965): 46.

8. Earl R. Wasserman, *The Finer Tone: Keats's Major Poems* (1953; rpt. Baltimore, 1967), p. 24. A strong argument for reading "essences" as "things" is presented by Newell F. Ford, " 'Fellowship with Essence' in *Endymion*," *Publications of the Modern Language Association of America* 62 (1947): 1061–76.

9. Katherine M. Wilson, *The Nightingale and the Hawk: A Psychological Study of Keats' Ode* (London: Allen & Unwin, 1964), p. 11; Anthony, Earl of Shaftesbury, *Characteristics of Men, Manners, Opinions, Times*, ed. John M. Robertson (1900; rpt. New York: Bobbs-Merrill, 1964), II, 98, quoted by Robert M. Ryan, "Keats's 'Hymn to Pan': A Debt to Shaftesbury?", *Keats-Shelley Journal* 26 (1977): 33.

10. Warren U. Ober and W. K. Thomas, "Keats and the Solitary Pan," *Keats-Shelley Journal* 29 (1980): 113.

11. Ian Jack thinks that Keats seems to have had Poussin's *Landscape with Orion* in mind, whereas "the image of Deucalion is probably of purely literary origin" (p. 156). Jack's suggestion would indicate that Keats requires no visual model for his verbal painting or for his effective Miltonic "stationing," the term he uses in a note on *Paradise Lost*, VII.420–23 (see H. Buxton Forman, ed., *The Complete Works of John Keats* [1900–1901; rpt. New York, 1970], III, 264).

12. E.g. by Jacob D. Wigod, "The Meaning of *Endymion*," *Publications of the Modern Language Association of America* 68 (1953): 787, and Stillinger, who links it to solitude versus love and to Shelley's Alastor (pp. 17–18).

13. Murry, *Keats*, p. 166.

14. Glen O. Allen, "The Fall of Endymion: A Study in Keats's Intellectual Growth," *Keats-Shelley Journal* 6 (1957): 37–57; Clarice Godfrey, "Endymion" in Muir, ed., p. 36; Ward, p. 145; Evert, p. 175; Dickstein, p. 128; Chatterjee, p. 260; Sperry, p. 112; Allen, pp. 46–47; Ende, p. 95, and see also Ende's article "Keats's Music of Truth," *ELH: Journal of English Literary History* 40 (1973): 90–104.

15. See Edward S. LeComte, *Endymion in England: The Literary History of a Greek Myth* (New York, Morningside Heights: King's Crown Press, 1944), pp. 30–31.

16. Northrop Frye, *A Study of English Romanticism* (New York: Random House, 1968), p. 129. Frye, however, sees Endymion moving from the second to the top realm by way of the two lower worlds (pp. 130–35).

17. The first allegorical reading of *Endymion* appeared only in 1880 in F. M. Owen's *John Keats: A Study* (London: Kegan Paul) but in the twentieth century the question of whether or not *Endymion* is an allegory has been repeatedly taken up. Bate gives a balanced judgment against attempts either to read the poem as "elaborate and planned allegory" (p. 171), especially one with a "systematic Neoplatonism" (p. 174), or "to deny any allegorical intention at all" (p. 172). The most persuasive representative of the minority view of the antiallegorists is Pettet, who is still unrepentant in his 1969 foreword to the second edition of his book on Keats. Pettet's approach provides a salutory antidote to the more abstruse allegorical readings which ignore or play down the basic love story. On the other hand even the most blatant eroticism in Book Two can be related to the wider context of a spiritual quest. We can therefore agree with Stillinger, who remarks at the end of a note listing twenty-one critics on *Endymion*, that "the main problem is (once again) the interpretation of the allegory" (p. 15). It might also be well to remember what Northrop Frye in *Anatomy of Criticism: Four Essays* (Princeton: Princeton University Press, 1957) observes about romance in general: "a suggestion of allegory is constantly creeping in around its fringes" (p. 304). But perhaps it is all a question of the definition of "allegory."

18. When Keats writes Taylor that the "fellowship with essence" passage

is his "first Step towards the chief Attempt in the Drama—the playing of different Natures with Joy and Sorrow" (I, 218–19), he probably means that joy and sorrow will be the subject of his future playwriting, but it is not impossible that "the Drama" may refer to *Endymion*.

19. Paul Sherwin, "Dying into Life: Keats's Struggle with Milton in *Hyperion*," *Publications of the Modern Language Association of America* 93 (1978): 389.

Chapter Five

1. See Alvin Whitley, "The Autograph of Keats's 'In Drear Nighted December,' " *Harvard Library Bulletin* 5 (1951): 118.

2. John Jones, p. 37.

3. Murry, *Keats*, p. 206.

4. For "Hell torment" (instead of "damnation") see *Letters*, I, 215. An autograph proves that Keats associates the oak forest with Shakespeare: see Porter Williams, Jr., "Keats' 'On Sitting Down to Read King Lear Once Again,' 11," *Explicator* 29 (1970): item 26.

5. Shakespeare, Sonnets 12, 64, 107. These three sonnets are perhaps the most influential for Keats's poem. Compare 12 and 64 for the repeated "When," 64 for the shore image, and 107 for "fears" and "the wide world." Lines 7 and 8 of Sonnet 12 are underlined in Keats's copy of Shakespeare's Sonnets. For this and other underlining and sidelining of Shakespeare's sonnets see Caroline F. E. Spurgeon, *Keats's Shakespeare: A Descriptive Study Based on New Material*, 2nd ed. (London, 1929), p. 40 and plate 16. On 22 November 1817 Keats had written into a letter to Reynolds (I, 188–89) the second quatrain of Sonnet 12. This quatrain epitomizes his favorite theme of the inevitability of natural process by carrying the past of the "canopy" of leaves and "Summer's green" into the autumnal present of leafless trees and harvested sheaves.

6. See H. W. Garrod, ed., *The Poetical Works of John Keats*, 2nd ed. (Oxford, 1958), p. 466, and Miriam Allott, ed., *Keats: The Complete Poems* (London, 1970), p. 297.

7. Ricks, p. 200.

8. Titian is mentioned in l. 19, and before the introduction of Claude's *Enchanted Castle* in l. 26 the descriptions bring to mind other Claude paintings. See Jack, p. 130, and Alan Osler, "Keats," *Times Literary Supplement*, 16 April 1971, p. 449.

9. See Matthews, ed., pp. 149–240, passim; Sidney Colvin, *Keats* (1887; rpt. London: Macmillan, 1964), pp. 148–52; Amy Lowell, *John Keats* (1925; rpt. [London,] 1969), I, 623; Murry, *Keats and Shakespeare*, p. 69; Ward, p. 174; Stillinger, pp. 37–43; Eve Leoff, *A Study of John Keats's "Isabella"* (Salzburg, 1972), pp. 55–56; Louise Z. Smith, "The Material Sublime: Keats and *Isabella*," *Studies in Romanticism* 13 (1974): 305–307.

10. George Bernard Shaw, "Keats," in *The John Keats Memorial Volume* [ed. George C. Williamson] (London, 1921), p. 175.

11. Though convincing on the whole, Jack Stillinger pushes his argument for "Isabella" as an "*anti*-romance" (p. 37) too far when he implies (pp. 41–42) that Keats treats the theme of love's immortality ironically.

12. First pointed out by Charles Lamb (see Matthews, ed., p. 158).

13. John Jones, p. 15.

14. Billy T. Boyar, "Keats's 'Isabella': Shakespeare's *Venus and Adonis* and the Venus-Adonis Myth," *Keats-Shelley Journal* 21-22 (1972–73): 167, is reminded of "Venus leading Adonis out of the underworld in spring."

15. Leoff, pp. 199–203, sees the invocation as part of a mystery rite.

16. Sidney Colvin, *John Keats: His Life and Poetry, His Friends, Critics, and After-Fame* (1917; rpt. New York, 1970), p. 426.

Chapter Six

1. For discussions of these poems see Bate, *John Keats*, pp. 351–62; Evert, pp. 214–24; Chatterjee, pp. 311–21; Dickstein, pp. 168–85; and Sperry, pp. 132–52.

2. Shiv K. Kumar, "The Meaning of *Hyperion*: A Reassessment," in his edition of *British Romantic Poets: Recent Revaluations* (New York: New York University Press, 1966), p. 309, writes: "There is hardly any critic who has not interpreted this poem, directly or by implication, as 'a poem of progress.'" More recently Sherwin has reaffirmed: "That *Hyperion* is a 'progress poem' is evident" (p. 385).

3. Keats owned this book but apparently had earlier read Andrew Tooke's *Pantheon*, which had appeared in 1698. See *Keats Circle*, I, 258; II, 148, and Jack, pp. 249, 282–83.

4. Harold Bloom, *Poetry and Repression: Revisionism from Blake to Stevens* (New Haven, 1976), p. 121.

5. See Bate, *John Keats*, p. 407; Bush, p. 103; and Pierre Vitoux, "Keats's Epic Design in *Hyperion*," *Studies in Romanticism* 14 (1975): 177.

6. Quoted in Jack, pp. 163–64.

7. But Ober and Thomas, p. 118, conjecture that in *The Fall of Hyperion* Pan was to supersede Apollo (and Mnemosyne-Moneta).

8. The defection of Mnemosyne is reminiscent of the aid to Zeus given by Prometheus (the Forethinker) against his fellow Titans.

9. Murry, *Keats and Shakespeare*, pp. 82–83.

10. Vitoux, pp. 179, 183. Vitoux conjectures that Saturn and Asia are reconciled to loss of power and become leaders of mankind (pp. 174–75) whereas Enceladus heads a rebellion (p. 176), and he discusses the problem of relating such epic action to Apollo's vision (p. 183).

11. Bate, *John Keats*, p. 406.

12. Brian Wilkie, *Romantic Poets and Epic Tradition* (Madison: University of Wisconsin Press, 1965), p. 182.

13. Keats's quotation has not yet been identified. Although I have not found the translation he might have seen or heard, I would hazard the guess

that Keats is perhaps alluding to Friedrich Schiller's poem of 1795 "Das Ideal und das Leben" [The Ideal and Life], stanza four: "Jugendlich, von allen Erdenmalen / Frei, in der Vollendung Strahlen / Schwebet hier der Menschheit Götterbild" (Here humanity's divine image [perhaps translated as "mankind's picture of the gods"] hovers youthful, free of all earthly signs, in the rays of perfection).

14. Bate, *John Keats*, passim; Bate, *The Burden of the Past and the English Poet* (New York: Norton, 1970); Sperry, p. 158.

15. See especially Bloom's *The Anxiety of Influence: A Theory of Poetry* (New York: Oxford University Press, 1973); *A Map of Misreading* (New York, 1975); and *Poetry and Repression*, p. 112: Milton and Wordsworth form "the composite precursor that both inspired and inhibited" Keats.

16. Sherwin, pp. 387, 391–93, 385.

17. Sperry, pp. 181–93, 164.

18. Leslie Brisman, *Milton's Poetry of Choice and Its Romantic Heirs* (Ithaca: Cornell University Press, 1973), p. 109; Ende, p. 115. Cf. also Homer Brown, "Creations and Destroyings: Keats's Protestant Hymn, the 'Ode to Psyche,' " *Diacritics* 6:4 (1976): 50.

19. Gittings, *John Keats*, p. 269; Bate, *John Keats*, p. 403.

20. M. R. Ridley, *Keats' Craftsmanship: A Study in Poetic Development* (1933; rpt. Lincoln, Nebraska, 1963), p. 93.

21. E.g. by Allott, ed., p. 438 and Bate, *John Keats*, p. 403. The phrase is quoted by Woodhouse (*Keats Circle*, I, 129).

22. See Keats's marginal gloss on *Paradise Lost*, I.321 (Forman, ed., III, 258).

23. *Keats Circle*, II, 277–78; see also above chapter 1, section IV, and the last note of chapter 1.

24. Pettet, pp. 102–104.

25. On the influence of Milton's versification on Keats see Bate, *Stylistic Development*, pp. 51, 57–58, 66–91, 108, 202–203, 209; and *John Keats*, pp. 409, 411–13.

26. Abrams, ed., *Romantic Poets*, pp. 37–54; Geoffrey Hartman, *The Fate of Reading and Other Essays* (Chicago, 1975), pp. 70–71.

27. Bush, p. 111.

28. By Marian Hollingsworth Cusac in "Keats as Enchanter: An Organizing Principle of 'The Eve of St. Agnes,' " *Keats-Shelley Journal* 17 (1968): 113, and the three critics she refers to (Wasserman, Finney, and Roger Sharrock).

29. Sperry, p. 206. Like Miriam Allott in Muir, ed., *Reassessment*, p. 56, and John Bayley, *Keats and Reality* (1962; rpt. [Folcroft, Pennsylvania,] 1969), p. 27, Sperry sees the poem as expressing wish-fulfillment.

30. See *Letters*, II, 19 and Jack, p. 99. The print from a fresco is entitled *Il trionfo della morte* [The Triumph of Death] and reproduced as plate 39 in Gittings's *John Keats*, which discusses several of its details in relation to "The Eve of St. Agnes" (pp. 280–81). Plate VIII in Jack identifies the painter as

Orcagna (1308–68). Gittings also finds traces of Keats's visit to Chichester in the poem (p. 277) and to Stansted Chapel in the colorful twenty-fourth stanza (pp. 283–84). Other probable influences: Mrs. Radcliffe's Gothic tales, Boccaccio's *II Filocolo*, Scott's *The Lay of the Last Minstrel*, Coleridge's *Christabel*, and Spenser (see Allott, ed., p. 451). R. S. White gives parallels in "Sidney's *Arcadia* as a Possible Source for 'The Eve of St. Agnes,' " *Keats-Shelley Journal* 28 (1979): 11–17.

31. Wasserman, p. 108.

32. Bayley, p. 30. Stillinger, who sees Madeline as victim of self-deception and Porphyro's stratagem, and the poem as satire on the idealistic dreamer, quotes from this stanza to illustrate "the folly of [Madeline's] delusion" (pp. 86–88), whereas David Wiener, "The Secularization of the Fortunate Fall in Keats's 'The Eve of St. Agnes,' " *Keats-Shelley Journal* 29 (1980): 121, uses the same stanza to illustrate "Madeline's dream world as a self-enclosed, stagnant Eden."

33. In the revision Keats wrote: "See, while she speaks his arms encroaching slow, / Have zoned her, heart to heart,—loud, loud the dark winds blow!" For Woodhouse's and Taylor's reactions see *Letters*, II, 163, 182–83.

34. See e.g. *Letters*, II, 163, and Stillinger, p. 81.

35. Michael Ragussis, *The Subterfuge of Art: Language and the Romantic Tradition* (Baltimore, 1978), p. 75.

36. Richard Harter Fogle, *The Imagery of Keats and Shelley: A Comparative Study* (Chapel Hill, North Carolina, 1949), pp. 66–67, 72–73; John Jones, p. 261.

37. Forman, ed., III, 7.

38. Bernard Blackstone, *The Consecrated Urn: An Interpretation of Keats in Terms of Growth and Form* (London: Longmans, 1959), p. 298; Judy Little, *Keats as a Narrative Poet: A Test of Invention* (Lincoln, Nebraska, 1975), p. 126; Walter E. Houghton, "The Meaning of Keats's Eve of St. Mark," *ELH: Journal of English Literary History* 13 (1946): 76–77; Sperry, p. 224; Bush, p. 117.

39. David Luke, "*The Eve of Saint Mark*: Keats's 'ghostly Queen of Spades' and the Textual Superstition," *Studies in Romanticism* 9 (1970): 173; Stillinger, pp. 97–98.

40. For a survey of possible influences see Francis Lee Utley, "The Infernos of Lucretius and of Keats's *La Belle Dame Sans Merci*," *ELH: Journal of English Literary History* 25 (1958): 105–107, and Allott, ed., pp. 500–506. For Celtic sources see Sperry, pp. 234–39.

41. Cf. David Simpson, "Keats's Lady, Metaphor, and the Rhetoric of Neurosis," *Studies in Romanticism* 15 (1976): 269; Evert, pp. 253–56; James Twitchell, "La Belle Dame as Vampire," *CEA Critic* 37 (1975): 31–33; Edward E. Bostetter, *The Romantic Ventriloquists: Wordsworth, Coleridge, Keats, Shelley, Byron*, rev. ed. (Seattle, 1975), p. 160; Utley, p. 121; Charles I. Patterson, Jr., *The Daemonic in the Poetry of John Keats* (Urbana, Illinois, 1970), pp. 138, 141.

42. Wasserman, p. 75; Richard Benvenuto, "La Belle Dame and the Pale Kings: Life's High Meed," *Michigan Academician* 2 (1969): 62.
43. Murry, *Keats and Shakespeare*, pp. 124–25; Jane Rabb Cohen, "Keats's Humor in 'La Belle Dame sans Merci,'" *Keats-Shelley Journal* 17 (1968): 12.
44. See above chapter 1, section IV, and chapter 1, note 8.

Chapter Seven

1. The best and most convenient selections of the countless critical essays on the great odes are by Jack Stillinger, ed., *Twentieth Century Interpretations of Keats's Odes: A Collection of Critical Essays* (Englewood Cliffs, New Jersey, 1968) and G. S. Fraser, ed., *John Keats: Odes* (London, 1971). Both collections reprint Kenneth Allott's fine essay on "Ode to Psyche" and several critics listed in the following notes. Joseph Sendry and Richard Giannone, *A Critical Study Guide to Keats: The Odes* (Totowa, New Jersey: Littlefield, Adams, 1968), give detailed, often stimulating stanza-by-stanza commentaries on "Psyche," "Nightingale," "Grecian Urn," "Melancholy," and "Autumn," comparative analyses, and a history of the ode.
2. Various paintings and sculptures mentioned by Jack (pp. 201–13) depicting Psyche in the arms of Cupid, three of which are reproduced as plates XXV, XXVII, and XXVIII, may have inspired the opening stanza. Jack's discussion shows how Keats creates an original work of art from diverse sources from literature (Spenser and Mrs. Tighe, in addition to Apuleius) and the plastic arts (Giulio Romano and Antonio Canova among others). Cf. chapter 4, note 11 above.
3. Dickstein, p. 197; Matthews, ed., pp. 171–72.
4. Homer Brown, p. 56. (See chapter 6, note 18.)
5. Sperry, p. 257; Bloom, *Map*, p. 152; and cf. Bloom's *Anxiety of Influence*, p. 5. In *Poetry and Repression* (p. 123) Bloom states that with the "Ode to Psyche" Keats "came to terms with his own belatedness."
6. Leon Waldoff, "The Theme of Mutability in the 'Ode to Psyche,'" *Publications of the Modern Language Association of America* 92 (1977): 410–19, links "Psyche" to the other odes by stressing the mutability of *the goddess*.
7. Mario L. D'Avanzo, *Keats's Metaphors for the Poetic Imagination* (Durham, North Carolina, 1967), p. 202.
8. David Perkins, *The Quest for Permanence: The Symbolism of Wordsworth, Shelley, and Keats* (1959; rpt. Cambridge, Massachusetts, 1965), p. 217.
9. Pettet, pp. 86–87.
10. Allen Tate, "A Reading of Keats (II)," *American Scholar* 15 (Spring 1946): 191; Dickstein, p. 209, note 17; Sperry, p. 264.
11. F. R. Leavis, *Revaluation: Tradition and Development in English Poetry* (1936; rpt. Harmondsworth: Penguin Books, 1972), pp. 230–31.

12. Colvin, *John Keats: His Life . . . and After-Fame*, p. 419; Lowell, II, 252; Garrod, p. 111; Muir, p. 69; Hough, p. 175; Cleanth Brooks and Robert Penn Warren, *Understanding Poetry* (1938; rpt. New York: Holt, 1966), p. 430; Andrew J. Kappel, "The Immortality of the Natural: Keats' 'Ode to a Nightingale,' " *ELH: Journal of English Literary History* 45 (1978): 273, 282.

13. Garrod, pp. 111–13; Victor J. Lams, Jr., "Ruth, Milton, and Keats's 'Ode to a Nightingale,' " *Modern Language Quarterly* 34 (1973): 432; and cf. the brief discussion by Sherwin, p. 383.

14. See Jack, *Keats and the Mirror of Art*, pp. 217–21 and plates XXIX–XXXVI and XXXIX.

15. Three famous interpretations which discuss paradox or the "mystic oxymoron" in the ode are those by Kenneth Burke, Cleanth Brooks (both reprinted in Fraser, ed.), and Earl Wasserman. These are attacked by John Bellairs and defended by Philip Waldron and Manfred Mackenzie in "Critical Exchange: Variations on a Vase," *Southern Review* (Adelaide) 1 (1965): 58–73. For additional critiques of Brooks, Wasserman, and others see Pettet, pp. 375–81; and Philip Hobsbaum, "The 'Philosophy' of the Grecian Urn: A Consensus of Readings," *Keats-Shelley Memorial Bulletin* 15 (1965): 1–7, includes Burke, Brooks, and Wasserman in a general survey.

16. Jack (p. 223) makes a strong case for taking the aphorism as an inscription on the urn. For convenient summaries of opinions on who addresses whom and how the words relate to the poem as a whole see Stillinger, pp. 167–73, and Allott, ed., pp. 537–38.

17. Garrod, p. 103; C. Maurice Bowra, *The Romantic Imagination* (1950; rpt. London: Oxford University Press, 1964), pp. 146–47.

18. Caldwell, p. 163; F. W. Bateson, *English Poetry: A Critical Introduction* (1950; London: Longman, 1966), p. 153, note 2; Jack, p. 287; Harry M. Solomon, "Shaftesbury's *Characteristics* and the Conclusion of 'Ode on a Grecian Urn,' " *Keats-Shelley Journal* 24 (1975): 89–101; Keith Brown, "A Short *Course of the Belles Lettres* for Keatsians?" *English* 27 (Spring 1978): 27–32. To Brown the aphorism means that "*only objects such as itself* express the highest truths" (p. 30).

19. See e.g. Bruce E. Miller, "Form and Substance in 'Grecian Urn,' " *Keats-Shelley Journal* 20 (1971): 66–69; Jack, p. 288; Sperry, pp. 277–78; Pratap Biswas, "Keats's Cold Pastoral," *University of Toronto Quarterly* 47 (1977/78): 103–104; James Shokoff, "Soul-Making in 'Ode on a Grecian Urn,' " *Keats-Shelley Journal* 24 (1975): 104–105. According to Biswas "Keats is here contrasting two kinds of beauty, the 'false beauty' of art and the true beauty of reality" (p. 107).

20. Muir, pp. 71–72.

21. John Jones, p. 85.

22. Janice C. Sinson, *John Keats and The Anatomy of Melancholy* (London, 1971), p. 35.

23. Bush, p. 146; Pettet, p. 307; Helen Vendler, "The Experiential Beginnings of Keats's Odes," *Studies in Romanticism* 12 (1973): 596 and note;

Horace G. Posey, Jr., "Keats's 'Ode on Melancholy': Analogue of the Imagination," *Concerning Poetry* 8 (Fall 1975): 67. Cf. also Sharp's comments that "beautiful things . . . make us embrace life even in our sorrow. The prerequisite, as always, is intensity" (p. 60); and that "it is the fact of transience that makes beauty meaningful" (p. 61).

24. See Robert Rogers, "Keats's Strenuous Tongue: A Study of 'Ode on Meloncholy [*sic*],' " *Literature and Psychology* 17 (1967): 5, and Aileen Ward's reply on p. 33.

25. Reid, p. 395 (see chapter 1, note 2).

26. John Jones, p. 263.

27. But William F. Zak, "The Confirmation of Keats's Belief in Negative Capability: The 'Ode on Indolence,' " *Keats-Shelley Journal* 25 (1976): 55–64, describes the poet's attitude here as "witty irony" (p. 63). Zak's article, which sees the three figures as trying to force the poet into activity before he is ripe for it, should help to raise the standing of this undervalued ode.

28. See Bate, *John Keats*, p. 528n.

29. The correct order and wording of the opening of the six stanzas is: I "One morn . . ."; II "How is it . . ."; III "A third time pass'd . . ."; IV "They faded . . ."; V "A third time came they by: Alas . . ."; VI "So. . . ." For a detailed discussion of the ordering of the stanzas see Stillinger, pp. 174–78. Our analysis clarifies Stillinger's two remaining "obscurities" (p. 177).

Chapter Eight

1. Cf. Sinson, pp. 31–34. In *Keats and the Dramatic Principle* (Lincoln, Nebraska, 1958) Bernice Slote gives a useful and balanced survey of the literary sources of *Lamia*, among them Burton and Philostratus, from whose third-century *Life of Apollonius of Tyana* Burton took the episode (pp. 140–46), and Wieland's *Oberon*, Ovid's *Metamorphoses*, Dryden's translations of Lucretius's *De Rerum Natura* and Ovid's *Art of Love*, La Motte Fouqué's *Undine*, the oriental tale and oriental play, and Potter's *Antiquities of Greece* (pp. 172–83). The influence of *Oberon* is discussed at length in Werner W. Beyer, *Keats and the Daemon King* (New York: Oxford University Press, 1947), pp. 192–238. For Keats's apparent acknowledgment of the influence of Dryden's versification, see *Letters*, II, 165.

2. Garrett Stewart, "*Lamia* and the Language of Metamorphosis," *Studies in Romanticism* 15 (1976): 30.

3. Gene M. Bernstein, "Keats' 'Lamia': The Sense of a Non-Ending," *Papers on Language and Literature* 15 (1979): 190–91.

4. Slote, p. 148.

5. D. G. James, *The Romantic Comedy: An Essay on English Romanticism* (1948; rpt. London: Oxford University Press, 1963), p. 150; Robert M. Ryan, "Christ and Moneta," *English Language Notes* 13 (1976): 190; Ward, p. 340.

6. Cf. Anya Taylor, "Superhuman Silence: Language in *Hyperion*,"

Studies in English Literature 1500–1900 19 (1979): 684, who visualizes the demythologized Titans of the earlier fragment wandering about "unnoticed except by poets who might reinvent them once again in the elaboration of metaphor."

7. Cooke, p. 177; Murry, *Keats and Shakespeare*, p. 186; Sperry, p. 333; James Land Jones, p. 195; Ende, p. 157; William C. Stephenson, "The Performing Narrator in Keats's Poetry," *Keats-Shelley Journal* 26 (1977): 67.

8. Bloom, *Poetry and Repression*, p. 131; Sherwin, p. 394.

9. Hartman, p. 65.

10. Annabel M. Patterson, " 'How to load and . . . bend': Syntax and Interpretation in Keats's *To Autumn*," *Publications of the Modern Language Association of America* 94 (1979): 449.

11. Arnold Davenport, "A Note on 'To Autumn,' " in Muir, ed., p. 96; William Walsh, "John Keats" in Boris Ford, ed., *From Blake to Byron* (1957; rpt. Harmondsworth: Penguin, 1962), p. 238; Robin Mayhead, *John Keats* (Cambridge, 1967), p. 95; John Jones, p. 268; Ricks, p. 208.

12. Virgil Nemoianu, "The Dialectics of Movement in Keats's 'To Autumn,' " *Publications of the Modern Language Association of America* 93 (1978): 205–14, discusses additional progressions and mutations, for instance an "evolution in *space*" (p. 206).

13. Ricks, p. 208. Ricks quotes three pages from Sartre's *Being and Nothingness* on "the slimy" which he describes as "the best criticism of Keats ever written not about him" (pp. 139–42).

14. For the season as boundary see Davenport in Muir, ed., p. 97. For the Ruth figure see Frederick L. Gwynn, "Keats, Autumn, and Ruth," *Notes and Queries* 197 (1952): 471–72, and Davenport, p. 98.

15. See *Letters*, II, 167, and above pp. 25–26.

16. Bate, *Stylistic Development*, pp. 183–84, and *John Keats*, p. 581 and note.

17. Murry, *Keats and Shakespeare*, p. 189.

18. Ward, p. 415; Matthew Arnold, "John Keats" (1880), republished in *Essays in Criticism: Second Series*, ed. S. R. Littlewood (1938; rpt. London: Macmillan, 1956), p. 71; Bate, *John Keats*, p. 699; Murry, *Keats and Shakespeare*, p. 220.

19. For more detailed discussions of *Otho the Great* see Slote, pp. 104–20 (especially pp. 109–13); Bate, *John Keats*, pp. 564–68; Bush, pp. 153–55; Chatterjee, pp. 100–104; and Harry R. Beaudry, *The English Theatre and John Keats* (Salzburg: University of Salzburg, 1973), pp. 178–90. Pettet, pp. 240–45, concentrates on Keats's self-projection into the hero Ludolph and on Aurenthe, the heroine, as femme fatale.

20. *King Stephen* is discussed by Slote, pp. 113–15, and Beaudry, pp. 178–80, 190–98.

21. For commentaries on *The Jealousies* see Bate, *John Keats*, pp. 623–24; Martin Halpern, "Keats and the 'Spirit that Laughest,' " *Keats-Shelley Journal* 15 (1966): 81–85; Gittings, *John Keats*, pp. 368–73; Chatterjee, pp.

135–38; and Howard O. Brogan, " 'The Cap and Bells, or . . . The Jealousies'?" *Bulletin of the New York Public Library* 77 (1974): 298–313.

22. For surveys of Keats's influence see George H. Ford, *Keats and the Victorians* (1944; rpt. London: Archon, 1962), and J. R. MacGillivray, *Keats: A Bibliography and Reference Guide with an Essay on Keats' Reputation* (1949; rpt. Toronto, 1968), pp. xi–lxxxi.

Selected Bibliography

PRIMARY SOURCES

ALLOTT, MIRIAM, ed. *Keats: The Complete Poems* (Annotated English Poets). London: Longman, 1970. Best all-purpose edition, with an introduction to each poem, textual variants, explanatory notes, sources, and parallels.

BARNARD, JOHN, ed. *John Keats: The Complete Poems*. Harmondsworth: Penguin Books, 1973. Much smaller format and cheaper than Allott's edition. Copious notes and useful appendixes.

BUSH, DOUGLAS, ed. *Keats: Selected Poems and Letters*. Boston: Houghton Mifflin, 1959. Contains nearly all the important poems and valuable notes.

FORMAN, H. BUXTON, ed. *The Complete Works of John Keats*. 5 vols. 1900–1901; rpt. New York: AMS Press, 1970. Revision of Forman's pioneering edition of 1883. Vol. III contains Keats's theater criticism and his notes on Shakespeare, Milton, and Burton.

FORMAN, MAURICE BUXTON, ed. *The Letters of John Keats*. 4th ed. with revisions and additional letters. London: Oxford University Press, 1952. The standard edition before Rollins.

GARROD, H. W., ed. *The Poetical Works of John Keats*. 2nd ed. Oxford: Clarendon Press, 1958. The complete variorum text. Now superseded by Stillinger.

GITTINGS, ROBERT, ed. *Selected Poems and Letters of Keats* (Poetry Bookshelf). London: Heinemann, 1966. Letters interspersed with poems in chronological order. Readable introduction and notes. Most of *Endymion* and part of "Isabella" omitted.

————, ed. *Letters of John Keats*. London: Oxford University Press, 1970. Contains practically all the major letters.

PETTET, E. C., ed. *A Selection from John Keats*. London: Longman, 1974. Useful Introduction and notes on poems and letters.

ROLLINS, HYDER EDWARD, ed. *The Letters of John Keats*. 2 vols. Cambridge, Massachusetts: Harvard University Press, 1958. Definitive edition. Contains also a 32-page "calendar" of events in Keats's life.

————, ed. *The Keats Circle: Letters and Papers and More Letters and Poems of the Keats Circle*. 2nd ed. 2 vols. Cambridge, Massachusetts: Harvard University Press, 1965. Letters, papers, and notes of Keats's family, friends, acquaintances, and earliest biographers. 350 carefully edited items.

STILLINGER, JACK, ed. *The Poems of John Keats*. Cambridge, Massachusetts: Harvard University Press, 1978. Should remain the standard scholarly edition for a long time. Detailed textual notes, the result of years of painstaking scholarship, inspire confidence.

THORPE, CLARENCE DEWITT, ed. *John Keats: Complete Poems and Selected Letters*. 1935; rpt. Indianapolis: Bobbs Merrill, 1975. Introductions and notes still valuable.

TRILLING, LIONEL, ed. *The Selected Letters of John Keats*. New York: Farrar, 1951. Contains an admirable Introduction describing the poet as "the last image of health" in Europe.

SECONDARY SOURCES

1. Bibliographies, Surveys of Criticism, and Concordance

BALDWIN, DANE LEWIS, et al., eds. *A Concordance to the Poems of John Keats*. 1917; rpt. Gloucester, Massachusetts: Peter Smith, 1963. Contains a valuable Introduction.

FOGLE, RICHARD HARTER. *Romantic Poets and Prose Writers* (Goldentree Bibliographies). New York: Appleton, 1967. Contains a section on individual poems.

GITTINGS, ROBERT. "Keats." In *English Poetry: Select Bibliographical Guides*. Ed. A. E. Dyson. London: Oxford University Press, 1971. Gives a critical survey in addition to bibliographical lists.

GREEN, DAVID BONNELL, and WILSON, EDWIN GRAVES, eds. *Keats, Shelley, Byron, Hunt and their Circles: A Bibliography: July 1, 1950–June 30, 1962*. Lincoln: University of Nebraska Press, 1964. Collected bibliographies of the *Keats-Shelley Journal* (see next item).

Keats-Shelley Journal: Current Bibliography. New York: The Keats-Shelley Association of America, 1952. Annotates articles and lists book reviews. Comprehensive.

MACGILLIVRAY, J. R. *Keats: A Bibliography and Reference Guide with an Essay on Keats' Reputation*. 1949; rpt. Toronto: University of Toronto Press, 1968. Classifies well over 1,000 items under 25 different sections, with entries in each category arranged in chronological order.

PERKINS, DAVID, and THORPE, CLARENCE D. "Keats." *The English Romantic Poets: A Review of Research and Criticism*. 3rd rev. ed. Ed. Frank Jordan, Jr. New York: Modern Language Association of America, 1972. Most useful general survey of studies on the Romantic period, as well as of works on aspects of Keats's thought and style and on individual poems.

The Romantic Movement: A Selective and Critical Bibliography. Appearing
annually in *ELH: Journal of English Literary History* 1937–49, *Philo-*
logical Quarterly 1950–64, and *English Language Notes* 1965–79. Lists
book reviews and gives notes on books and articles published the
previous year. Beginning with the Bibliography for 1979, the work is
now brought out by Garland Publishing, Inc., 136 Madison Avenue,
New York. A cumulation for 1936–1970 in 7 volumes with index was
edited by A. C. Elkins and L. J. Forstner and published by the Pieran
Press, Ann Arbor, 1973.

VIEBROCK, HELMUT. *John Keats*. Darmstadt: Wissentschaftliche Buch-
gesellschaft, 1977. In the series "Erträge der Forschung" (Proceeds of
Research). Survey of criticism 1818–1976. In German.

2. Biography and Criticism

ABRAMS, M[EYER] H., ed. *English Romantic Poets: Modern Essays in Criti-*
cism. 2nd ed. London: Oxford University Press, 1975. First-rate essays on
the period and individual poets, including Keats.

BATE, WALTER JACKSON. *The Stylistic Development of Keats*. 1945; rpt. New
York: Humanities Press, 1962. Detailed analysis of Keats's prosody.

―――. *John Keats*. 1963; rpt. New York: Oxford University Press, 1966.
Outstanding work on Keats's life and art. Gives a superb general survey
and fine discussions of nearly all poems of importance. Not only integrates biography with criticism, but also combines literary history,
history of ideas, critical theory, psychology, and stylistic analysis.

―――, ed. *Keats: A Collection of Critical Essays*. Englewood Cliffs, New
Jersey: Prentice-Hall, 1964. Some of the best twentieth-century criti-
cism, including essays by Eliot, Bush, Fogle, Bate, Stillinger, Bloom,
Perkins, Wasserman, and James.

BAYLEY, JOHN. *Keats and Reality*. 1962; rpt. [Folcroft, Pennsylvania:] Fol-
croft Press, 1969. Incisive, brief study reevaluating specific passages.

BLOOM, HAROLD. *The Visionary Company: A Reading of English Romantic*
Poetry. Rev. and enlarged ed. Ithaca, New York: Cornell University
Press, 1971. Close readings of Keats's chief poems. Stimulating
throughout.

―――. *A Map of Misreading*. New York: Oxford University Press, 1975.
Expands the theory of poetic influence formulated in Bloom's *The*
Anxiety of Influence (1973). Analysis of "Ode to Psyche" shows Keats
making distinctive contribution in reaction to Milton and Wordsworth.
Ideas original but difficult.

―――. *Poetry and Repression: Revisionism from Blake to Stevens*. New
Haven: Yale University Press, 1976. Discusses the two *Hyperion* frag-
ments. Contrasts Bloom's own earlier conventional interpretation of
Keats with a "revisionary" reading. Original but difficult.

BOSTETTER, EDWARD E. *The Romantic Ventriloquists: Wordsworth, Cole-*
ridge, Keats, Shelley, Byron. Rev. ed. Seattle: University of Washing-

ton Press, 1975. Discusses imaginative failure in major unfinished Romantic works, among them *The Fall of Hyperion*.

BROOKS, CLEANTH. "Keats's Sylvan Historian: History without Footnotes." In *The Well Wrought Urn*. New York: Harcourt, 1947. Explores the paradoxes and ambiguities of the "Grecian Urn." Influential essay.

BUSH, DOUGLAS. *John Keats: His Life and Writings*. New York: Macmillan, 1966. A brief scholarly and readable critical biography relating Keats's life to his work with excellent discussions of individual poems.

CALDWELL, JAMES RALSTON. *John Keats' Fancy: The Effect on Keats of the Psychology of His Day*. 1945; rpt. New York: Octagon, 1965. The influence of associationist theories culminating in Hartley.

CHATTERJEE, BHABATOSH. *John Keats: His Mind and Work*. New Delhi: Orient Longman, 1971. Comprehensive, scholarly, unbiased work with detailed, sensitive analyses of individual poems. Contains three chapters on the comic in Keats.

COLVIN, SIDNEY. *John Keats: His Life and Poetry, His Friends, Critics, and After-Fame*. 1917; rpt. New York: Octagon, 1970. Most balanced comprehensive interpretation before 1963 of Keats's life and works.

COOKE, MICHAEL G. *The Romantic Will*. New Haven: Yale University Press, 1976. Romanticism as "the metaphysics of action, a constant engagement." Distinguishes between Keats's "personal" and "artistic" will.

D'AVANZO, MARIO L. *Keats's Metaphors for the Poetic Imagination*. Durham, North Carolina: Duke University Press, 1967. Discusses images of poetic flight and disillusionment. Interesting interpretations of "La Belle Dame" and "Ode to Psyche."

DICKSTEIN, MORRIS. *Keats and His Poetry: A Study in Development*. Chicago: University of Chicago Press, 1971. Perceptive discussion of Keats's work in the light of the schism between "self-consciousness and vision."

ENDE, STUART A. *Keats and the Sublime*. New Haven: Yale University Press, 1976. Discusses Keats's poetry in the Freudian terms of ego-development from narcissim to relationship with otherness. Difficult.

EVERT, WALTER H. *Aesthetic and Myth in the Poetry of Keats*. Princeton: Princeton University Press, 1965. Apollo as the informing spirit of Keats's poetry. Detailed analysis of *Endymion*.

FINNEY, CLAUDE L. *The Evolution of Keats's Poetry*. 1936; rpt. New York: Russell, 1963. Still valuable for its comprehensiveness and its investigation of sources.

FOGLE, RICHARD HARTER. *The Imagery of Keats and Shelley: A Comparative Study*. Chapel Hill: University of North Carolina Press, 1949. Fine discussion, supported by statistics, of Keats's synaesthetic and empathic imagery, its sensuousness, spontaneity, and intensity.

FRASER, G. S., ed. *John Keats: Odes*. London: Macmillan, 1971. Includes, besides earlier commentary, eleven of the best twentieth-century essays.

GARROD, H. W. *Keats*. 2nd ed. 1939; rpt. Oxford: Clarendon Press, 1957.
Sees Keats as poet of pure sensation rather than philosopher. Some fine
insights.

GITTINGS, ROBERT. *John Keats: The Living Year, 21 September 1818 to 21
September 1819*. 1954; rpt. London: Heinemann, 1968. Influence of
day-to-day events and reading on Keats's poems.

———. *John Keats*. London: Heinemann, 1968. This carefully researched
biography corrects several errors of its predecessors and admirably
demonstrates how closely Keats's life and works are linked.

GOLDBERG, M. A. *The Poetics of Romanticism: Toward a Reading of John
Keats*. Yellow Springs, Ohio: Antioch Press, 1969. Relates isolated
passages from poems and letters to a wider context.

HARTMAN, GEOFFREY H. *The Fate of Reading and Other Essays*. Chicago:
University of Chicago Press, 1975. Contains penetrating analyses of
Hyperion and "Ode to Autumn."

HEWLETT, DOROTHY. *A Life of John Keats*. 3rd rev. ed. London: Hutchinson, 1970. Sound and straightforward biography.

INGLIS, FRED. *Keats*. 1966; rpt. New York: Arco, 1969. "For that elusive
figure, the common reader."

JACK, IAN. *Keats and the Mirror of Art*. Oxford: Clarendon Press, 1967. An
abundance of convincing examples of images and passages in Keats's
poetry suggested by particular pieces of sculpture, paintings, and
prints. 43 plates.

JONES, JAMES LAND. *Adam's Dream: Mythic Consciousness in Keats and
Yeats*. Athens: University of Georgia Press, 1975. Based largely on the
theories of Ernst Cassirer. Perceptive analysis of "Ode to a Nightingale."

JONES, JOHN. *John Keats's Dream of Truth*. London: Chatto and Windus,
1969. Defends Keats against the implications of Arnold's phrase "the
merely sensuous man." Keats as poet of "feel," of intensity, of picture-
making, of dreams that come true and dreams that disappoint. Full of
brilliant insights.

KNIGHT, G. WILSON. *The Starlit Dome: Studies in the Poetry of Vision*. 1941;
rpt. London: Methuen, 1964. Contains an influential essay on Keats,
particularly valuable for its treatment of the imagery.

LEOFF, EVE. *A Study of John Keats's "Isabella."* Salzburg: University of
Salzburg, 1972. Thorough stanza-by-stanza analysis.

LITTLE, JUDY. *Keats as a Narrative Poet: A Test of Invention*. Lincoln:
University of Nebraska Press, 1975. Detailed discussion of structural
use of imagery in several of the poems of the 1817 volume and in the
completed and fragmentary narratives of 1818–19.

LOWELL, AMY. *John Keats*. 2 vols. 1925; rpt. [London:] Archon Books, 1969.
Though not free from faulty conjecture (e.g. on the composition of the
two *Hyperions*), contains some sensitive discussions of individual

poems. Influential in its time, now superseded by the critical biographies of Bate, Ward, and Gittings.

LUKE, DAVID. "Keats's Letters: Fragments of an Aesthetic of Fragments." *Genre* 11 (1978): 209–26. Relates Keats's concern with "fragmentary experiences" to his idea of the "camelion Poet."

MATTHEWS, G. M., ed. *Keats: The Critical Heritage*. London: Routledge, 1971. Indispensable as source for the reception of Keats's three volumes of poetry by the reviewers of his time. Contains criticism up to 1863.

MATTHEY, FRANÇOIS. *The Evolution of Keats's Structural Imagery*. Bern: Francke, 1974. Sees the structural pattern of the early verse as down and upward and of the later poetry as up and down.

MAYHEAD, ROBIN. *John Keats*. Cambridge: Cambridge University Press, 1967. Brief critical study with detailed, often stimulating discussions of selected passages.

MUIR, KENNETH, ed. *John Keats: A Reassessment*. 2nd ed. Liverpool: Liverpool Univeristy Press, 1969. Ten articles on various aspects of Keats, all of high quality.

MURRY, JOHN MIDDLETON. *Keats and Shakespeare: A Study of Keats' Poetic Life from 1816 to 1820*. 1925; rpt. London: Oxford University Press, 1964. Enthusiastic reading of Keats as "pure poet," an example of human triumph. Highly subjective, but full of brilliant insights.

———. *Keats*. 4th ed. 1955; rpt. [London;] Minerva Press, 1968. Fourteen essays, including a polemic against Gittings.

OBER, WARREN U. and THOMAS, W. K. "Keats and the Solitary Pan." *Keats-Shelley Journal* 29 (1980): 96–119. Best explanation to date for Saturn's address to Pan in *The Fall of Hyperion* (i.411), but the suggestion that Keats planned a role for Pan comparable to Cynthia's in *Endymion* is highly conjectural.

PATTERSON, ANNABEL M. "How to load and bend . . . : Syntax and Interpretation in Keats's *To Autumn*." *Publications of the Modern Language Association of America* 94 (1979): 449–58. Skeptical "counterhypothesis" to the poem's traditional optimistic readings.

PATTERSON, CHARLES I., JR. *The Daemonic in the Poetry of John Keats*. Urbana: University of Illinois Press, 1970. This investigation of Keats's "daemonic" world, the imaginative realm which is neither good nor evil, works best for "La Belle Dame."

PERKINS, DAVID. *The Quest for Permanence: The Symbolism of Wordsworth, Shelley, and Keats*. 1959; rpt. Cambridge, Massachusetts: Harvard University Press, 1965. Explores the tension between Keats's awareness of orderly process and the claim of the visionary imagination.

PETTET, E. C. *On the Poetry of Keats*. 1957; rpt. Cambridge: Cambridge University Press, 1970. Sensitive discussions of Keats's artistry such as sound effects and characteristic images. Plays down Keats's metaphysics and sees *Endymion* as nonallegorical. Useful antidote to Wasserman.

RAGUSSIS, MICHAEL. *The Subterfuge of Art: Language and the Romantic Tradition*. Baltimore: The Johns Hopkins University Press, 1978. Contains chapters on the *Hyperions* and "St. Agnes."

RICKS, CHRISTOPHER. *Keats and Embarrassment*. Oxford: Clarendon Press, 1974. Highly original and sensitive study of the humanizing effect achieved in the poems and letters by Keats's acceptance and manipulation of embarrassability.

RIDLEY, M. R. *Keats' Craftsmanship: A Study in Poetic Development*. 1933; rpt. Lincoln: University of Nebraska Press, 1963. Keats's methods of composition. Scholarly, yet entertaining.

RYAN, ROBERT M. *Keats: The Religious Sense*. Princeton: Princeton University Press, 1976. Concentrates on the letters and throws new light on key concepts such as "negative capability," "the truth of Imagination," and "Soul-making." Aware of Keats's skepticism, yet maintains that he "believed in the existence of a Supreme Being." An important study.

SHARP, RONALD A. *Keats, Scepticism, and the Religion of Beauty*. Athens, Georgia: University of Georgia Press, 1979. Keats offers a "humanized religion" in which beauty and poetry provide consolation, but not salvation. *Endymion* demonstrates "that the heavenly, immortal realm is a fiction," and the religious imagery in works like "St. Agnes" serves to demolish traditional beliefs in a transcendental reality. Penetrating analyses of poems and letters support a vigorous, lucidly presented argument which should be weighed against Ryan's.

SHERWIN, PAUL. "Dying into Life: Keats's Struggle with Milton in *Hyperion*." *Publications of the Modern Language Association of America* 93 (1978): 383–95. A rich article, which, among other things, makes Bloom's concept of a poet's revisionary strife with his precursor accessible to a wider audience.

SIMPSON, DAVID. "Keats's Lady, Metaphor, and the Rhetoric of Neurosis." *Studies in Romanticism* 15 (1976): 265–88. Explores the poet's quest for ontological certainty. Relates "La Belle Dame" to "overdetermination" in Freudian dream analysis, and to Coleridge, Locke, Hume, Kant, and Hegel.

SINSON, JANICE C. *John Keats and The Anatomy of Melancholy*. London: Keats-Shelley Memorial Association, 1971. Speculates that Keats read through two volumes of Burton in April 1819.

SLOTE, BERNICE. *Keats and the Dramatic Principle*. Lincoln: University of Nebraska Press, 1958. Scholarly study, not only of the theatre of Keats's time and his attempts at play-writing but of his Shakespearean temper.

SPERRY, STUART M. *Keats the Poet*. Princeton: Princeton University Press, 1973. Focuses on Keats's preoccupation with the poetic process and gives penetrating analyses of all the major works and many lesser known poems such as those written during the northern walking tour. Takes into account different recent trends in Keats criticism and makes its own distinctive critical and scholarly contribution. Profound, yet clear and readable.

SPURGEON, CAROLINE. *Keats's Shakespeare: A Descriptive Study Based on New Material*. 2nd ed. London: Oxford University Press, 1929. Shows and discusses Keats's underlinings, sidelinings, and marginal comments.

STEWART, GARRETT. "*Lamia* and the Language of Metamorphosis." *Studies in Romanticism* 15 (1976): 3–41. Ambivalent language bridges dream and reality.

STILLINGER, JACK, ed. *Twentieth Century Interpretations of Keats's Odes: A Collection of Critical Essays*. Englewood Cliffs, New Jersey: Prentice-Hall, 1968. Fine essays by Kenneth Allott, Fogle, Brooks and Warren, Charles Patterson, Wigod, Gérard, Bate, Perkins, and Bloom. Also contains brief "view points" and an excellent Introduction by Stillinger.

———. *The Hoodwinking of Madeline and Other Essays on Keats's Poems*. Urbana: University of Illinois Press, 1971. Eight lucid independent essays united in emphasizing Keats's firm grip on reality. With his constantly stimulating arguments, Stillinger, who sees satire where others have seen dreaming escapism, has probably done more than any other critic to restore the balance against "metaphysical" readings such as Wasserman's.

TAYLOR, ANYA. "Superhuman Silence: Language in *Hyperion*." *Studies in English Literature 1500–1900* 19 (1979): 673–87. The poem moves from "a rendering of myth as it dies" in Books I and II "to the deployment of myth as psychology" in Book III.

THORPE, CLARENCE DEWITT. *The Mind of John Keats*. 1926; rpt. New York: Russell, 1964. Influential study, establishing Keats as thinker though not claiming a systematic philosophy for him.

TING, NAI-TUNG. "Chatterton and Keats: A Reexamination," *Keats-Shelley Journal* 30 (1981): 100–117. Chatterton's influence was greatest in the spring of 1818 and in those later poems which are "tranquil in mood."

WALDOFF, LEON. "The Theme of Mutability in the 'Ode to Psyche.'" *Publications of the Modern Language Association of America* 92 (1977): 410–19. Keats accepts mutability of a goddess and affirms his own spiritual growth.

WARD, AILEEN. *John Keats: The Making of a Poet*. 1963; rpt. New York: Viking Press, 1967. Scholarly, psychologically oriented approach, exciting reading.

WASSERMAN, EARL R. *The Finer Tone: Keats's Major Poems*. 1953; rpt. Baltimore: Johns Hopkins Press, 1967. Influential readings of "Grecian Urn," "La Belle Dame," "St. Agnes," *Lamia*, and "Nightingale" in terms of the contraries between mortal and immortal realms.

WIENER, DAVID. "The Secularization of the Fortunate Fall in Keats's 'The Eve of St. Agnes.'" *Keats-Shelley Journal* 29 (1980): 120–30. Madeline falls from a stagnant world of innocence into the vale of soul-making.

[WILLIAMSON, GEORGE C., ed.] *The John Keats Memorial Volume*. London: John Lane, 1921. Contains articles by de Selincourt, Bradley, Colvin, Shaw, and many others.

Index

Abbey, Richard, 17, 35
Abrams, Meyer H., 102, 163n9, 165n7, 169n26, 178
Adam, 94, 121. *See also* Letters: "Adam's dream"
Adonis, 66, 68, 71, 73, 77, 168n14
Aeschylus, 98
allegory, 74, 159–60, *166n17*, 181
Allen, Glen, 72
Allott, Kenneth, 171n1, 183
Allott, Miriam, 163n11, 167n6, 169n21, n29, 170n30, n40, 172n16, *176*
Alpheus, 61, 66, 71, 77
Angela, 105, 108, 109, 110
Apollo, 22, 24, 26, 27, 54, 57, 61, 62, 74, 81, 85, 91, 92, 93–94, *95–102*, 117, 143, 144, 145–46, 149, 150, 151, 162n7, 165n6, 168n7, n10, 179
Apollonius, *140–43*, 158, 173n1
Apuleius, 119, 171n2
Arethusa, 61, 66, 71, 77
Argus, 116
Ariadne, 30
Aristotle: *Poetics*, 131
Arnold, Matthew, 154, 180
art and life, 26, 37–39, 42–43, 47, 60, 62, 63–64, 68, 71, 75, 87, 90, 96–97, 100, 109–110, 121–27, *128–34*, 143, 150, 153, 157–58, 163n12, 172n19: creative process, 21, 22, *58–62*, 122–23, 141, 143, 149, 157, 182; drama, 34, 42, 60, 82, *155–56*, 167n18, 182; imagination, 22, 23, 24–26, 30–31, 33, 37–46, 50, 55, 56, 60, 64, 70, 74–76, 78, 85, 86–87, 91, 96, 110, 111, 115, *122–24*, 128–32, 137, 141–42, 146, 148–50, 154, 157, 181. *See also* Letters: "truth of Imagination"; painting and sculpture, 17, 21, *29–30*, 42–43, 58–60, 63–64,

art and life—continued
71, 86, 101–102, 106, 120, 128–34, 144, 149–50, 151–53, 163n9, *166n11*, 171n2, 180; sensation, 21, *23*, 25, 28, 29, 30, *33–34*, 39–40, 42, 48, 59, 61, *80–81*, 86, 88–89, 99, 114, 121, 123, 124, 125, 129, 136–38, 180. *See also* Letters: "Sensations, O for a Life of"
Asia (in *Hyperion*), 168n10; (in *Prometheus Unbound*), 95
aspiration. *See* dream and reality
Augustan, 156
Aurenthe, 174n19
Aurora, 121

Bacchus, 30, 75
Bailey, Benjamin, 17, 31, 34, 36, *37–40*, 41, 42, 44, 48, 49, 69, 74, 99, 101, 122, 131
Balboa, Vasco Nuñez de, 54,
Baldwin, Dane Lewis, 177
Balslev, Thora, 163n11
Barnard, John, *176*
Bate, Walter Jackson, 31 42, 98, 99, 100, 153, 154–55, 162n9, 163n9, 164n4, 166n17, 168n1, n5, 169n21, n25, 173n28, 174n19, n21, *178*, 181, 183
Bateson, F. W., 172n18
Batteux, Charles, 132
Bayley, John, 107, 169n29, 178
Beadsman ("St. Agnes"), 105–106, 109, 110
Beatrice, 145
Beaudry, Harry R., 174n19, n20
beauty: ephemerality and, 24, 26, 61, 72, 83, 89, 92, 97, 100, *104*, *134–137*, 153–54, 158, 160; fatality of, 115, 140; passions creative of, 38, *74–75*, 97; religion of, 122, 182; sense of, 42, 43, 45,

184

Index 191

Mnemosyne. See Moneta
Moneta (Mnemosyne), 25, 96–98, *144–50*, 168n7, n8
mortality. See time and timelessness
Muir, Kenneth, 127, 132, 163n9, *181*
Murray, E.B., 165n2
Murry, John Middleton, 51, 60, 72, 87, 98, 115, 149, 154–55, 161n5, 163n11, 165n4, 167n3, *181*
mutability. See time and timelessness

Narcissus, 57
nature, 22, 25, 34, 43, 44, 52–53, 61, *63–70*, 77–78, *80–81*, 88, 90, 115, 116, 121, 126–28, 137, 143, 156; bower, 22, 24, 28, 52, 56–57, 58, 61, 63, *73–78*, 97, 100, 120, 122, 126, 134, 143, 158; destructiveness of, 47, 64, *86–87*, 112; cycle of, 28, 53, 73, 84, 88, 95, 128, *152*, 154; harvest, 22, 26, 28, 55, 57, 63, 68, 82, 83, 115, 117, 128, 133, *151–54*, 155, 167n5; inspiration of, 28, *55–58*, 63, 64, 97; process of, 24, 26, 43–44, 53, 61, 63, 70, 89, 96, 97, 105, 106, 107, 109, 112, 116, 128, 133, 137, 139, 140, 145, *151–54*, 157, 158, 167n5, 181; ripening, *21–22*, 28, 43, 45, 46, 55, 57, 63, 67, 75, 82, 88, 89, 90, 95, 105, 111, 117, 133, 147, *151–54*, 157; supernatural, 25, 27, 71, 77, 105, 106, 109, 110, *112–15*, 126, 142–43
Nemoianu, Virgil, 174n12
Neptune, 66, 71, 91, 95, 147
nereids, 71
nightingale, 52, 68, 74, 85, 86, 103, 127. See also "Ode to a Nightingale"; Philomela
Norris, Marjorie, 55

Ober, Warren U., 70, 168n7, *181*
Oceanus, *92–97*, 100, 146
Oedipus complex, 16
Ophelia, 16
Orcagna, Andrea: *The Triumph of Death*, 169–70n30
Orion, 71, 166n11
Osler, Alan, 167n8
Ovid: *Metamorphoses*, 66, 140, 173n1; *Art of Love*, 173n1
Owen, F.M., 166n17

Pan, 57, 61, 65, *69–70*, 77, 91, 168n7, 181. See also "Flora and old Pan"
paradox, 23, 27, 45, 48, 50, 57, 61, 71, 76, 79, 81, 82, 83, 87, 97, 101, 103–104, 106, 107, 117, 122, 124–26, *129–34*, 135, 137, 139, 145, 158, 159, *172n15*, 179; joy/pain, *23*, 27, 43, 61, 75, 86, 97, 101, 107, 117, 123, *124*, *136–38*, 140, 142, 144, 156, 167n18; "unperplex," 27, 66, 101, 107, *142*. See also Letters: "beauty" and "truth"
Parthenon, 63
Patterson, Annabel M., 150, *181*
Patterson, Charles I., Jr., 170n41, *181*, 183
Peona, 65, 67, 108
Perkins, David, 123, 177, 178, *181*, 183
Pettet, E.C., 67, 102, 125, 162n13, 166n17, 172n15, n23, 174n19, 176, *181*
Petrarchan simile, 84–85; sonnet, 26, 27, 82
Philomela, 74, 85. See also nightingale
Philostratus: *Life of Apollonius of Tyana*, 173n1
Phoebe, 65, 68. See also Cynthia
Phoebus, 68. See also Apollo
Plato, 76, 132, 166n17
Pluto, 147
Polyphemes (Polyphemus), 59
Pope, Alexander, 26, 54
Porphyro, *105–110*, 120, 170n32
Posey, Horace, 135
Potter, John: *Antiquities of Greece*, 173n1
Poussin, Nicolas, 128: *Autumn*, 162n11; *Landscape with Orion*, 166n11; *Realm of Flora, The*, 60, 61
Pre-Raphaelites, 111, 156
process. See art and life; nature
Prometheus, 95, 98, 168n8

quest. See dream and reality
Quietude, Cave of, 23, *66–67*

Radcliffe, Ann, 170n30
Ragussis, Michael, 110, *182*
Ready, Robert, 163n9
reality. See dream and reality
Reid, Stephen, 137, 161n2